# Workers and Narratives of Survival in Europe

SUNY series in the Anthropology of Work

June C. Nash, editor

# Workers and Narratives of Survival in Europe

*The Management of Precariousness at the End of the Twentieth Century*

Edited by
Angela Procoli

STATE UNIVERSITY OF NEW YORK PRESS

Published by
State University of New York Press

© 2004 State University of New York

For information, address State University of New York Press,
State University Plaza, Albany, NY 12246

Production by Kelli Williams
Marketing by Micheal Campochiaro

Library of Congress Cataloging-in-Publication Data

Workers and narratives of survival in Europe : the management of precariousness at the end of
    the twentieth century / edited by Angela Procoli.
        p. cm — (SUNY series in the sociology of work)
    Revised versions of papers presented at the fifth and sixth meetings of the European
Association of Social Anthropologist (EASA), held respectively in Frankfurt-am-Main,
Germany, in Sept. 1998 and in Krakow, Poland, in July 2000.
    Includes bibliographical references and index.
    ISBN 0-7914-6085-1 (alk. paper)
        1. Structural unemployment—Europe. 2. Labor market—Europe. 3. Industries—Social
aspects—Europe. 4. Europe—Economic conditions—1945–    I. Procoli, Angela.
II. European Association of Social Anthropologists. III. Series.

HD5708.47.E5W67    2004
331'.094–dc22
                                                                                    2004045398

10   9   8   7   6   5   4   3   2   1

# Contents

**Part III.  Continuity or Discontinuity with the Past?**

# Acknowledgments

Most of the chapters in this volume are revised versions of papers read at the fifth and sixth meetings of the European Association of Social Anthropologists (EASA), held respectively in Frankfurt-am-Main, Germany, in September 1998 and in Krakow, Poland, in July 2000. Some of them were presented in the two workshops I convened on these occasions. The general topics of the two meetings were, respectively, "The End of Work, Illusion or Reality, Nightmare or New Utopia: What Do Anthropologists Have to Say About It?" and "Extreme Situations: Case Studies in Survival."

Susana Narotzky, Sophie Day, and Italo Pardo could not attend the EASA conferences but they have prepared chapters for this collection that significantly enhance its range and value. I would also like to thank those in attendance who made a significant contribution to our discussions, although they have not written chapters for this volume.

I am also grateful to the Wenner-Green and the Deutsch Forschung Gesellschaft foundations and to the Laboratory of Social Anthropology in Paris for financially supporting my two workshops.

My thanks to the organizers of the EASA meetings, to the EASA editorial board, and, particularly, to Marilyn Strathern for her excellent advice. I am grateful to Jocelyne de Viry and to my husband François Rochet—had it not been for their assistance, I would never have dared to attempt to write this book in English.

# Introduction

ANGELA PROCOLI

The purpose of this book is to describe, from an anthropological standpoint, how work has evolved in contemporary European society. Particular stress will be placed on the trend to greater precariousness, which has
emerged in "affluent" Europe (i.e., the north and center of the community) against a backdrop of radical changes involving the world of work
and employment: the economic crises of the 1970s and 1980s; the technological revolution involving manufacturing activities, which is driving
millions of jobs to redundancy; globalization, at an ever-increasing pace
of financial services, production, markets, strategies, and firms; changes
have occurred in the pattern of society (decline of the working class,
weakening of the middle class, a higher proportion of older people).
The crisis in the welfare state (the United Kingdom was the first country
to experience it) has brought about a radical change in the social landscape of western Europe. Full employment polices have been dropped;
unemployment benefits have been reduced. As employment becomes
more precarious and as layoffs are on the rise, newfangled forms of work
appear (part-time, limited intime, interim, subcontracting on a large
scale, and so forth) so that firms can meet the demands of free trade and
the logic of competitiveness, cutting down on production and manpower
costs (Gruppo di Lisbona 1995).

As work undergoes such changes and becomes a "rarer commodity,"
the following issue emerges in the debate among intellectuals: Is work, up
to now a core value in Western society, about to fade from the scene? As in
any time of crisis, a feeling that the future is uncertain fosters the emergence of utopias. Thus, in the mid-1990s the eschatological concept of the
"end of work" finds its way to a number of media-friendly philosophical
and sociological essays. This blooming utopian literature forecasts a society in which man would be freed from the slavery of work, as Karl Marx
imagined (Rifkin 1995). It mirrors the so-called global economic model

1

that, breaking with the past, would lead to a destruction of the local modes of organizing work. An attempt is made to show that the building up of work as an institution occupying a focal position is a slow historical process, set on its course by the industrial revolution and coming to an end along with industrial societies (Gorz 1989; Méda 1995, 1996). The possibility is also evoked for any individual to choose an activity he finds congenial and for which, whatever his choice may be, he is allocated such a sum of money as will allow him to survive on acceptable terms (a kind of lifeline allowance, a negative tax) (Gorz 1999).

The whole issue, thought-provoking as it appeared to us, justified our organizing in 1998 (in Frankfurt-am-Main, Germany) and in 2000 (in Krakow, Poland) two international workshops in connection with the biennial of the European Association of Social Anthropologists (EASA). Researchers were scrutinizing work problems in Europe, focusing on the symbolic imaginary of workers in their field, in an attempt to weigh the relevance of the very notion of the end of work. In these two EASA workshops, ethnographic surveys, carried out over a long period of time in different European societies, were presented. The surveys analyzed affluent societies, areas of the community where unemployment is endemic (the Italian Mezzogiorno), groups in society torn apart by the repatterning of industry (Welsh miners), and eastern European societies brutally dragged into a market economy with all of its well-known consequences on employment and the status of workers.

Research has shed light on the ambiguous nature of the expression of the end of work. The "end of salaried work" would be a more adequate formulation. It is understandable that the expression the end of work is widely used in a society where officialdom and the media see nothing more in work than its economic function and profitability. The end of work image appeared unjustified for a number of reasons. First, wherever a utopian ideology prevails, those who advocate a freely chosen activity financed by a "negative tax" are prone to describe it as "work." Second, it overlooks the fact that the attrition of employment in our world has brought about the growth of employment "elsewhere." As June Nash (1995, 188–211) has made clear, a working class is emerging in the Third World, while Alain Touraine doomed it to disappearence in the wake of technological progress (cited in ibid., 1995). Last but not least, as they focus on the developped and affluent West, they overlook those areas in the European Union (EU) where for some time, and well before the so-called economic crisis, a structural form of chronic unemployment was officially recognized and involved 30 percent or thereabouts of the active population, as opposed to the 10 percent EU average. If utopian theories were to be believed, work would have already vanished from those areas. The example of Naples, Italy, to be developed further, goes to show that this is not at all the case. To understand how people have managed to survive, one must look beyond statistical data and explore the underground of unregulated work and trafficking in one form or another. Hence, the relevance of qualitative investigation.

These remarks shed light on the complex nature of the very notion of work. As it referred to the end of work, in fact the end of salaried work, the most usual form in western Europe until then, utopian thinking has had the great advantage of reminding us that work is not limited to the economic sphere in which it has been enclosed by traditional Western philosophy since the eighteenth century (work to produce uselfuness, and carried out by the individual worker as an obligation). Anthropological surveys, on the other hand, have for some time insisted on the necessary inclusion of work in a semantic field covering more than its economic aspect. As Frederick Gamst (1995, 1–45) stressed a few years ago, work connotes far more than the mere production of goods and services. A survey of remote societies has shown that work is indiscernible from other human activities. Production cannot be considered an economic process isolated from its background in society; nor can a producer be insulated against forces at work encompassing his area of activity (Sahlins 1972).

Work as a value has to be reconsidered so that work can be reassessed in all of its semantic complexity (Wallman 1979). Work as a reality is a complex notion since it can fit into areas in apparent opposition in the economic, social, and political fields. As will be shown further, work fits into the "formal and the informal," the "lawful," "semilawful," or "illegal." But is there really cause for surprise? Anthropologically wise, identity is built up, it is assumed by interacting material and nonmaterial factors, as Sandra Wallman and Italo Pardo will elaborate on in this book; consequently, work is to be taken in a broader sense encompassing the various compartments into which, in conventional terms, social reality is divided. These conventional terms are challenged, however, as research gives pride of place to qualitative investigation, whose objects are followed over a long span of time in various areas of the social field where they develop their activities (work, family, neighborhood).

The "moral community" of workers looms much larger than the sociological community of workers with a salaried job. A fresh assessment should be made of work carried out in areas unexplored so far. Thus, an ethnographic survey I carried out in France (Procoli 2000) among humanitarian nongovernmental organizations, where salaried workers work side by side with volunteers, shows that work does not boil down to "paid employment" and "obligation." The sociological barriers between workers and volunteers or, indeed, between workers and the unemployed (since associations tend more and more to provide opportunities for reconversion to the unemployed or workers on the brink of retirement) break down as all concerned work out a collective notion of what real work is, unsullied by economic profit (Procoli 2000). Reasoning in anthropological terms, and taking into account the symbolic imaginary of those concerned, it is important to look beyond hallowed sociological categories (work/unemployment, formal/informal, lawful/ illegal). Thus, the loss of a job is not enough to exclude a worker from the community of workers. When Cato Wadel (1973) analyzed the figure of George, an unemployed worker of a small rural community of Canada, he showed that his identification as a worker, in the eyes of other people who had known him for a long time, as well as in his own eyes, persisted because of his long past as a logger. More recently, Leo Howe (1990) also demonstrated this, showing that in a community in Ulster, Ireland, where employment is precarious, the "deserving" unemployed still rank with other workers, sharing their ideology of individual endeavor, in opposition to the "undeserving" unemployed, frowned upon as shirkers and parasites. This goes to show that beyond the sociological divide a moral community of workers is shaping up. Such communities develop survival strategies and produce a narrative about survival by which events become meaningful for human groups and enable them to cope with the violence of extreme situations.

This book deals with work and the complex task of attempting a definition. It shows the degree to which identity (intimacy, the family) meshes with work (part I). Further contributions analyze the discourses and survival strategies developed to confront precarious employment. The situation, as employment goes, in the European Union (part II) is put in parallel with the one prevailing in post-communist societies. In the latter case, the role of memory, in a situation where a clean break has occurred in a historical process, is studied with particular care.

## Part I:  Identity and the Experience of Work

In part I, the authors show that when the issue of the precariousness of work is examined, full account must be taken of the complex nature of identity where the professional and the personal, material and nonmaterial inputs are closely intertwined. Sandra Wallman also shows that the negative impact of precariousness is all the stronger where identity has been most heavily invested in the area of work. While prevailing ideology tends to consider social and family considerations as subservient to economic factors, Sophie Day and Susana Narotzky lay stress on the tensions that arise as the former are made the instruments of the latter; the areas observed are as wide apart as prostitution in London and small-scale firms in Spain.

In chapter 1, Wallman points out how work is an activity made meaningful by combinations of time and identity invested in it by the worker. The disruption caused by job loss can be as much—even more— about loss of the structure of time and/or of the sense of self as it is about the crude realities of money. She demonstrates that systems (i.e., communities and individuals) characterized by diffusion and diversity are inherently less precarious than any more homogeneous, more tightly closed ones. Communities built on flexible local labor markets are better placed to adjust to the shutdown of formal employment; similarly, individual well-being will be best assured when time and identity are spread across the whole of life than when narrowly invested in a single domain.

In chapter 2, Day analyzes precarious work in an "unregulated" sector, the object of her ethnographic study: prostitution in London. As work goes, it defies description, as prostitutes cannot give an account of their activities. The lack of a social status and occupational hazards might well doom them to unmitigated precariousness. Two main strategies are deployed by sex workers, one in which work is definitely separated from all other aspects of life, the other in which both are intermingled—the relation with Wallman's contribution on time, identity, and work is worth noting. The author shows that "career" sex workers seek a more secure and stable living as they associate with regular clients who eventually become friends or business partners, so that sex work can provide a springboard for other enterprises. In such cases prostitutes give up any notion of separating professional considerations from personal ones. Day shows that such an option is to be taken as arising in the context of a political situation in which the welfare state has been dismantled and the ideology of the "self-made" man or woman has become prevalent, that is, he or she will be able to rise to success on his or her own and will be ready to give up his or her personal life to conform to the dictates of the market.

In chapter 3, Narotzky also deals with the personal and the professional as intertwined—so they appear in her survey of the Vega Baja, near Valencia (in southeast Spain) an area of small factories and unregulated workshops. People there rely heavily on family labor, kin, and neighborhood networks to access work and labor. Following recent sociological and economic models, the area has been described as an "industrial district" where social considerations are no longer excluded from, but put to use by, the world of economy. This model is increasingly acquiring a hegemonic role in the agendas of institutional policy-makers including Eurocrats or World Bank advisers. The crucial component of the new industrial district model is the concept of "social capital," highlighted as the main asset to be developed in order for development policies to succeed. Social capital refers to the idea of the embeddedness of economic rationality within the fabric of a wider social experience. Noneconomic social relations are deemed increasingly necessary for the local establishment of dynamic entrepreneurial practices and flexible relations of production. However, the hegemonic discourse of an organic and culturally defined economic region misrepresents the harsh realities of Vega Baja. What ethnography reveals is a complex and conflict-ladden space where deep tensions are generated by the embeddedness of production relations in the social fabric of the community, the family, and the self.

## Part II: Liminality and the Narrative of Survival

Part II develops the topic of a "moral community" shaping up and producing a survival narrative encompassing values with a clear cultural profile: self-sacrifice for the sake of others, honesty, to work with a will, competitiveness, "entrepreneurialism." The thorny problem arises from the complex relationship of such a narrative with the all "dominant ideology" (i.e., ideology of wide acceptance, as obvious and morally unimpeachable, and, to a large extent, conveyed by the mass media); it may well embrace some of its concepts; it can also twist them around or subvert them.

In chapter 4, I present an ethnographic survey I carried out in an upper-crust French institute for professional training, where middle- and high-level managers seek to retain their employability. Training courses in the management of human resources, fraught with the ideology of "happy flexibility," provide an exceptionally good vantage point from which to observe the imaginary of a destabilized middle class. The training method giving pride of place as it does to change fosters strong group dynamics, the impact of which goes well beyond the professional goals as initially planned. Deep-set alterations in identity are thus brought about, along with the emergence of symbolic narratives and spontaneous rituals. Former equilibria may well have disappeared, professional and social life been repatterned; it does not follow that the notion of permanent adaptability has triumphed—much to the contrary. If Change (motto of the training institution) is to be accepted, it must move in the direction of higher stability and deeper entrenchment. It may seem paradoxical that in the very place where the ideology of permanent adaptability is taught, a counternarrative of resistance should emerge. In fact, participants define of their own accord what good management should be, based on altruistic values. Within the group, they define what is evil (bad management based on individualism) and drive it away in a ritual scene evocative of the scapegoat.

In chapter 5, Richard-Michael Diedrich proceeds to a survey of mining communities in South Wales where the radical economic restructuring of the 1980s has driven them to severe unemployment, weakened as they already were by the decline of the industry over the years. In such a group, to belong to the community of "real men" a sine qua non condition is to have a job in the mine. The loss of such a job involves the loss of membership. Indeed, the workplace was an extremely important space for the construction of gendered difference and men who no longer worked were excluded from a prominent arena for the negotiation of male identities. The scope of this identity crisis is expressed in terms of unemployment seen as a case of liminality, or withdrawal from public life, to last forever, or the entrance into a "no-man's-land." Diedrich shows that the community survives thanks to a narrative in which male hegemony and work remain core values. This narrative, however, has not arisen *ex novo* since it has matured through trade union struggles against overbearing bosses in the mining industry; paradoxically enough, it borrows the values of respectability and deservingness embedded in the individualistic ideology of capitalism. Mining-community culture was constituted by a political discourse of the working class that linked lines of distinctions, expressed as class differences, with concepts of work, community, and gendered difference. So even at a time when the mining industry declines and is finally wiped out, male hegemony is safeguarded in a narrative when the community of real men—miners still in jobs or the "deserving unemployed"—have some experience, past or present, of work in the mine as opposed to "scroungers" excluded from the community, and whose inferior position is similar to that of women. It is worth noting that the re-creation of identity—eventually by borrowing elements of the dominant ideology—brings to mind some aspects of the retraining/reidentifying program that is the issue of chapter 4. The concept of work, which enabled working class men to construct positive male identities in a situation characterized by exploitation, ultimately involves negative identities when work "disappears."

In chapter 6, Italo Pardo studies the case of Naples, Italy, a town in the Mezzogiorno, where industrial development has been low throughout its history, where organized crime is present in various sectors of the market, and the official unemployment rate is high. In such a situation, fraught with so many difficulties, where the local powers that be are quite unable to face up to the south's crucial social problems, the object of the survey display their resilience to a surprising degree as they manage the precariousness of their lives. Contrary to derogatory stereotypes concerning southerners and despite official statistics, genuine unemployment affects only a minority—numerically slight. The present ethnographic work, grounded in episodes of these peoples' lives and narratives, goes to show that survival is built on a system of values where entrepreneurialism and mutual assistance—in a network of family, neighbors, and friends—play a key role. Given these moral tenets, work means more than a form of activity geared to material needs; it is also to be considered in a symbolic field where individuals can defy the powers that have relegated them to an inferior position. Thus, the dichotomy formal/informal, legal/illegal is denied by those concerned, even though it is used by local officialdom when describing social reality as it sees it. As they see it, "legitimate work" is to be found in a "gray area." It may be "outside" the law, but it is never seen as unlawful, since according to their moral code, organized crime alone is responsible for social evils such as drugs and prostitution.

## Part III: Continuity or Discontinuity with the Past?

Examining the case of workers from former communist countries (East Germany, the Czech Republic, the USSR, Poland) or migrants from those countries who have settled in the West (German Russian returnees), part III of this book shows how the very concept of work has been drastically modified as the changeover from planned to market economy was taking place. The authors lay particular stress on the feeling of insecurity brought about by the new work ideology. A repatterning of memory, as they show, helps to survive. The constrast between "before" (socialism) and "after" (market economy, a move to the West) may well be dramatic, but the way the survival narrative shapes up shows that the relationship to the past does not amount to a clean break—far from it. Thus, categories from the socialist past may be called upon to reinterpret the capitalist present and resist the new managerial policy when a firm has been bought out by a Western multinational. The ability (or lack of it) to become part of the new economy may well be attributable to varying conceptions of work already in force in a number of social groups under socialism (chapter 8). Finally, history's tragic turns and twists and the decision to emigrate are fully accounted for in a mythical narrative linking the opposite poles of East and West.

In chapter 7, Birgit Müller examines the concept of productivity in central and eastern European countries. Increasing the productivity of labor has been the prime concern in both the planned and the market economies. The aim to produce more in a shorter time was therefore familiar to the workers of the south Moravian factory who needed to adapt to the enterprise politics of their new employer, a multinational combine producing elevators. Fieldwork data from this Czech enterprise, compared to material collected in its Russian and East German subsidiaries, shows how the arguments and strategies with which the combine attempted to extract a maximum productivity from its workers at a minimum cost, contradicted the workers' socialist idea of productivity—defined as a political act of the workforce on behalf of the whole socialist society. Indeed, the combine promoted in the factory a capitalist concept of "productivity" as a category of identity and personal worth. Observing interactions on the shop floor and interviewing managers and workers, Müller finds out how workers and employees respond to the attempt of redefining their identity through the criteria of productivity and how they react to the restructuring of their enterprise as a low-cost factory, where salaries are pushed down to the absolute minimum and where a decent income can only be assured through overtime and a second job. She analyzes the active and passive mechanisms of resistance of the members of the enterprises against this policy and how the workers make use of categories of their socialist past to give sense to the capitalist present.

In chapter 8, Michal Buchowski presents the anthropological fieldwork he has conducted in the village of Dziekanowice in the Wielkopolska region of western Poland. It shows how different social groups within the community of four hundred people adapt to a changing economic and political situation in the 1990s. Four such social classes can be distinguished: white-collar workers, agricultural workers, nonagricultural workers, and farmers. For all of them, pragmatism is the most striking feature. However, economic, social, and symbolic assets that various groups possess shape the way people deal with a new structural context. In the process of domesticating capitalism, people develop their own strategies for survival and reshape social relations within the community. Culture and class are intertwined in a dynamic relationship and their characteristic features can be observed in various domains, such as ways of facing everyday difficulties, dependence/independence with regard to the state welfare system, the ways in which different groups perceive each other, and, last but not least, the way work-related issues are conceptualized and performed. The new economic model has brought into life phenomena that were unknown in the socialist past, such as unemployment, migrant labor, private entrepreneurship, and hired work in private enterprises and farms, which are often expanding, deeply involved in market production, some of them in transnational cooperation. All these factors redefine social structure, village solidarity, and the meaning and value of work itself.

In chapter 9, Regina Römhild looks into the case of Russian German immigrants who represent a specific segment in German "multiculture." Officially, they are perceived as late returning ethnic Germans from the former Eastern bloc. Entering the German labor market, however, this privileged immigrant status enters into conflict with experiences of ethnicization, social devaluation, and unemployment. As far as men are concerned, what they chiefly experience is a drop in their professional status since their erstwhile training and qualifications are not recognized; women, on the other hand, are excluded all together from the labor market, since the new situation does not play in their favor, particulary when they have children. In everyday social practice, the Russian Germans come to represent just another clientele of postsocialist easterners, namely "Russians," who seek jobs in the "Golden West." The chapter explores the ways Russian German immigrants react to this precarious situation and how they themselves try to make sense of Eastern histories in relation to their presence in Germany. The author sheds particular light on their careful seclusion from other east European migrant communities. In this segregated area, leaving Russia is woven into a mythical narrative as a "transnational" move linking rather then dividing East and West.

The different ethnographic studies collected in this book may well show that the issue of work precariousness must be seen against the backdrop of societies where it appeared (its import is not the same everywhere). However, the development of survival strategies takes the necessary course of a symbolic narrative embodying the key concepts that define a group's identity. This symbolic narrative may be developed in contrast to the discourse of the powers-that-be as they define work and divide up society, and it may challenge dichotomies such as work/unemployment, formal/informal, legal/unlawful. In post-socialist societies, threatened as they are by precariousness, survival takes the course of a repatterning of memory, where elements from the past provide explanatory clues to the present. When all is said and done, it is in all cases around a survival narrative that individuals congregate. Such a community, in contrast with the "world outside," split up as it is, provides the tools to face up to the crisis.

# References

Gamst, F. C. 1995. Considerations of work. In *Meanings of work*, edited by F. C. Gamst. Albany: State University of New York Press.

Gorz, A. 1989. *Critique of economic reason*. London: Verso

———. 1999. *Reclaiming work: Beyond the wage-based society*. Cambridge: Polity.

Gruppo di Lisbona. 1995. *I limiti della competitività* (a cura di Riccardo Petrella). Rome: Manifestolibri.

Howe, L. 1990. *Being unemployed in Northern Ireland: An ethnographic study*. Cambridge: Cambridge University Press.

Méda, D. 1995. *Le travail. Une valeur en voie de disparition*. Paris: Aubier.

———. 1996. New perspectives on work as value. *International Labour Review* 135 (6): 633–643.

Nash, J. 1995. Post-industrialism, post-fordism, and the crisis in world capitalism. In *Meanings of work: Considerations for the twenty-first century*, edited by F. C. Gamst. Albany: State University of New York Press.

Procoli, A. 2000. Le travail "pur" des faiseuses de l'adoption: étude d'un groupe de bénévoles d'une ONG française. *Anthropologie et Société* 24 (3), 133–152.

Rifkin, J. 1995. *The end of work: The decline of the global labor force and the dawn of the post-market era*. New York: Tarcher/Putnam.

Sahlins, M. 1972. *Stone age economics*. Chicago: Aldine–Atherton.

Wadel, C. 1973. *Now, whose fault is that? The struggle for self-esteem in the face of chronic unemployment*. Toronto: University of Toronto Press.

Wallman, S. 1979. *Social anthropology of work*. London: Academic.

# PART I
# Identity and the Experience of Work

# 1

# The Hazards of Overemployment

*What Do Chief Executives and
Housewives Have in Common?*

SANDRA WALLMAN

## Introduction

Concerns about work fluctuate with changes in technology and economy—
regional, national, and global—and with the political stance of governments or commentators. But consistently it is the shortage, absence, or
loss of "formal employment" that dominates the agenda of popular and
parliamentary debate. Two questions predominate it: What shall we do
about unemployment? What drives the trends? The facts and figures of
unemployment are the same whether caused by the unintended consequences of industrial policy or by mindless evolutionary process. But at-
tributions of cause govern who/what is blamed for unemployment, and
the shape of measures taken to help households and national economies
to weather it. Because they also reflect fundamental assumptions about
what work itself is/should be/has been, it is significant that public debate
continues to envisage the future of work as a one built around industrial
employment.

The optimistic view is that full employment will come back when industry "recovers," and all will be well when it does. This view neglects the
fact that the massive economic growth that sustained full employment is
more likely to have been the aberration of a couple of decades than the
beginning of an endlessly progressive upward curve; it patronizes the
many people whose experience of employment has been neither normal

15

nor delightful; and it ignores the increase in popular criticism, even the rejection, of formal employment (I will discuss this later).

In effect the old developmental assumptions remain unchallenged—that is, economic growth and full employment are normal and they are good; any hitch in the "natural" development process is bad and must be explainable, blameable, removable (Wallman 1977). These assumptions are historically and ethnographically wrong, and they are politically misleading. Only by suspending them can we begin to understand what it is about employment and unemployment issues that makes them so obsessively important in our time.

This chapter is not about the accuracy of employment figures or the politics of unemployment as such. It is an attempt to account for contradictions in the meaning of work in advanced industrial society by broadening the notion to include other-than-economic aspects of the work experience.

## What Do the Figures Mean?

Fifteen years ago approximately 3 million people were claiming unemployment benefits in Britain; by this count then, more than 10 percent of potential workers were out of work. Despite an average 2.7 percent annual economic growth rate over the previous five years—a sure sign of economic recovery by classic industrial measures—the total number unemployed continued to rise by more than one hundred thousand a year. Economists explained this with a model borrowed from physics. They claimed that just as reversing the forces applied to certain metals does not return those metals to their original state, so it is not possible to engineer a return to the "original" level of unemployment after years in which it has been well above its "natural" rate. Their conclusion was that high unemployment is self-perpetuating (Smith 1986). On the face of it they were wrong: Since April 2001, the total claiming benefit has been under one million, equivalently about 3 percent (National Statistics Office 2001). But it is hard to gauge what the error might mean. For one thing, the figures are not strictly comparable: crude totals obscure internal variation by industry, region, and gender;[1] and governments everywhere adjust the way unemployment is calculated so that the number of people on the register is reduced without altering the number actually out of work.[2] For another, not everyone who is out of a job is enumerated as unemployed; maybe the last job they had was too part time or too "informal" to be officially recognized as employment and they would have no right to unemployed status even if they wanted it. Or perhaps they expect the procedure of registering to bring too little advantage and/or too much hassle.

Equally, the totals may be exaggerated: some among the registered unemployed are economically very active. A minority may be double-dealing to cheat the system, but most do not register their work as employment because it matches neither their own nor the bureaucrats' definition of what employment should be (cf. Wadel 1979). Inevitably, women figure importantly in this category. It is instructive that the justification for being registered while working is substantially the same as the reason for not being registered when not working: in both cases the realities of economy and identity are outside the official system. The official categories are narrower than experience because the implications of "employed" or "unemployed" status depend on other things happening in people's lives.

All of this noted, still the good news is that Britain's unemployment rate is now the lowest it has been in twenty years. The bad news, however, according to a recent account, is that a number of employment-related problems have become worse over the same period (Dickens, Gregg, and Wadsworth 2001). The optimistic aggregate figure masks huge inequalities in the distribution of work—by area, by age, sex, and skill; and it "overlooks the unprecedented rate at which people have simply dropped out of the labour market entirely" (ibid., 11).

There are very different dropout categories. Most crucial is the degree to which people choose—or feel they choose—to be unemployed; what their options are; what they lose or gain by the absence of a job. In my view, the variation along these parameters can overshadow class difference entirely.

The article cited above is called "Non-working Classes: Britain's New Chronic Unemployed," and it documents the extreme plight of the 2.3 million men of working age (not counting students) who are economically inactive: "This figure is twice that for the registered male unemployed and 20 years ago was only 400,000. . . . Inflows into unemployment are now only a fraction above those in the late 1960s, but the duration of unemployment spells is more than double. . . . Those entering unemployment have a history of past unemployment." And most telling: "The bulk of unemployment falls on a minority of individuals . . . [and] by far the worst concentrations . . . are in our social housing estates" (ibid., 11–13). The combination leads the writers to consider the special deprivation of "workless households," the implications for child poverty, and the likelihood of continuing cycles of disadvantage.

These last points begin to take account of other things happening along with the absence of a job. It is in this holistic perspective that the disadvantaged may be compared to the relatively elite. If the former are the "chronic unemployed" and consistently vulnerable, the affliction of the latter (pursuing medical terminology) can be called "acute." Unemployment hits them suddenly, unexpectedly, maybe only once, but often with disastrous damage to present self-esteem and future well-being. The category includes highly skilled professional people whose work ultimately is controlled by the forces of globalization. It numbers the thousands made redundant by structural change, recession or—most recently—terrorism. Even before the New York Twin Towers disaster it was common to see press notices of jobs "axed" for want of profits or cheap labor. Since September 11, 2001, so many airlines have downsized that highly specialized pilots laid off by one company will not be able to find the same job with another.

   This is a very new circumstance. It used to be said that specialization at any level paid dividends in money, job security, and self-esteem. In this era the more narrowly specialized the job, the more vulnerable the worker on all three fronts. Here again, exactly as in reference to employment, public attention has shifted to the *social* shock waves of unemployment and its relation to the wider context of the one-time worker's life.

## Employment and Work

Official figures are quoted to indicate the numbers "out of work," but they actually represent people registered as being without a particular kind of employment. The inference is that work is the same as employment, that working is about having a job. And because the most measurable aspect of a job is the money it earns, discussions of joblessness, at least in the political arena, tend to proceed on the assumption that work is primarily about earning money. If that were the whole story, then the effect of unemployment would be confined to the pocket, which clearly it is not. Although some among the jobless do suffer terrible financial hardship, money is never the only loss. Even in welfare systems more generous than that of the United Kingdom, money payments cannot seem to cure the pain of unemployment. So what else is work about?

   Marie Jahoda's classic studies of unemployment have direct bearing on the answer (Jahoda, 1982; Jahoda, Lazarsfeld, and Zeisel 1972). Comparing the circumstances and welfare systems of recession in the 1930s and the 1980s, she identifies five sociopsychological effects of unemployment common to both. They make a useful agenda for discussion here. Thus, in the long term, people who have lost a job suffer also loss of *the structure of time*, the absence of *regular activity*, the reduction of *social contact*, the lack of participation in *collective purposes*, and the absence of an acceptable status and its consequences for *personal identity*. These five elements, in Jahoda's analysis, are common functions of employment—perhaps even of employment in mindless and dispiriting jobs. In the context of this chapter, Jahoda's inventory is doubly useful. By listing the things that people lack when they are unemployed, it indicates how unemployment affects the whole of livelihood; and because secure industrial employment, skilled or unskilled, is increasingly less available in the industrialized world, she also gives us a first-stage insight into serious shortages that may come in future.

But there is a familiar ring to this list that has nothing to do with unemployment, whether chronic or acute. It covers exactly the kinds of items that go out of joint in the lives of the overemployed—that is, the things that highly paid and high-status people are said to suffer during and because of their employment. Notice particularly the first and last. Shortages of time and personal identity are widely and specifically cited as symptoms of the so-called workaholic, and as reasons for people to give up lucrative and high-status jobs to become "rat-race refugees."[3]

Of course there are differences between unemployment and overemployment, but the similarities are instructive. Even with the advantages of public status and relative affluence, an overemployed chief executive may have no more control over his personal time and identity resources than an unemployed factory hand. Economic benefits, as I have said, are never more than half the story. Time and identity begin to fill out the whole.

## Time

In some cultures, at least in the performance of some tasks, no time cost is computed: time as such apparently has no value. The scope for using time as a measure of economic value as an alternative to money is, in any case, very limited (Belshaw 1954; Firth 1979), and even the use of time expenditure to evaluate precisely the things that money cannot buy has been disappointing (Brenner 1979). Time and money belong in different equations because they represent essentially different kinds of value. The real problem is that time is not a singular measurement. We know it is different when applied to history, to calendar and clock intervals, to the life cycle, or to the working day, but we have trouble putting the differences into words. Nor is the same measured quantity of time consistently valued, not even by the same person in the same culture. It is experienced as a dimension of quality, not quantity, and its value depends on other things happening, on other things that could be happening, and on things that have happened in the past or may happen in the future.

Thus, when people talk of having too much or too little time without specific reference to something like boiling an egg or catching a train, they are using the sense of time to describe the quality of experience. In this perspective time is equally a burden when not "filled," like an existing vessel, and when not "structured," as though the vessel were still to be constructed. When time goes too slowly, it must be "killed," although the real "tyranny" of it is in the speed of its passing. As qualities of experience, the goodness and the badness of time are not always distinct.

In industrial society there is commonly too much or too little of it—perhaps both at once: the two complaints refer to the same malaise. I have already suggested that some part of that malaise is caused by changes in the relation between time and work. Four aspects of the relationship are implicated. First, the time cost of work varies according to when it is done because it depends on what else the worker could have been doing. What is called "overtime" is paid at "time-and-a-half" or "double time" to reflect the fact that some parts of the daily, weekly, or annual cycles are "more social" and so more valuable than others. All industrialized countries find that some among the young are reluctant to take on jobs their elders consider appropriate because, in time terms, the opportunity costs of the employment are too high. These youngsters, like the rat-race refugees mentioned in the previous section, are finding "better things to do with time"—which is to say that the quality of time is "better" outside the available job than in it.

Second, the time it takes to do a given piece of work is affected by technology because tools extend or replace the energy and efficiency of the worker. An item of physical work done by hand "costs" so much time to complete, but when improved technology is brought to the same task, the input of time is reduced—indeed it is often the time "saved" that is the very criterion of improvement. The same is true of mental work assisted by computer, even after the time it takes to design, build, and program the machine is taken into account. In both cases human time and energy are replaced by nonhuman versions and some of the input of the human worker becomes redundant—whether because the productive task is changed or because control of the machines that now perform it requires different skills and passes into other hands.

Third, the control of time is crucial because the machine or the person who controls the timing of work also controls the worker. The power that bureaucrats and doctors wield is essentially the power to control their clients' time (Frankenburg 1988; Wadel 1979). At the very least, the power to delay another demonstrates a simple status difference. In more extreme circumstances, the control of a person's time is tantamount to control of that person's self.

Finally, the sense of time and the sense of self are not readily distinguished in experience. This follows directly on the last point and leads into the discussion of identity that follows. The bridge is built on Elliot Jaques (1982) separation of the sequential and the enduring dimensions of time. I depend here on one element of Jahoda's interpretation of his work: "Jaques' concept (of time) contains two dimensions of experience: the experience of succession, of earlier or later, before and after; and the experience of the enduring present, *the continuity of existence*" (Jahoda, 1988). The last phrase expresses—better, it accounts for—the effects of age on the time-self entity. Individual life is finite and each of us knows it. The further on in the life cycle, therefore, the sharper the experience of time as a scarce resource. And just as the continuity of time is or represents the continuity of self, so the fact of time "getting shorter" may be experienced as a progressive reduction of the scope of the self.

But chronological age is not the real issue. At any age, work that effectively fills the hours or structures the days will still be described as "a waste of time" if it feels like a diminution or a waste of the person. So how is it that the performance of even the most grueling task can sometimes be such a positive experience? Here, again, the wider concept of work is a key. Jaques (1982) describes the more enduring of the time dimensions as "intentional," suggesting it to be the force behind all those purposeful activities and involvements we experience as "good" work.

Confusion arises in industrial society to the extent that only work in the narrow sense of occupation is considered a proper focus of intentionality and purpose; work outside employment is officially invisible and widely undervalued. Anyone without an occupation tends equally to be undervalued: the old, the unemployed, and the housebound are assumed, even by themselves, to be without goals or purposes, and so, in these terms, without continuity. But cultural continuity has always been a proxy for personal continuity, and involvement in cultural and social purposes can focus intentionality just as well as a job. Indeed, to the extent that its value survives the individual lifespan and outlives the individual self (Kotre 1984), it provides more effectively for "the continuity of existence" than conventional formal employment can. People without occupational commitments are potentially no worse off than the employed in this dimension, although so far only the rat-race refugees seem to have realized it.

## Identity

Identity issues come up whenever the question "Who Am I?" is asked or answered. There is no answer to it because no one entirely identifies with any one feature of themselves. While there is no logical limit to the number of identity options open to ordinary individuals, or to the number of ways the question "Who Am I?" might be answered, popular reference to social identity in industrial society is dominated by three domains: local community or place, ethnic or family origin, and work in the narrow sense of occupation or employment. (It is in these arenas that the abstractions of race, nation, and class are played out). The three domains are integrated through personal experience and it is possible that the identity strength of each depends on the identity strength of the others—that is, more self-investment in work, less in the family; more local involvement, less ethnic consciousness (as Wallman et al. 1982); more of either of these, less social or psychological dependence on the job—and maybe, by extension, less pain in the event of job bereavement or unemployment.

In every case, a person can take the option of identifying with one domain by minimizing or denying his or her investment in others, and, logically at least, he or she can shift that identity investment from one domain to the other according to the opportunities and constraints of circumstance. The shift is probably easiest in complex industrial society where the domains of life are curiously discrete, but it is not always without cost. Each domain needs attention—occupational status is not ascribed, it must be achieved; marriage must be worked at; political concern should be demonstrated, and so forth—and each is somehow vital to the composite identity structure of the individual. Too narrow a focus of time or self, therefore, creates other problems. Where overidentification with one domain occurs it is diagnosed as pathology. The workaholics referred to earlier are, by definition, too closely identified with the domain of their employment. In popular as well as clinical expectation, they are, therefore, bound to be neglecting other obligations and are probably suffering from stress. The healthy balance would seem to be spread of identity—of time and the self—across all of livelihood so that each domain gets and gives its due.

## Versions of Unemployment

Financial implications apart, the experience of employment and unemployment is governed by the patterns of time and identity investment that each job or no-job situation entails. The members of an occupational group are not entirely alike in any respect, and there are important comparisons to be made among individuals whose objective circumstances are similar (as Fagin and Little 1984; Marsden and Duff 1975; Wallman 1984). But there are also useful contrasts to be drawn at the level of occupation. They are demonstrated in the series of figures that follow.

The implications of the previous section are sketched in figure 1. In ideal or "best-case" circumstances, an individual's time and identity resources are diffused across the three most vital domains of livelihood—namely, occupation, domestic group, and local community (Wallman 1996). If one of those domains falls away, the self who was invested in it is readily translated into another domain. When, for example, a person becomes unemployed, the time and identity previously spent on occupation can be redistributed across family or local community interests. The

**Figure 1**
**"Best Case": Time and Identity Diffused Across Livelihood**

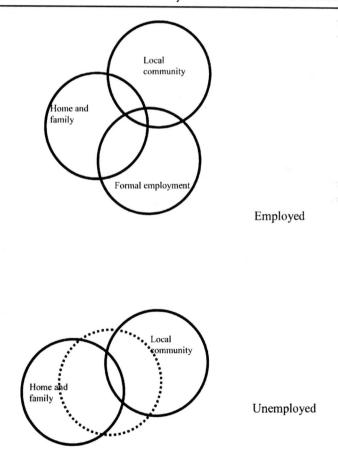

shift is feasible because this individual is already rooted in the other domains; and the reinvestment is safe because the other domains are sufficiently distinct from occupation to be unaffected by the job loss as such.

Figures 2 and 3 by contrast illustrate two "worst-case" examples. Figure 2 shows first the pattern of time and identity investment in mining, dockworking, and single industry/Marienthal-type communities, and then the disaster brought about by the collapse of the industry concerned. The crucial points in this case are that the occupational domain is/has been dominated by one industry and some combination of culture, infrastructure, and the technology of that industry has caused the three domains to be closely overlaid. In traditional docklands for example, men who worked together lived as neighbors within walking distance of their employment, and even the social life of their wives was focused around

**Figure 2**
**"Worst Case": Domains Overlaid—Miners, Dockers,**
**Marienthal-Type Communities**

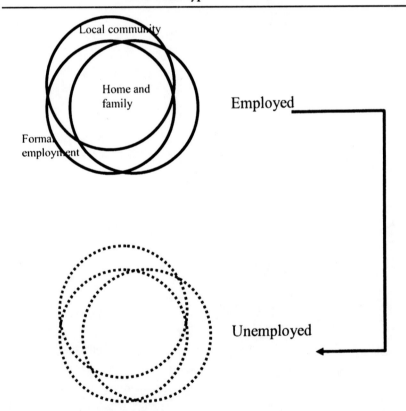

the concerns of the docks. The effect of generations of this pattern was to tie dockers to each other by employment, locality, and kinship, whether directly as brothers and cousins, or indirectly through the links of their wives and children, and to create a tightly bounded, locally distinct, and fiercely conservative occupational group. In these circumstances, the collapse of the employment base is experienced as the destruction of community and continuity at a blow.

Figure 3 is similar but different. While figure 2 shows what can happen when a community is dominated by one industry, figure 3 shows

**Figure 3**
**"Worst Case": The Self Invested in Only One Domain**

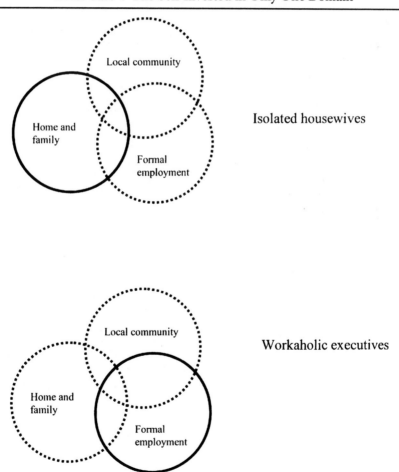

individuals monopolized by a single domain. By so doing it answers the riddle of the subtitle to this chapter. Stereotypical housewives are "only" involved in family matters; workaholic chief executives are obsessed by their jobs—each at the cost of neglecting other domains. Deprived of the monopoly domain—the housewife when her children grow up and leave home, the executive when illness or redundancy lays him off— each will have lost the locus of time and identity that had underpinned the sense of self.

## The Work of Livelihood

Everyone knows that work is never just a matter of finding shelter, trans- acting money, and preparing food to put on the table or exchange in the marketplace. The tasks of meeting obligations and securing identity, sta- tus, and structure are as fundamental to livelihood as bread and shelter.

By the most minimal definition, work is a goal-oriented activity in- volving the expenditure of energy and with it some "sacrifice of comfort and leisure" (Firth 1979, 192). The goals and purposes of activities that are experienced as work are fueled by necessity—moral or economic or both (Godelier 1972, 266; Schwimmer 1979). The goals may be incom- patible: it is normal to want to be a good mother but still be a free woman (as Gullestad 1984); to be publicly recognized and yet privately anony- mous. Further, the values of different kinds of work may be contradic- tory: actions that are optimally moral are rarely optimally economic (and vice versa), and shortages of one kind of resource are not compensated by abundance of another. Despite the durability of the old adage, for ex- ample, time is not money. We speak of them as mutually convertible— money "buys" time, time "costs" money—but they remain quite different kinds of resources.

Because people in employment and out of employment may be frus- trated by similar contradictions, shortages, and inflexibilities, they may suffer a similar malaise. The experience of having or of not having a job in the formal economy is governed by other things happening in the life of the person employed or unemployed. Both employment and unem- ployment are elements in a system of livelihood, and neither can be un- derstood outside the whole. We need a model that puts the specifics of time and identity in modern society into a more general context.

Suppose we define work as the production and management of all the resources necessary to livelihood; and that, for present purposes, we assume those necessary resources to be six (Wallman 1984). The quan- tifiable necessities are represented (in figure 4), as they always have been, by *land, labor,* and *capital,* but they are complemented here by *time, information,* and *identity,* representing necessities that are equally vital but much less measurable. Because livelihood is a system, the scope of the whole is constrained by each of its separate parts. And because the viability of any system is limited by the availability of the least available resource, the whole of livelihood will be jeopardized by mismanagement or shortages in any one of the six domains. Making the same point in more humanistic terms, a contemporary essayist writes, "Our attention attaches to that which is not there" (Rosenblatt 1985). In effect it is the things we lack that we want, not those that we have in abundance.

The six resources can be valued in the same variety of ways and they are, in the right conditions, interchangeable. But in other respects the two sets of three remain distinct. Land, labor, and capital-type resources are not only material, they are structural. They provide the framework for action by deciding which options are available in a given setting. Time, identity, and information-type resources have more to do with organization. It is these which limit the conditions of possibility within the objective structure (as Bourdieu 1977). In so doing they account not only for the capability of the structure itself (Wallman 1997), but also for who does better within the constraints of a single environment—who finds the opportunities, who solves the problems, and who takes best advantage of the options available (see further Wallman 2001).

**Figure 4**
**The Whole of Livelihood**

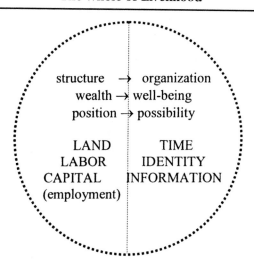

The narrow definition of work as employment in paid jobs of particular kinds takes in only the material/structural half of the picture (the left-hand side of figure 4). The wider concept covers the whole of livelihood and takes the nonmaterial qualities of life into equal account. It is the narrow version, like too narrow a focus of time and identity, that will be experienced as a burden or diagnosed as pathology (figures 2 and 3). On the other hand, wherever "good" work is at issue (as, eponymously, Schumacher 1980), it applies to circumstances in which energy and effort are widely invested across the separate domains of livelihood (figure 1). Paradoxically, the "better," in this sense, that the job has been, the easier will be the experience of unemployment when the job goes (see further Fagin and Little 1984).

## Changes in the Meaning of Work

This model of the work of livelihood requires only that the nonmaterial/organizing resources be given as much weight as the material/structural kind, but writers in various disciplines have implied that their prior importance is a characteristic of advanced industrial society. It is no surprise therefore to find that time and identity have become the focus of contemporary concern. Scholars and nonscholars alike are observing the limitation of the least available resource in operation. Housing, services, and money resources are not scarce in industrial welfare states in the way they too often are in nonindustrial settings. In the former, there is no overall shortage: the well-being of individuals or communities is limited more importantly by access to information and the control of time and identity than by any poverty of the industrial system. It is not a coincidence that it was Big Brother's total control of information, time, and identity that enslaved industrial man in George Orwell's vision of 1984.

## Notes

This chapter is adapted and updated from one appearing in a Festschrift for André J. F. Kobben, which appeared in *Wetenschaap en Partijtigheid* [Science and Partiality], ed. Frank Bovenkerk, Frank Buijs, and Henk Tromp (Assen, Ger.: Van Gorcum, 1990), 499–510.

1. In 1986, the 15.5 million European Economic Community total "concealed" a crucial drop in the number of men and an increase in the number of women registered as unemployed (*Le Figaro*, 25 July).

2. For example, the 1986 figure for Britain was "the sixteenth adjustment to date" (*The Economist*, 26 July).

3. As I prepare this piece, BBC Radio 4 reports a survey of British general practitioners in which one-quarter are so "profoundly dissatisfied" with conditions of work that they plan early retirement and/or a change of job.

# References

Belshaw, C. 1954. *Changing Melanesia: Social economics of culture contact.* Melbourne, Australia: Oxford University Press.

Bourdieu, P. 1977. *Outline of a theory of practice.* Studies in Social Anthropology. Cambridge: Cambridge University Press.

Brenner, Y. S. 1979. *Looking into the seeds of time.* Assen, Ger.: Van Gorcum.

Dickens, R., P. Gregg, and J. Wadsworth. 2001. Non-working classes: Britain's new chronic unemployed. *CentrePiece* 6(2): 10–19.

Fagin, L., and M. Little. 1984. *The forsaken families.* Harmondsworth, Eng.: Penguin.

Firth, R. 1979. Work and value: Reflections on ideas of Karl Marx. In *Social Anthology of Work*, edited by S. Wallman, Association of Social Anthropologists Monograph No. 19. London: Academic Press.

Frankenburg, R. 1988. "Your time or mine?"—An anthropological view of the tragic temporal contradictions of biomedical practice." In *The rhythms of society*, edited by M. Young and T. Schuller. London: Routledge.

Godelier, M. 1972. *Rationality and irrationality in economics.* London: New Left Books.

Gullestad, M. 1984. *Kitchen table society.* Bergen, Ger.: Universitetsforlaget.

Jahoda, M. 1982. *Employment and unemployment.* Cambridge: Cambridge University Press.

———. 1988. Time: A social psychological perspective. In *The rythms of society*, edited by M. Young and T. Schuller. London: Routledge.

Jahoda, M, P. Lazarsfeld, and H. Zeisel. 1972. *Marienthal: The sociography of an unemployed community.* London: Tavistock.

Jaques, E. 1982. *The forms of time.* London: Heineman.

Kotre, J. 1984. *Outliving the Self.* Baltimore: Johns Hopkins University Press.

Marsden, D., and E. Duff. 1975. *Workless: Some unemployed men and their families.* Harmondsworth, Eng.: Penguin.

National Statistics Office. 2001. *Claimant count for Great Britain, January 1986–August 2001.* London: Labour Market Statistics Helpline.

Rosenblatt, H. 1985. Essay. *Time*, 14 January.

Schumacher, E. E. 1980. *Good work*. London: Abacus.

Schwimmer, E. 1979. The self and the product: Concepts of work in comparative perspective. In *Social anthology of work*, edited by S. Wallman. Association of Social Anthropologists Monograph No. 19. London: Academic Press.

Smith, D. 1986. Economic briefing: Why high unemployment is selfperpetuating. *The Times* (London), 24 July.

Wadel, C. 1979. The hidden work of every life. In *Social anthology of work*, edited by S. Wallman. Association of Social Anthropologists Monograph No. 19. London: Academic Press.

Wallman, S. 1977. Introduction. In *Perceptions of development*, edited by S. Wallman. Cambridge: Cambridge University Press.

———. 1984. *Eight London households*. London: Tavistock.

———. 1996. Ethnicity, work, and localism: Narratives of difference in London and Kampala. *Ethnic and Racial Studies* 19(1): 1–28.

———. 1997. Appropriate anthropology and the risky inspiration of "capability" Brown: Representations of what, by whom, and to what end? In *After writing culture: Epistemology and praxis in contemporary anthropology*, edited by A. James, J. Hockey, and A. Dawson. Association of Social Anthropologists Monograph No. 34. London: Routledge.

———. 2001. Global threats, local options, and personal risk: Dimensions of migrant sex work in European cities. *Journal of Health, Risk, and Society* 3(1): 75–87.

Wallman, S., with I. H. Buchanan, Y. Dhooge, J. I. Gershuny, B. A. Kosmin, and M. Wann. 1982. *Living in South London: Perspectives on Battersea 1871–1981*. London: Gower.

# 2

# Secret Enterprise

*Market Activities among London Sex Workers*

Sophie Day

> I just want to do the work I know the best that gives me the most
> money, the most autonomy and the most mobility. I am a prostitute.
>
> —Gail Pheterson, *The Prostitution Prism*

## Introduction

In a collection of chapters about work in Europe, it is important first to
clarify different perspectives on the status of prostitution.[1] Nonprosti-
tutes have great difficulty in considering prostitution a job and the
stigma attached to the occupation makes this a very particular form of
work. Sex workers themselves value what they do in contrast to wage
labor and poorly paid service jobs, the great majority having had some
experience of formal work that paid little and was humiliating, boring,
and time-consuming. A single woman's career may include a bewilder-
ing array of jobs before, during, and after prostitution. Accordingly, the
job has to be situated in the context of the life course as well as a
chronological time frame.

   I have conducted long-term research with sex workers in London
since 1986, including two main periods of fieldwork and interviews, first
in the late 1980s and again in the late 1990s. My anthropological research was part of a larger collaborative project with a clinical epidemiologist based in a clinic for sexual health and in the locality where
women worked, lived, or came into contact with the criminal justice
system. Research led to the development of clinical and nonclinical

services, including a drop-in and advice center established in 1991, known as the "Praed Street Project."[2] During these fifteen years (1986–2001), there have been significant developments in the London sex industry leading to greater diversity in the workforce, which now includes more women from other countries, particularly the Newly Independent States and countries of central and eastern Europe. Today, some sex workers appear to work for shorter periods or in combination with other jobs in conditions of increasing insecurity and with less access to welfare services. In general and for the majority, work has become more precarious. But, in this chapter, I focus on women I knew in the late 1980s, predominantly white and British, who I have been able to meet again or learn something about in the late 1990s. These women have enjoyed certain advantages, both because they have been in the industry for longer and because they have privileged access to welfare and citizenship as "locals." Some of these women have done well; some have failed so far to realize their dreams or goals. Some still work in the sex industry; others have left. The group of women we have followed up on over the years is diverse and heterogeneous just like the industry itself, and I focus only on a handful of women in this chapter so as to explore their success over a relatively long period in a precarious and insecure industry. These are women who have left "work" behind for a period of years as understood in the terms of formal employment relations with relatively fixed work routines and strong hierarchical relationships. They do not consider prostitution a temporary interlude in their working careers, as many do, and have no intentions of "reintegrating" themselves in the mainstream.[3] Such sex workers typify the flexibility that Emily Martin (1994) attributes to contemporary work requirements, which is a major theme of the current collection. These women are highly mobile, socially and geographically; they are also very discreet, few people know what they do for a living.[4]

I base this chapter on research discussions that took place in 2001 among a few sex workers with long experience in the industry. In the next section, the major issues in sex work that these women discussed are presented, ranging from stigma to criminality and economic insecurity. Subsequently, I focus on regular clients, who visit the same sex worker repeatedly, and argue that these women had built their successes largely through relationships with regular clients. Some women cultivate such relationships while others avoid them. I argue that this contrast indicates differences in women's views of work and characterize two of the most important "models" of the market.[5] One of these models corresponds to views of a virtually disembodied, impersonal rationality thought to be so important in Western economies (see, for example, Schneider 1980, for one anthropological account of the contrast between work and kinship).

Anthropologists have argued that this model should not be taken for granted either for comparative purposes, in researching non-Western economies, nor as a tool for ethnographic research in Western contexts (see, for example, Kahn 1997). I hope to contribute to these debates by describing how views of impersonal rationality at work are located in everyday conversations and activities, and by contrasting them with a second model of a far more personal relationship to the market, on which I focus. Although one and perhaps both models may be very familiar, the specificities of the sex industry also make them look less obvious because the two models that I shall outline constitute a form of political opposition to the devastating legal and social penalties attached to sex work in London. In this way, the models both resemble and contrast with those in other occupations. As a number of anthropologists have argued, research at home must situate "our" practices and beliefs more effectively in both historical and comparative terms. For example, "We need to anthropologise the West: show how exotic its constitution of reality has been; emphasise those domains most taken for granted as universal . . . ; make them seem as historically peculiar as possible" (Rabinow 1986, 241). In what follows, I deal exclusively with sex work and I focus on just one aspect, namely, relationships with regular clients, but I hope that this specific case may illuminate more general concerns.

As these few comments show, I use the term *work* in two senses, both as an overall gloss for income generation and more specifically as an exchange of wages for labor and services. While prostitutes generally said they worked in the first sense, they commonly contrasted waged work in the second sense with the business that they themselves conducted. On the whole, waged work was devalued in comparison with business.

# The Research Discussions: Advantages and Disadvantages of the Work

In 2001, we held research discussions about the sex industry, specifically the changes in women's lives at the end of the twentieth century. Participants were women we had known over a period of years, who had previously contributed to our research.[6] As these were "semipublic" accounts (in which formal consent was obtained for research purposes) in which issues were clarified relatively explicitly and reflexively, they provide an appropriate introduction to sex worker views of clients, the law, and the state more generally. They illustrate the dangers and risks of the work as well as its advantages, and the particular benefits of self-employment in the informal economy.

## Using Money

In one discussion, four women (A, B, C, and D) talked about the process
of earning and saving from the perspective of unusual success; all four
earned more than enough to live on, owned property and, in one case,
supported a family. As C noted, "[Y]ou have to do everything, more or
less, if not actually illegally, at least in the grey area." She had obtained a
mortgage and references from a second, legal job in order to acquire her
property.[7]

B:     The point is, I know a lot of girls who earn a lot of money but
       because they don't have the ability to bring it into the main-
       stream, one of the reasons they end up at the age of forty or
       whatever, and they have spent all the money, because they
       don't know how to put it into . . .

D:     Because there's nowhere to put it.

C:     And you want to do something with it. And it hasn't all gone
       on drugs. It's gone on stuff like, they want a nice life. But I'm
       sure if there was a way of putting it into a property. They just
       keep saying to me, how can you do that? The point is because
       my accountant is dodgy, he'll do it for one person, but he's
       not going to do it for fifteen. . . .

D:     How do you do it without declaring it? It really has to go on
       record if you're going to take advantage of good banking
       systems.

A:     Everyone is doing cash. . . .

    In another research discussion, A explained to K how to buy prop-
erty with a slightly more expensive nonstatus mortgage commonly taken
out by the self-employed and she gave K the number of her solicitor.

A:     . . . I bought my first [house] twenty years ago, . . . but I did it
       slightly differently then. They didn't ask for wage slips and
       stuff and I got this guy to say, "yes, she works for me" and I
       typed my own letter that said, "yes, she works for us and she's
       been working here for no matter how long and she earns x
       amount of pounds per week." And we sent it off and they said
       fine. But I've recently bought another one, I completed in
       November, and that was a whole different kettle of fish [situa-

tion]. I had to lie and say I was working as a god knows whatever and I was earning god knows whatever and how long had
I been there, I had been there for five and a half years. And
that guy had another friend and, for the sake of £100, if they
ever ring him up, he will say, "yes, its all true, everything
you've got on there is true," and it went through. But I am
paying 1 percent more.

K was advised to take her money home to another country in cash every
year and bring it back to the United Kingdom in the form of a check so
that it would be easier to raise a mortgage.

I have argued that it is easier to earn your money than to use it productively in the London sex industry (Day 1994). The women in these research groups noted in passing that sex workers might spend a lot on
nice things or even drugs, but it was the law fundamentally that made it
hard to save and invest. Some women insist on earning in cash; some
women avoid banks. Many do not know how to obtain the services of professionals such as accountants to launder their earnings. Therefore, sex
workers can end up with nothing to show for years of work.

### Record Keeping

A complained,

In so many ways we have to duck and dive because we are not supposed to exist. Because we're not supposed to be doing what we
are doing, so we have to lie low in so many respects. The thing that
really annoys me now that I am older and so much more experienced at it—I just admit it and I don't give a damn what people
say—but . . . you walk into a pub, you get on an aeroplane whatever, and the first thing someone asks you is, what's your name and
what do you do?

I mean you two [the facilitators] can stand up proud and say
I'm a—whatever. I have to look at this person and think, "Oh my
god, are they going to shout and scream and say, Oh my god, not a
hooker?" And then everyone knows. Or are they going to think, oh
good, we can get a freebie [sex for free] here or what? Or, if it's a
woman, is she going to think, she's obviously after my husband. You
know, in that split second, you have to look at that person and judge
can they handle it? And that's wrong. I am quite proud of what I do.

D was particularly concerned about her children and B noted sympathetically how vulnerable mothers were to state interference. C agreed but emphasized that children were not the only issue. She had another profession and, if it were known that she was a prostitute, she would be unable to return to this work.

A changed her name regularly, "for everywhere that I have used in the past for advertising I have used a different name. So as soon as they call up and ask for Martha I know exactly where they are calling from. . . . Just by that first hello, my brain starts ticking and I know how much, roughly how long ago it was, because I might have changed names a few times since then."

> D:　　The name that's on my birth certificate is not the name on my fingerprints. It's a totally different name. My first ever conviction was a totally different [that is, yet another] name.

B reflected on this aspect of their conversation: "Do you find that a lot of women in this business are very resourceful? In the way you make your life fit together? And the strategies you come up with and the details you have to remember to tell people. To tell your story right. There's just so much going on in this job."

This sense of "ducking and diving," multiple identities and secrets is central to sex work in London. Women have to attach their work to distinctive identities in order to minimize state interference and many preferred to keep their work separate from the rest of their lives to minimize the stigma as well. Criminalization and stigma led women to distance work from their sense of self and to invest it with distinctive rationalities and behaviors (as I shall discuss further in the section "Consequences of Cultivating Regular Clients"). Yet, in this conversation, a contrasting reaction can be glimpsed as well. B's reflections suggest that the necessity for pretense and constant inventiveness also made women resourceful and skilled in handling different stories and multiple threads to their lives. The positive and negative aspects of informal and illegal work were a constant topic of conversation in these research discussions and more informal conversations at the project drop-in center alongside assessments of the most profitable forms of work.

### Earning Money

The London sex industry is classified and ranked largely in terms of the prices that clients are charged and the degree of privacy. Secondary literature suggests that street workers occupy the bottom rungs of a hierarchy while those who work with personally selected clients in the privacy of their own homes or in hotel rooms occupy the top rungs. Rank is constructed in terms of the prices charged each client, state interference, and also the relative amount of financial and social capital needed to work in different ways, which is sometimes represented in terms of the women's own social status. This hierarchy is extremely misleading to an understanding of the everyday conduct of sex work.

The advantages and disadvantages to any form of sex work change over time with fluctuations in the money supply, new technologies such as the mobile phone and the Internet, different patterns of law enforcement, and client preferences and it is never clear where the best conditions are to be found. Participants in the research discussions had worked in many ways, including apparently low- and high-status work. In the past, they had struggled to find clients, to expand their business, and to make their money. While the secondary literature suggests that money is available in some types of prostitution and not others, the women I knew found no recipe for tapping into these sources of wealth, and their practices sometimes changed on a daily basis (Day 1994). No one knew which sector was most profitable, nor who would succeed and who would fail. Since money is so elusive in the short term, concepts of success or failure require a longer-term analysis. Over time, experiences varied and the women to whom I have referred occupied the successful end of the spectrum where conversations were more likely to concern processes for turning pots of money to new ends and milking the market than the everyday business of making ends meet and avoiding the state. As I have noted, these women had done well: they earned an income from property as well as sex work, planned pensions and other investments. Two, both in their early forties, had very little financial need to work at all and only saw clients when they wanted to. Even though none felt the same pressures to make their money as they had in the past, they nonetheless continued to play the market and search out new ways of making money.

### Clients

Clients provided the last major topic of discussion that I shall summarize in this background section. It was hard to minimise exposure to violent or difficult men and, in the first research discussion, C said, "[O]ne of the reasons I am careful about saying what type of work I do, is that, you know, like prostitute, there are some people who think that gives them a license to murder you, or to stalk you or to treat you badly." She objected to the term *whore*: "It's what guys say before they slice, before they hit you. It's the, you've put in the groundwork for saying you can treat this person as less than a human being."

B explained how the stress of this disregard had led her to stop working by telephone and move to the Internet, where men thought and checked what they wrote before they sent their messages. She refused to do "free telephone sex" with "time wasters." C agreed about the need to be in charge and in control: "The more you feel in control and—because control for me relates to safety—the more safe you feel. To me the stress is about safety. It's not about the stress of working hard. I don't really consider it hard work. For me, it's not the stress of doing something I don't want to do. The thing always is the safety."

D conveyed similar concerns as she explained why she preferred working from her car,

> It's just something you develop over the years. You know. I feel much safer in my car, knowing I'm there, I'm driving the car, rather than getting into someone else's car and being driven to wherever you're going to go, or stood on a street corner, being totally vulnerable to the outside world. At least in my little car, it's my little space. . . . You can look at somebody. I can't describe what it is but you could just look at somebody and . . . you could turn round and say, "OK I'll chat him" and another one, you could turn round and say, "Oh no, I'm not touching that."

In discussing safety with strangers, these women emphasized their experience and intuition, the need to make rapid assessments and to enforce certain kinds of behavior. Safety and earnings are seen to derive from prostitutes' skill and mastery of the environment. Moreover, clients and the market more generally are represented as though they were positively built through these activities. It is not always easy to create these sources of money or to make them observe the appropriate norms. For example, clients refused to pay the going rates,

A:   They just don't think. Everything in life goes up except hookers. And that baffles me. Why?

D:   Basic disrespect—they [clients] take you for granted.

If new clients posed a risk, regulars could prove more taxing. B talked of clients' narcissism: "That's one of the worst parts of the mental health in this work, their own narcissism—their incredible self-involvement. It's one

of the most wearing things about this job. They are in love with themselves."
Long lists emerged about the stress caused by men who fell in love with you
and treated you as though you were a girlfriend, who became obsessed and
stalked you, who might hit you when they could not have an erection, who
treated you as friends and told you who had died, whose wife had fallen ill,
and all the details of their daily life. C, for example, complained of being
taken for granted:

> I don't mind a bit of discussion. This guy I've been seeing about ten
> years goes to the sideboard, runs his hand in the dust and goes, "my
> God, the housekeeping isn't up to standard." "I'm not your . . .
> wife." What does he think he is? This other guy, he's Italian, we go to
> a restaurant and he starts kicking me under the table because I am
> talking to the waiter and I suddenly [lose my temper] outside. I said,
> "Don't you ever . . . tell me who I can or cannot talk to." And he just
> said, "[M]y wife doesn't talk to me like that." "I'm not your . . . wife."
> Jealous!

Everyone spoke at once. The worst was:

A:  They start thinking they are in love with you and you should
    be like a girlfriend and that you should give it for free. And
    they think they can call you up and chat about the weather
    and that their cat's died.

C:  [He even] sat down with a calculator and . . . worked out how
    much money [he had] spent on me.

B:  Or they don't have to behave well.

D:  That's why some women don't want regulars.

Regular clients were difficult but they had provided three of the
four women in this discussion with regular sums of money through
which they met expenses and, more significantly, had provided unexpected windfalls which meant that two of the three did not really need
to work. B had bought her first house through a client and, later, discussing the difficulties they faced with regulars, C reminded her, "What
I am saying is that a lot of people if they didn't have a client helping
them or someone helping them . . . you got a lucky break that's what I
am saying." D, by contrast, had not spoken about regular clients. Perhaps her comment, "that's why some women don't want regulars," referred to her own preferences. Like other women, she may have found

them too much effort to be worth the gamble of some extraordinary possible fortune.

Although I have not summarized all that was said in these research discussions,[8] it can be seen that regular clients offer a particular means of dealing with a precarious and dangerous job. These men, it is hoped, will yield some sort of living (and perhaps too the longed-for windfalls) and prove trustworthy as well. In the next section, I look at regular clients in greater detail, bearing in mind the contrast between D and the other three women I have noted.

## Regulars: Security, Lucky Breaks, and Trouble

Regular clients are important to many sex workers in all sectors of the London industry. They provide women with some financial stability and security through regular payments and sometimes loans that tide women over through bad times. They pose less of a risk to women's physical safety than strangers. They provide business opportunities by introducing sex workers to new clients and also helping them diversify into other activities. For example, lawyers, accountants, doctors, and other professionals provide services that their colleagues avoid because of the questionable status of sex work. Sometimes, regular clients provide new markets in which they become not only clients of sex workers but also of sales, rental services, or services of other kinds such as nursing. Women I knew had received help from clients in establishing enterprises ranging from small-scale freelance work, selling goods for example, to large ventures backed by significant amounts of capital drawn from regulars and their contacts, such as West End clubs. Above all, regulars might yield substantial additional sums enabling women to move on at last: to buy property, attend college, and, commonly, leave the business altogether. As C said, a regular provides that "lucky break."[9]

Men appeared to visit the same woman repeatedly for different reasons. Some sought specialist services from a particular woman while others sought introductions to a wider network of colleagues. Some sought endless innovation in the services sold, often glossed in terms of fantasy. Others looked for domesticity and for a relationship that mimicked conventional marriage. Interviewing clients during the earlier period of fieldwork (Day et al. 1993), I was struck by one man's account of a sex worker he had visited for fifteen years in a flat that they had established: "We're old friends." He described how they had enjoyed tea and toast together that morning: "Well, we have become friends and we talk on the phone now and again, so she is a friend as well as I am a client." They gave each other Christmas presents.

The most regular of regular clients are sometimes known as "sugar daddies." The term conjures up a complicated situation for sex workers where neither partner is altogether clear of their status. In theory, the sugar daddy is a man who does not know of his partner's business and expects to be treated as a friend or quasi husband. Therefore, the sex worker acts as though she were a girlfriend while considering the relationship in purely instrumental terms. This state of affairs can cause acute difficulties in earning money and ensuring an appropriate emotional and physical distance. It is difficult to guard against the penetration of substances, such as semen, at work or to connect the working persona to a particular look and biography that can be remembered from one visit to the next. Such men may pay erratically, through gifts rather than cash, and they may refuse to use condoms. They may introduce their "girlfriend" to their families, take her on holiday, and escort her to dinner, all of which takes so much time that the sex worker may lose money overall because she is unavailable for other work. While regulars hold the promise of substantial subsidies, they may also fail to yield any profit at all.

Different skills are cultivated in the management of regular, as compared to new, clients. Business is personalized and men are singled out for special and favored treatment in a performance requiring extensive dissimulation, captured in a felicitous phrase, "the managed heart," by Arlie Hochschild (1983) in describing comparable work among air hostesses. In the first research conversation cited, the four women talked about "faking": they never knew whether the continual faking would be worth the effort as some regulars turned out all right and others did not, and they could only ever know after the fact which was which. With sugar daddies, neither partner knows who is really faking. Should a regular make a sex worker look like a girlfriend, is it not also possible that he is acting a part? In acting a part, does he succeed in getting his sex cheap or for free, and who then is in charge? Moreover, faking is dangerous for it may lead to a "true" passion. Several sex workers I have known became close friends with or lovers of their clients and several subsequently had a falling out with these men.[10] I illustrate the difficulties by reference to one of the participants in the 2001 research groups, who I call Sarah.

In the later 1980s, Sarah planned to work for another two years, keeping open her options for a day job. She would return to secretarial work and start a family. She was working for particular targets, namely, a car and a house. Sex work was a temporary and somewhat unpleasant in-

terlude in her life. During several meetings in 1990, Sarah came to talk of
work differently. She talked especially of a single man, a sugar daddy
who, she said, was no longer a client. We had talked of him before but it
transpired that he had not been a client for a year; he had fallen in love
with Sarah and promised to leave his wife. As a client, he had been so
worried about AIDS that he hardly had sex; he paid the best and all "the
girls" wanted to see him. Sarah did not want to live with him but she had
obviously become involved in a very different relationship.

They had an argument, and he started to see other prostitutes because, he said, she was still working; "he says it's only fair," but "it's difficult not to work when I know he is at home with his wife and children.
[It's] not the money or anything, [I] don't know what else to do. He says
he'll help me set up in business. But, what would you[11] do if you suddenly
stopped what you were doing?" Sarah retaliated with what she considered
the worst possible insult for this man, throwing all his money back with
the comment, "If that's all you've got to give." She was less sure now
whether he was a client or a boyfriend. As a client, she should have kept
his money. It would have made good business sense to accept his offers of
help and to set up some enterprise. As a boyfriend, she had new jeal-
ousies and problems of demarcation to resolve: her friend still lived with
his wife and yet attempted to take over Sarah's life and to shame her out
of prostitution. She resented her friend's double standard.

Sarah cast this relationship in both positive and negative terms during an interview in 2000, when I heard what had happened subsequently.
It seemed that this man had pursued Sarah vigorously when she moved
abroad. On her return, he matched her income and persuaded her away
from prostitution. They quarreled, made up, and she stopped the phone
line that she used for work. For three weeks, she said, she saw him alone
at her own flat. Then she panicked. He was seventeen years older than
she was, "and instead of going to the local disco and getting [drunk] like
all my [friends], I was having to go to Claridges [a smart hotel] in my little Chanel suit and watch my [manners] and I was like, I can't bear this,
I travelled the world and did all that." Sarah said that she could not stop
the phone ringing: "A lot of my then clients were friends and the guys
who took me out for dinner, for lunch, for gambling were fun, they
would come round and bring a bottle of champagne and we would have
a laugh, and I would miss all that, so I couldn't stop and a couple of times
over the course of the years I was with him, he found out and I said, "OK,
I will stop" [but] I never did, it got a little less but it never stopped."

Sarah's friend/client left his wife and lost his money; "he squan-
dered his; he flunked it. That's his problem but I saved mine, and people
used to say [I was] an old miser but thank god . . . and because of that, I

have built on it." The threat of bankruptcy led this man and his wife to live together once more, and Sarah has since lent him money. They are still friends of a sort.

Sarah spent a total of nine years with her friend/client and, for a while, this man approximated the ideal. He was wealthy, generous, and rarely around. It takes enormous luck and skill to find and keep such a man, but examples spanning the research period as a whole indicate that many women did in fact bring the ideal to life. As Sarah's and other histories suggest, relationships often soured after a while. Sometimes regulars lost interest or stopped yielding riches; sometimes the difficulties of combining business and sentiment proved intractable. As noted, some women avoided regular clients and Sarah's history suggests why. While these men sustained sex workers and their businesses, they also subverted working personae and undermined professional practice and, often, profits. Some women found it much harder to work with regulars than with new clients because of the acting or faking where you had to pretend, at least minimally, to like your customer while, with new clients, sex could remain impersonal, quick, and distant.

In summary, regular clients may provide a stable income, professional advice, and business introductions; they may also bankroll women and create apparent mistresses, kept women, and wives out of what were initially commercial contacts. In this account, I have focused on a particular type of regular, sometimes described as a sugar daddy, who provides enough support over time to enable a woman to establish herself successfully inside and outside the sex industry. Some women such as Sarah have not had to worry about money since. The attention required by these men has further implications that I explore in the next section.

## Consequences of Cultivating Regular Clients

Regulars could rarely be confined to strictly demarcated times and places of work. But the fostering of carefully selected relationships, luck, a good sense of timing, and discernment can all make the difference between good and bad business and, at the extreme, wealth and poverty. The cultivation of regular clients typifies one approach to sex work, which I call life "on the game." A few women, D perhaps among them, sustained sharp distinctions between work and the rest of life and more often expressed contrasting attitudes to the market, which I call "simply working." D seems to belong to a small minority who not only avoided regular clients but also continued to work in the sex industry and indeed to flourish.[12]

Early in this research, I came to associate representations of work with a particular rhetoric: work was simply work, there was nothing else to say about it. In fact, over hours of discussion, it transpired that research participants had a lot to say about their work in explicit opposition to claims that prostitution is morally wrong. These women insisted that what they did was legitimate, and involved the use of a public and alienable aspect of their persons comparable to all sorts of other uses of the body in the workplace. This stance suggests that prostitutes are all too familiar with popular rhetoric, where the status of sex work is constantly questioned. Media images, childhood memories, academic and official reports, and other people seem to assume that sex should not be sold; it belongs to the "private" person. To sell sex, it seems, is to give your inner self away to the lesser domain of the market; you become merely a "public woman" (a common epithet for prostitutes). To sell sex is to confound the separation between a public realm of work and the private realm of socially significant relationships, often in the family or the home. In this view, the realm of the market is contaminated by women who live their private lives in public and the realm of the home is likewise threatened by the introduction of money and economic thinking.[13] Thus, it is not just the status of work that is called into question but the status of life outside work too and the person as a whole. The accounts of work I collected can be understood as a reaction to popular stereotype, involving a conventional "splitting" of the person into two parts, one public and one private. When sex workers said they were simply working, they were also asserting a separation between these two aspects, as I have described previously with reference to contrasts between different parts of the body, the places in which these were located, nonreproductive as opposed to a reproductive sexuality, market calculations, and control as opposed to intimacy, love, fate, and the absence of a utilitarian rationality (see, for example, Day 1990). In making these distinctions, women rejected the stigma attached to "lazy" and "immoral" prostitutes.

I heard about work first and primarily in the clinic that sex workers attended as patients. I was an unknown entity, apparently neither medical nor an official of the government. Since these women knew I was studying, they sought in good faith to explain how their work was both like and unlike other people's. Yet, I do not mean to imply that this representation of work was a mere public relations exercise. For many women, it was critical to insulate commerce within the boundaries of place, time, attitude, and motivation. In claiming to work just like other people, in separating work from the rest of life and in distancing work from a sense of self, women made extensive use of a widespread view of the market as a place in which services are timed, priced, and circumscribed; in which costs are calculated against benefits, and instrumental considerations are uppermost. The fact that they worked with sex rather than factory products, food and drink, or computers was purely incidental and in no way compromised their capacity to form significant relationships and families, to build a home, and to have a future. Or, at least, this would be true were it not for the prejudice faced every day that led women to work secretly, and the illegality that made it difficult to use earnings productively: buy homes and keep children.

While the conversations that I have cited in this chapter addressed the stigma of prostitution in similar ways through references to simply working, they also suggest another way of working. Many comments revealed an intense interest in predicting the market; dealing with uncertainty, competition, and innovation; and assessing when and where to move to avoid violence and/or interference by state agents while tapping into the wealth that no one else had yet noticed. The stereotype was often repeated to me, "prostitution is easy money." I do not understand this cliché to mean that prostitution is easy work; to the contrary, it is not work (labor) at all but rather an activity involving chance, risk, and skill. I have used the phrase "on the game" as a central metaphor in sex work (Day 1999). For English (UK) speakers, this phrase immediately evokes a contrast: on the game as opposed to "on the job," a colloquial way of describing noncommercial sex. The term describes how women make their money through selling sex rather than giving it away for free. It also has further connotations as far as many sex workers were concerned because experiences on the game were evaluated in terms of previous experiences on the job in ordered work hierarchies of class, gender, times of the day and the month, pension plans, and so forth. On the game thus evokes a view of the market itself as a playground where wit, intellect, guesswork, and imagination can yield rewards that contrast favorably with the drudgery of wage labor. Women talked of becoming wholly engrossed in the business of duping their customers as though the money were virtually a "free" gift. The metaphor, on the game, thus combines shifting senses of both sexual and working lives.

It must have been hard initially to convey this more pragmatic, implicit, and situated knowledge of market trading to someone outside the industry with no obvious experience of informal, let alone illegal, work. Once they knew me, however, and especially once they knew who else I knew, I might be asked in the clinic, where's the money at the moment, do you know anyone who needs a relief worker?[14] As with views about simply working, the business activities that I came to understand through growing familiarity with individuals and through more informal discussions among groups of sex workers had a general significance. Ideas about entrepreneurs and small businesses have been explored in a range of situations and historical periods in relation to concepts of the "self-made" man or woman whose success is often attributed to a freedom of, and ability to, maneuver outside class and other traditions. She or he is often credited with new inventions, forms of wealth, or ways of being in the world (see, for example, Dilley 1992; Heelas and Morris 1992; Keat and Abercrombie 1991).

During the 1980s, such images of enterprise became prominent under the government of Margaret Thatcher in an effort to deregulate and disinvest older traditions of work identified with the welfare state. While it soon became clear that economic salvation was unlikely to be found in the growth of small businesses, most of which collapsed, the rhetoric of initiative and innovation attached to enterprise has remained central to Labour as well as Conservative governments in the twenty-first century. This set of views about morality and success enabled sex workers to value their work in a different way. If simply working places economic life at a certain distance and ultimately serves primarily to facilitate a more satisfying personal life outside work, life on the game engages the person herself if not in the sex (although some were), then in the skills and stakes attached to the front, theatricals, sense of timing, and dealing. Some became wholeheartedly caught up with hustling a living in that archetypal free market, the informal economy, where the state simply does not penetrate: you can work as you like without a boss and series of rules on how to behave; you can work on your own and bring to life the untold riches that are the stuff of fairy tales, which you will be given "freely," like fruit picked from trees, by gullible men. In brief, business on the game provided a way of making money, making a market, and making oneself.

Both views of work provide creative, productive ideologies and practices that counter the overwhelming social stigma and legal sanctions of sex work in Britain today.[15] As I have noted, these two views were initially elicited in different situations but, I suggest, both were relevant more generally to women's lives. However, the material in this chapter suggests that they can prove incompatible. Women who avoided regular clients or any sense of fluidity in their working relationships often found themselves "stuck" in a job that should have allowed them to move on rapidly. Most such women complained that their money had simply disappeared. The extracts from the research discussions indicate how earnings are swallowed up in the costs of working, especially those associated with criminalization such as state fines and fraudulent advisers who steal your money. Women also found that they spent a great deal on friends, family, and trivia. It becomes difficult to save and to invest. Women we have known simply stopped sex work without meeting their targets and goals, in short, with "nothing" to show for their work.

Women who cultivated regular clients tended to soften the boundaries between different activities, and these more permeable boundaries were associated with a sense of opportunity. Clients presented a challenge because they were all potential goldmines who might be turned into regulars and who might ultimately enable their prostitute girlfriends to stop working forever: then money will simply be taken from "the bank" and replenished through rent, shares, dividends, and the other payments that money yields. Yet, in the process of cultivating these men, a rational calculation of mutual benefit is subverted. Regular clients seemed to cheat. Over time, the sense of control that initially seemed so clearly in the hands of the sex worker, who set terms for an exchange, dissipated. It was no longer clear who was duping whom, who was the ingénue, who was in charge, and a sense of artifice spread to other relationships and activities. Moreover, once the barriers were down, these women made friends and lovers out of clients who they could never fully trust. Sarah refused to be bought when she threw back the money, because friendship was not the same as commerce. Flattered and seduced, she was, in the end, frustrated and irritated by this man and subsequent regulars who fell in love with her. Relationships with regulars can lead work to become less and less invested in one part of life, one part of the body, and one set of relationships, all governed by strict accounting, distance, and pretense. Business and a sense of artifice come to permeate much of life.

I have presented two models and suggested their relevance to earning a living, counteracting stigma, and a positive identity or sense of self. I have suggested that both models are relevant to the same people, albeit in different situations and at different times, but they may come into conflict. My references to Sarah's career suggest that this conflict is resolved over time: women who make a career out of sex work are more likely to have cultivated the regular clients who so often cause a shift from one model, simply working, to another, on the game.

## Sarah's Biography

Sarah used to talk of sex work as an unfortunate interlude, which would nonetheless finance a better future. She made radical distinctions between work and the rest of life, what she did now and what she planned to do in the future when she returned to an "ordinary" day job and family. She acquired her money from a single man who crossed between public and private; a client and then an ex-client and then a "kind-of" client. In the early 1990s, Sarah tried to make this relationship a private affair before putting it back in the domain of work. As she reacted against playing the wife or girlfriend, a scenario that struck a good many women with horror when it became a possibility or, indeed, reality, and moved back to work, she came to value her skills more highly. I suggest that her positive attitude to sex work can be attributed to her success both in dealing with money and in managing stigma. Work is no longer, if it ever strictly was, simply work, a source of money with which to sustain a real life outside. Sarah does not consider herself to come in two discrete parts: public and private. Work has a far more valued content in which the skills of hustling can be developed and reapplied. The present is no longer marked off from some radically different and respectable future.[16] Although this particular relationship with her sugar daddy had ended, as most do, the effects of a thoroughgoing and most likely mutual artifice continued. Having pretended to take business back home, there was no particular reason not to capitalize on or commercialize these more intimate realms of life. Sarah came to talk about sex work as though it would simply carry on and unfold: full of respectability, success, and youth.

In 2000–2001, Sarah was relatively wealthy, in the process of buying a third property, and she expressed no desire to return to her previous day job or, indeed, any other form of work except, she said, she would like to write a book. At the same time, she talked of living alone and I had the impression she was lonely. She said,

> I am now thinking it might never be, I have never wanted it but it is a bit frightening to think that suddenly someone is saying that's it, you had your chance and you blew it. . . . I hope I don't wake up at ninety-three and say, "God why did I stay a hooker for all those years and have a big fat bank balance, I mean what have you got?" You're lonely, you have got no kids, you have got a big fat bank balance but so what? . . . I am comparing myself with my mother at my age and my grandmother at my age, I mean . . . my grandmother, when she was forty-one; she had had it by then . . . whereas now you can go and trek the Himalayas when you are sixty-five if you want. . . . So your life doesn't have to finish, you don't have to be in your rocking chair when you are sixty-five but twenty, thirty, forty years ago you were. . . . You had your blue rinse and you were in your rocking chair and you were about to zip.

Should she freeze her eggs?

If I do meet Mr. Wonderful in ten years time and I think, God, I really want kids with you, I don't want to adopt . . . if I had the equipment there any more, then we could plant those eggs and his sperm into a surrogate, and then she can do all the dirty work for nine months, at least then I will know it will be my eggs and his sperm.

Yet, Sarah was uneasy about manipulating nature, "[I]f nature's way is saying right, OK, you have had your turn, you adapt, you get used to it, and you think what was." And she went on to talk about her position now: "I am used to this business, I know I do it well and I know it works for me." She described herself as a lady of leisure, tanned, expensively dressed, younger than her years, with a small clutch handbag and a mobile telephone that rang incessantly. As she said, "I don't look my age, so I'm doing something right."

Just as women made their very own market through attracting men and their money, so could they have families if and when they wanted, and maintain their youth. Women such as these spent significant amounts of time and money on regimens of health, fitness, and beauty; in cosmetic surgery; and other changes to their appearance that extended beyond the standard trappings of multiple identities that most women cultivated at work in different names, legal identities, wigs, makeup, and biographies. It becomes possible to spend on oneself and renew the resources though which money is attracted, in other words, to invest in the future. Such spending is no more "wasteful" than (other) ascetic bodily exercises on the part of sportsmen, artists, or monks. In fact, it can become one of several strategies for saving or investing in which women may feel less of a conflict between spending on "nothing" and saving for the long term.

Sarah's concerns about aging were echoed in a research discussion where participants were asked, Is prostitution a job for life? A had mentioned an older, unmarried woman she knew living in a tiny flat in a smart part of central London with two cats. B said, "[I]t's my idea of heaven," and C responded to A's concerns about aging on your own, "[S]he might be having a fabulous life for all you know." These two women considered that she might enjoy working: "[S]he might like her clients enough for that to be a way of having extra spending money." C explained how older women modified their services[17] and said how appalled she had been by a television program about the legalization of prostitution, in which it was implied that a woman who had worked as a prostitute, saved her money, and had gone back to college had moved on in life. "This guy is saying you know, the cliché, well now we've heard from a working girl who's gone on to better things, . . . I mean I have been to college but I have chosen this. I am trained in a profession. . . . Other people I know are trained in a profession—nursing, teaching, or whatever—and they choose. I choose to do this work and I see it as a profession and I see it as something I continue to do." B responded in agreement.

During our interview in 2000, Sarah's only complaint was, "prostitution is the only job or profession that you have to give up on marriage. . . . Either you have to lie and say you're not working, and they think you're a lazy cow or you have to make something up and get found out." She used to talk about her sugar daddy to friends but still they thought she was lazy. "It's not like being a baker or a road sweeper, you just can't say what you do." Recently, she had decided to be more open and told her family and friends what she did although she was doubtful about having a personal relationship while working. In the first research discussion cited, all four women talked about their work with pride. No one seemed to think that the stress of working with clients got worse or better over time but the stigma and enforced isolation had taken a heavy toll. B had worked secretly for seven or eight years and more "openly" for the remainder of her fifteen-year career. The double life had proved intolerable but now she said that "it is so much easier than having to lie and remember what you lied about." C agreed: "I used to have recurring nightmares about being found out. And they stopped when I came out to people." These two women described the boost to their self-esteem that came from finding friends who even accepted their work and treated them well. Other women have also described how they kept their secrets for years before testing the water little by little and telling friends or family what they did. They gradually came to share their secrets selectively and to restore a broader sociability to their lives. If Sarah still felt lonely, she was nonetheless in the process of recovering her biography in a public realm, within relationships that she had selected.[18]

## Conclusion

In this chapter, I have addressed strategies of work among a handful of successful women with extensive experience in the sex industry. I particularly wanted to convey a sense of sex work as a longer-term pursuit: the women I have described have survived and prospered; they may work another twenty years. They liked their work, and continued even though they had independent financial resources, primarily in property, and other possible jobs or professions. None worked long hours and none worked "hard" any longer. Relationships with regular clients provided crucial financial, and sometimes social, security in a difficult environment, and over time, as I have shown, these relationships tended to be associated with a view of life on the game in which work approximates less and less to the impersonal and instrumental rationality so often associated with markets in Western economies and attracts more and more of a personal investment, in which the emotions are implicated alongside intellectual calculations of costs and benefits, and where private affairs intermingle with the public.

As others have argued (Dumont 1977; Gudeman 1986; Sahlins 1976), the language of economics provides a way of talking about culture but the terms are so familiar in the United Kingdom and elsewhere that it can be hard to see how talk of work speaks to the morality of making money, relations with the state, and a sense of self, and it can be hard to see the diversity and heterogeneity of these views (Carrier 1997; Friedland and Robertson 1990). Sex work provides a good forum in which to explore the language of economics because of the unfamiliar way in which terms and values are used, in part, to counter widespread stigma.

Ideas about simply working enable sex workers to create a sphere that produces the wherewithal to subsist and, hopefully, to prosper; it suggests that sex workers do what everyone else does to get by. At the same time, the stigma of prostitution is dissociated from a sense of self because work is both separated from and devalued in relation to a more personal and private realm of life. Albert Hirschman (1977) has argued that the idea of the economy has provided a major space through which to dream universal reason and knowledge. Prostitutes too may dream a rational economy when they are simply working and, in contrast to life on the game, this space is rather bare, engaging neither the passions nor the self. Women seemed to celebrate a contrasting sense of creativity and self-invention in this game, constructed in explicit opposition to attempts to order social life and, specifically, attempts by the state to discipline prostitutes. This game is the object of passionate involvement where skill, a sense of timing, feats of endurance, illusion, and intuition all assume importance. A skilled player has to bring all her senses with her to compete effectively and thereby come to live, at least momentarily, within that game.

I have argued that prostitutes employ multiple views and strategies of work and, in doing so, construct different views of self and society. At times, these strategies and ideas come into conflict, as I have shown, with reference to the regular clients who provide one of several possible perspectives on the interplay between views of work, stigma, and success. In cultivating regular clients, women commonly relinquished the bald characterization of work as a simple variation on what everyone else did in order to make a living. Some women softened distinctions between work and home, one part of their body and another, what they do now and an imagined future respectability as they became involved with individual clients. This general blurring of distinctions, which are so important at times and to so many women, rebounds on other aspects of life including the contrasts I have described between different aspects of business, such as saving and spending, and, of course, between paid and unpaid sex and between friends or families as opposed to buyers and sellers. In other words, the contrast I have drawn between two models of the market can also be situated within different age groups and career stages.[19]

The latter half of this chapter suggested that the cultivation of individual men (notably sugar daddies) exacts high costs even if it makes business viable. Sarah and other women created a web of artifice that extended to their significant relationships; these were rarely considered to be either dependable or trustworthy. Constant invention and performance, I have argued, led women to feel lonely for they had created everything of value through their own activities and efforts. These women had individually and independently made not just successful businesses, but also homes, children, bodies, and identities. As shown toward the end of the chapter, some found the continual artifice too much of a burden ultimately. Women continually refashion their views and activities in relation to changing circumstances; this particular example indicates that apparent successes came to be questioned over time, and artifice was dropped through the sharing of secrets.[20] This shows that the contrasts I have drawn need to be situated within a wider context that attends to the life course and other factors that I do not have space to present, such as social class. In conclusion, however, I wish to draw attention to a related point concerning the way in which this wider context affects workers and businesswomen in a similar rather than distinctive fashion.

In this chapter, I have not discussed material that illustrates how prostitution reproduces gendered inequalities. On the game (a critique of giving sex away) suggests a striking ambivalence about stereotyped gender relations. Other comments, however, indicate that sex workers reproduced relationships in which men could "buy" two or more homes and "consume" endless sexual fantasies while women had to please and flatter their men in order to get by. These gender inequalities also affect the extent to which women can build their lives and futures. Neither the self-made career woman, created through her own artifice and effort, nor the worker, who engages in a short-term occupation, has a wife at home and few have much paid help. If you come in two parts, private and public/present and future, you may become stuck less because of the difficulties of earning a living than because of the absence of this "wife" at home, through whom to launder your money, bear and care for your children, and create a local sense of community. If you come in just one part, bringing to life that gold-mine of a regular who yields riches, you may end up creating everything of value through your own person, alone. In this sense, becoming stuck in prostitution as a worker balances the loneliness of the entrepreneur: both strategies are limited by wider gender relationships.

In this context, the gradual process of coming out I have described provides a powerful critique of gendered work and sexual arrangements and, particularly, the relationship between the two. In sharing their se-crets, the women I have described claimed some public or semipublic recognition for themselves and their profession. They also put limits on the artifice of their lives by refashioning social relationships to create new communities and collectivities of their own choosing.

## Notes

1. In this chapter, prostitute is a synonym for sex worker and prostitution for sex work or the sex industry.

2. I have worked closely with Helen Ward, a clinical epidemiologist, throughout the period. Kate Cooper and Anna Green have been working on our recent project, Changes in Prostitution, 1985–2000, supported by the Wellcome Trust from 1998–2002. I would like to thank them and the Praed Street Project staff as well as participants in the research. I would also like to acknowledge the support of AVERT, the Medical Research Council, the Wellcome Trust, the NHS Executive, North Thames, and the Jefferiss Trust from 1986 to the present. The Praed Street Project is funded by the National Health Service. (See Ward and Day, 1997, for a brief historical account and description of the services.)

3. *Reintegration* is a term commonly used to describe the retraining or education of sex workers, and includes both the rescue attempts classically asso-ciated with religious organizations and more recent community efforts to pro-vide the language resources, information technology training, and access into the formal sector requested by sex workers.

4. While contemporary economies may increase the value or necessity of flexibility, the literature on sex work suggests strong resonances with strategies in other times and places. The poor and disenfranchised have long dealt with situ-ations that are increasingly affecting other classes and core countries. (See Nu-gent, 2000, for comments about Ulrich Beck's ideas of risk society in the context of Brazil.)

5. These models are heuristic devices that will hopefully clarify contrasting strategies among sex workers (for example, between those who do and do not value relationships with regulars) without doing violence to the shifting visions of

work described by the majority of women, who tend to employ both models at different times, and indeed others that I shall not have space to present.

6. These research discussions were familiar in form and content to more informal discussions in the project drop-in center where women met to talk about work issues and other matters with a staff member present. Women were invited to participate through the project as well as our own contacts, and consented to the research. Thanks to Anna Green and Kate Cooper who facilitated the discussions.

7. A, B, C, and D corresponds to the order of speakers in this discussion. An ellipsis indicates passages I have omitted. Brackets indicate additions intended to make the sense clear. Double quote marks indicate taped transcriptions while single quote marks indicate more approximate transcriptions from notes. I have changed details about these women to preserve confidentiality, and have slightly altered wording to suit written rather than spoken conventions.

8. Other topics included health and service provision, particularly in relation to broken condoms, stress, and help for women starting the work. Stigma was discussed in great detail and some references were made to love and marriage (I shall discuss romance at work, but not outside, later).

9. This regular who provides a lucky break has also been noted in historical studies. For example, Judith R. Walkowitz (1980) said of Victorian England that concubinage "was not only the door into prostitution but also the door out" (197). Concubinage is comparable to relationships with sugar daddies, as I shall describe.

10. On the other hand, some sex workers married or set up home with ex-clients. One, for example, described her clients as her friends and family. After some time, I realized that her boyfriend was the brother of one of her best clients.

11. That is, Sophie Day.

12. I judge prosperity in relative terms: D owned a house, rented a flat, and supported her family.

13. This is the dogma; of course, a great many activities bring money into kinship and personal life into the workplace. The fiction of societies divided into two realms of public and private has long been challenged by a variety of critics and, in anthropology, especially from feminist perspectives.

14. This is a fill-in, part-time, or temporary worker in the flats/apartments where the majority of London prostitutes now work.

15. These passages summarize parts of a book in preparation tentatively entitled *On the Game* (Pluto Press).

16. Ideas about respectability are key to these women's images of their future lives and can also be understood in terms of social class (see Giles 1995; Skeggs 1997). However, many women refused notions of respectability altogether and developed strategies that I have been unable to discuss in this chapter such

as "stealing" rather than "working" or "doing business." Some women enjoyed sex work because it accommodated a wide range of "unrespectable" gendered roles outside the household and family. Such women included artists, counter-cultural practitioners of various kinds, those who identified with alternative sexualities, drinkers, and others. Sex work is extraordinarily diverse in London and the value attached to domesticity is variable.

17. In similar interviews, women talked of advertising as mature ladies and establishing lucrative businesses.

18. See Kath Weston (1997) on how lesbians choose and create their own families and communities through coming out.

19. These models were not the only ones expressed, nor was the gradual displacement of work (simply working) by a more successful business (on the game) universal: D, it will be recalled, did not talk of regulars but had nonetheless achieved significant financial security. Moreover, these models have other sociological correlates, in particular, the images, issues, and practices of social class, that qualify the generalized "career" I have presented.

20. While women who had sustained rigid distinctions between work and the rest of life tended to keep their secrets, whether they continued to keep these secrets in the long term is unclear due to a lack of comprehensive data, whish is due partly because I did not ask everyone and partly because so many I knew in the late 1980s had left sex work by the late 1990s and thus were difficult to contact again.

# References

Carrier, J., ed. 1997. *Meanings of the market: The free market in western culture.* Oxford: Berg.

Day, S. 1990. Prostitute women and the ideology of work in London. In *AIDS and culture: The global pandemic,* edited by D. A. Feldman. New York: Praeger.

———. 1994. L'argent et l'esprit d'enterprise chez les prostitutees à Londres. *Terrain* 23: 99–114.

———. 1999. Hustling: Individualism among London prostitutes. In *Lilies of the field: Marginal people who live for the moment,* edited by S. Day, M. Stewart, and A. Papataxiarchis. Boulder, Colo.: Westview.

Day, S., H. Ward, and L. Perrotta. 1993. Prostitution and risk of HIV: Male partners of female prostitutes. *British Medical Journal* 307: 359–361.

Dilley, R., ed. 1992. *Contesting markets: Analyses of ideology, discourse, and practice.* Edinburgh: Edinburgh University Press.

Dumont, L. 1977. *From Mandeville to Marx: The genesis and triumph of economic ideology.* Chicago: University of Chicago Press.

Friedland, R., and A. Robertson, eds. 1990. *Beyond the marketplace: Rethinking economy and society.* New York: Aldine de Gruyter.

Giles, J. 1995. *Women, identity, and private life in Britain, 1900–1950.* London: Macmillan.

Gudeman, S. 1986. *Economics as culture: Models and metaphors of livelihood.* London: Routledge.

Heelas, P., and P. Morris, eds. 1992. *The values of the enterprise culture: The moral debate.* London: Routledge.

Hirschman, A. 1977. *The passions and the interests.* Princeton: Princeton University Press.

Hochshild, A. 1983. *The managed heart: Commercialization of human feeling.* Berkeley and Los Angeles: University of California Press.

Kahn, J. 1997. Demons, commodities, and the history of anthropology. In *Meanings of the market: The free market in western culture,* edited by J. Carrier. Oxford: Berg.

Keat, R., and N. Abercrombie, eds. 1991. *Enterprise culture.* London: Routledge.

Martin, E. 1994. *Flexible bodies: Tracking immunity.* Boston: Beacon.

Nugent, S. 2000. Good risk, bad risk: Reflexive modernisation and amazonia. In *Risk Revisited,* edited by P. Caplan. London: Pluto.

Pheterson, G. 1996. *The prostitution prism.* Amsterdam: Amsterdam University Press.

Rabinow, P. 1986. Representations are social facts: Modernity and post-modernity in anthropology. In *Writing culture: The poetics and politics of ethnography,* edited by J. Clifford and G. Marcus. Berkeley and Los Angeles: University of California Press.

Sahlins, M. 1976. *Culture and practical reason.* Chicago: University of Chicago Press.

Schneider, D. 1980. *American kinship: A cultural account.* 1969. Reprint, Chicago: University of Chicago Press.

Skeggs, B. 1997. *Formations of class and gender: Becoming respectable.* London: Sage.

Walkowitz, J. 1980. *Prostitution and victorian society: Women, class, and the state.* Cambridge: Cambridge University Press.

Ward, H., and S. Day. 1997. Health care and regulation—new perspectives. In *Rethinking prostitution,* edited by G. Scambler and A. Scambler. London: Routledge.

Weston, K. 1997. *Families we choose: Lesbians, gays, kinship.* New York, Columbia University Press.

# 3

# The Political Economy
# of Affects

*Community, Friendship, and Family in the Organization*
*of a Spanish Economic Region*

Susana Narotzky

## Introduction

This chapter is based on an ethnography of the Vega Baja del Segura (Valencia in southeast Spain).[1] It is an area of small- and medium-size family firms, some of which, however, are among the more profitable in their sector (shoewear). Following recent sociological and economic models, the area has been described as an industrial district, in reference to its dynamic and flexible economic structure and its entrepreneurial culture. The industrial district or economic region model was first defined for northern Italy as an optimistic developmental model based on the relevance of a shared culture and the use of noneconomic social networks. This model is increasingly acquiring a hegemonic role in the agendas of institutional policymakers including Eurocrats or World Bank advisers. Now the concept of "social capital" is highlighted as the main asset to be developed in order for development policies to succeed. Social capital refers to a vague idea of the importance of embeddedness (as defined by Mark S. Granovetter rather than Karl Polanyi) for a successful economic organization. The dominant model of economic development now incorporates the importance of "noneconomic" social relations that are deemed increasingly necessary for the local establishment of dynamic entrepreneurial practices and flexible relations of production.

What the ethnography reveals, however, is a complex and conflict-laden space where increased embeddedness of labor/capital relations produces increased tension within the "traditional" boundaries of identity: the self, the family, and the community. Moreover, far from supporting the idea of a fairly homogeneous access to the local pool of social capital on the part of local agents, our ethnography shows how different people have, for historical reasons, very different capabilities in this regard. However, the hegemonic discourse of an organic and culturally defined economic region misrepresents these harsh realities. Last, this chapter will address the political problems that this new developmental model poses: namely, the implosion of a social space where labor rights might be claimed.

## Concepts and Models: Industrial Districts, Embeddedness, and Social Capital

Before exploring the ethnographic material, I want to present the methodological issues that are raised by the concepts that have been used by social scientists to analyze spaces of social interaction such as the Vega Baja in southern Alicante. My concern is that the social reproduction of these regional economies, which means the historical production of particular forms of livelihood where the personal is in a very deep way economic, hinges on the production of a hegemony that, I think, can be partially unveiled in the scholarly use of these concepts (Smith 1991). The three concepts I have chosen here are particularly significant for the region I did fieldwork in, but they are not the only ones and others such as "entrepreneurship" or "community" might have as much weight.

Alfred Marshall (1964) first described the "industrial district" (151–155) as "the concentration of specialized industries in particular localities" (151). He was describing the industrial districts as different from large-scale manufacture but still highly economic and profitable. This first use of the concept of "industrial district" was descriptive. The development of the concept of industrial district that interests me here appears in the early 1980s and is based on the observations of some Italian economists and sociologists about decentralized forms of production (*economia diffusa*), small-firm dynamism and an unregulated labor market, after the apparent demise of the Fordist model of large-scale, stable employment and mass consumer market economic organization following the first oil crisis (Bagnasco 1988; Becattini 1994; Bellandi 1989).

Michael J. Piore and Charles F. Sabel (1984) present an alternative economic development theory based on the Italian material and on a reinterpretation and reevaluation of Marshall's industrial district description, stressing his vague reference to a particular "industrial atmosphere." They propose the industrial district now as a model of dynamic economic development in the post-Fordist context where *fluidity, flexibility, innovation,* and *deregulation* are the key words enabling economic growth, but unlike the grim prospects set forth by the shrinking of the welfare state, the informalization of labor/capital relations, and, in general, neoliberal reforms in economic policies, Piore and Sabel create a positive model for flexible specialization. This optimistic view of the new industrial districts in an era of economic de-structuration is based on the fundamental role of the community as the main support structure of economic relations (265).

The basic morphological character of the model is its flexibility: links between production units change continuously and this enables the production process to reorder itself frequently. On the other hand, belonging to a community is the main relational basis that permits competitive interaction to take place in the system while preserving cooperation and a place to all those which belong to the community: "No firm or individual has a right to any particular place within the community, *but all have a claim to some place within it*" (269, emphasis added). But it is also the community aspect, which protects economic actors from external competition:

> A second characteristic of these organizations of flexible specialization is that they limit entry. This follows from the fact that *communities are bounded,* and the boundaries identify those with claims to the provision of social welfare. . . . Many (though not all) of the restrictions to entry are informal: *getting a job depends on whom you know, and whom you know depends on who you are.* (269–270; emphasis added)

Thus, local economic agents rely on communal institutions, which are not directly "economic" in their purpose (the family, cultural associations, political parties, religious base groups, and so forth) for the construction of their industrial cooperation networks.

As Bennett Harrison (1992) has pointed out, the crucial component of the new industrial district model is the idea of embeddedness of economic rationality within the fabric of a wider social experience. Here it is interesting to note that this concept of embeddedness of economic action is bounded to a notion of an individual oriented agency, whose logic "runs from *proximity to experience to trust to collaboration to enhanced regional economic growth*" (Harrison 1992, 478). This use of embeddedness, however, is a particularly restrictive interpretation of the vaguer "culture and community" thickness of economic rationality that the Italian scholars perceived and began to theorize in the late 1970s. The concept of embeddedness that has become hegemonic in the industrial district's more recent literature is ambiguous. One aspect is closer to Granovetter's idea of embeddedness, a very instrumental notion of the production of trust through recurrent social interaction among particular individuals. In fact, Granovetter (1985) is very critical toward an "oversocialized" idea of economic action in which individuals would be endowed with a "generalized morality" (we would say "culture"). From this point of view, economic action is embedded in an articulated network of personal social transactions. Social relations, here, become transactional experience, and economic action would involve choice between alternative partners in order to maximize the unwritten "trust" element of contracts. This we might, I think, define as a "formalist" (in anthropological jargon) version of embeddedness, which is a completely different version from the original "substantivist" idea of embeddedness that Polanyi (1957, 1971) put forward for societies other than those integrated by the market system: one where "human economy, then, is embedded and enmeshed in institutions, economic and non economic" (1957, 250), whereas in societies where the market system integrates economic activities, the "economy" appears to be disembedded from other social relations. For Polanyi, then, embeddedness was a fundamental aspect of the way in which economic processes where integrated into society as a whole. He very clearly stated that it did not concern the form of individual transactions. He also spoke of patterns of institutionalization of economic activity (the main patterns being reciprocity, redistribution, exchange, responding to social and political structures of the society). If Polanyi saw a break in societies integrated by the market system, it was not so much in that embeddedness was mystified or appeared to disappear, it was that the direction of embeddedness was reversed and, with it, the moral landscape where economic action took place: "Instead of economy being embedded in social relations, social relations are embedded in the economic system" (1971, 57). The Italian scholars seem to have retained originally more of the "organic" spirit of the "substantivist" idea of embedded economic activities in their descriptions and theorizing of the Italian cases (Bagnasco 1994). However, as the model becomes more and more an instrument of economic policies, the "formalist" version of embeddedness seems to weight more, if only because it responds better to the process of abstraction and modelization and to the purported objective of applied social engineering (Woolcock 1998). There remains, however, a basic ambiguousness that is built in the meaning of embeddedness and with it in the new theoretical concept of industrial district both as it is used by scholars and as it is integrated in economic development policies by national governments and international institutions.

The concept of social capital is a development of the idea of embeddedness, and Ben Fine (1999) has described its vagueness: "[I]t seems to be able to be *anything* ranging over public goods, networks, culture, etc. The only proviso is that social capital should be attached to the economy in a functionally positive way for economic performance, especially growth"(5; emphasis in original). Two complementary aspects of social relations have defined social capital: embeddedness and autonomy. Autonomy describes the ability of certain individuals within the community to forge and sustain social relationships with individuals and institutions outside the community. Autonomy would enable some economic agents in a community to overcome the centripetal forces and closure that are generally attributed to social and cultural proximity. Autonomy, then, would be as necessary as embeddedness for social links to successfully work as social capital (Woolcock 1998, 175). The insistence on both embeddedness and autonomy as basic aspects of social capital points to the need to incorporate forms of social and economic differentiation within the model, for successful capitalist development. The assumption being, however, that community integration will contain disruptive individualist tendencies of entrepreneurial success that would cause social anomie.

One of the main questions about the concept of social capital is Why should the concept of capital be separated into different forms—social and economic—as if "economic" capital was not social, as if it was a "thing," an object devoid of social content? (Fine 1999, 16). Other issues are also at stake: The concept of social capital is tied to the surreptitious way in which life in general, all sorts of social relations, is (1) transformed into capital, that is, into a "dead" (stable and reliable) factor for the production of commodities with the aim of increasing "economic growth" (capital accumulation) and (2) capital—a market-based concept—is allowed to invade and kidnap the space of nonmarket social interaction and use it as a force structuring relations of production. What is very interesting about this concept, however, is that it works. That is, on the one hand, it makes a selective description of the reality of informal and personalized relations of production, while on the other hand, it is a crucial element of their reproduction. In other words, it is a concept with a political agenda. It blocks the possibility of looking at the tensions and articulations between market- and nonmarket-mediated relationships between persons as an integral part of processes of social reproduction, of processes of differentiation yielding power and structuring particular forms of exploitation.

What I will try to show in this chapter is that (1) the reality of the social relations that concur in a particularly "successful" economic region in Spain have to be approached in an unromantic way; (2) history is necessary for understanding the construction of particular forms of social interaction; and (3) scholarly models of social capital in economic processes might become part of a hegemonic agenda geared toward a corporatist structuring of society.

## The Ethnography

The area of the Vega Baja del Segura is located to the southeast of Spain, in the autonomous community of Valencia. It is located in the province of Alicante, bordering the region of Murcia to the south. The nearest largest city is the port of Alicante (272,432 inhabitants in the 1998 census) to the northeast of the Vega Baja. The Vega Baja del Segura is the irrigated plain in the basin of the river Segura, near its mouth. This area comprises the region between the towns of Elche (191,713 inhabitants) to the north, Crevillente (23,945 inhabitants) to the northwest, and Orihuela (50,581 inhabitants) to the west.

## History and Regional Work Relations

The present-day regional economy of the Vega Baja is grounded in past social relations of production that presented a highly differentiated, while strongly interdependent social and spatial structure. The Vega Baja a century ago was heavily agricultural, although Elche to the north was an industrial town centered on the manufacture of *alpargatas* (rope sandals). The Vega Baja was the main producer of hemp, the industrial fiber used for the manufacture of alpargata. Indeed, Elche attracted lots of labor from the neighboring rural area. Trade unions were strong there and had a tradition of labor struggle (a nine-month-long strike in 1903, for example; Moreno Saez 1987). Elche industrialists used cheap and docile labor from the Vega Baja as home-based workers in manufacturing rope sandals, pitting them against unionized factory workers. Labor unions responded by trying to educate and organize rural homeworkers, but without much success.

    In the Vega Baja, the structure of landownership before 1936 was still one in which large absentee landlords, mostly aristocrats or urban bourgeois, managed their property through a few very large tenants.

These were in charge of hiring landless day laborers and also of establishing annual subtenancies for tiny plots of land with peasants working as day laborers on the owner's land. Social relations of production in agriculture were structured through a series of links of patronage that articulated landowners with large tenants, and the latter with landless workers. However, the degree of "dependence" and political submissiveness was very different for "free" labor (i.e., day laborers without land) and "dependent" workers who were "favored" with tiny plots of land on informal annual leases. For these, the tensions of having to blend personal, affective, and work risks and responsibilities was a very important aspect of their experience of labor/capital relations. On the contrary, free day laborers were highly mobile and this made them aware of wider regional and national labor struggles organized around trade unions and the use of public politics to forward their claims. Most of the free day laborers and dependent workers also worked in one way or another for the rope sandal industry, one structured through subcontracting and putting-out networks (Municipal Archives, Derramas).

Overall, the situation before the onset of the Spanish Civil War and the following Francoist regime, was one of strong ties between industrial and agricultural activities both on the capital side and on the labor side of social relations of production. On the other hand, dependent or free worker relationships with capital produced different strategies both from employers and from labor to try to further their interests and claims. The general context in those years was one of economic, political, and institutional instability. In the contractual setting of free market relations, struggles took place around the limits that civil society, through the state, would set to regulate the de-structuring social effects of unregulated market forces. This took place through public politics and the use of organized collective confrontation. In the dependent relations setting, making a living or forwarding claims took, for laborers, the form of personalized relations, the construction of affective and reciprocal ties of patronage responsibilities. Likewise, these affected employers who chose to rely on household labor organization, kin, and friendship networks to secure and control labor and capital. Thus, two very different and overlapping processes were linked in a dialectical tension between security and uncertainty, private versus public politics, in the social reproduction of this regional economy.

With the advent of the Francoist regime in 1939 the national-Catholic organic model of social relations was imposed on all aspects of society, supported by a violent repression and a closed and state-administered economy, the *Autarquía* (Richards 1998). In this new context corporatist institutions, economic policies, and an ideology imposed through fear supported highly personalized networks of social relations of production. This produced a totalitarian closure of the social space.

In the later years of the regime things began to change, in part due to the Cold War international context and the increasing and open support of the United States to the Franco regime. Large-scale industrialization of a Fordist type took place after 1952, class unions began to organize within the "vertical" corporatist state-unions of the regime, and collective spaces of dissent slowly opened at great personal risk. However, the weight of forty years of a culture of fear that foreclosed the use of public politics to forward claims and institute civil rights had pushed people to rely on practices of dependency, couched in a paternalist and social-Catholic moral discourse of proportional justice, reciprocal responsibilities, and essentialist duties.

For the past thirty years, the particular mix of agricultural and industrial activities that characterized making a living in the Vega Baja, since the end of the nineteenth century, has strongly tilted toward the industrial sector, particularly shoe manufacturing. During the 1960s and early 1970s large factories were established in the towns of Elche and Crevillente that relied on labor from the villages in the Vega Baja (Bernabé 1975). In those years, many men and women migrated to reside in the towns where the factories were located. However, during peak production seasons, home-based piecework was a complementary device to increase production capacity in the more labor-intensive parts of the process, mirroring putting-out practices of old. Generally, foremen in the factory became intermediaries distributing outwork, using their kin and local networks to get the extra work done.

After Franco's death in 1975, the increased capacity of the labor unions to organize for collective action gave them more bargaining leverage and resulted in higher wages for workers. This, together with other economic changes, including the increased competition made possible by advances in transportation, information technologies, and the international division of labor, restructured production into a decentralized pattern that can be described as a regime of flexible accumulation (Harvey 1989). Locally, this took a form resembling the Italian industrial districts, although with a clear hierarchical subcontracting articulation nested in networks of personalized relations centered on large commercial firms that often only retain marketing and packaging processes (Becattini 1994; Sabel 1989; Ybarra 1991).[3]

The present-day structure of industrial production in the area comprises large factories; small, family firms; unregulated workshops; middlemen; home-based workers; and industrial wage workers. Only factory workers tend to have some kind of legal contract. Small factories, workshops, middlemen, and homeworkers rely heavily on family labor, kin, and neighborhood networks to access work and labor. Firms, workshops, and middlemen try to diversify their clients and directly control market outlets when possible. Homeworkers lack this flexibility, instead they are highly dependent and loyal to particular middlemen. Industrial wage workers, on the other hand, feel free to move between different factories and workshops, and between different jobs locally, as well as within the region. This seems to be associated with a higher incidence of protest and to the high failure rate of most small local entrepreneurial ventures. Industrial wage workers, then, are in a similar position to the free day laborers of old; while homeworkers, middlemen, unregulated workshops, and small, family firms seem to reproduce a structure of dependence and subordination strongly reminiscent of the personalized web of patronage that pervaded agriculture and industry in the region in the previous period.

Indeed, it is important to note that, except for the largest factories, which have flexible location practices and are able to use information technologies to their benefit,[4] the middlemen, small-scale entrepreneurs, and workers are tightly bound to one another and frequently merge or emerge from one another. Locally, there is a perceived and extremely differentiated network of shifting but necessary alliances expressed in the subjects' characterization of the region as a coherent space with an "entrepreneurial culture," meaning by this the continuous movement of emerging (and declining) economic destinies. Moreover, the instrumental weight of personal and affective relations in the construction and maintenance of these hierarchical networks of production has its corollary in the stress produced on these affective relations, induced by the tension of differentiation within the realms of shared belonging; that is, the family, the community, or fellow workers. Distributive and retributive problems, issues of equity and equality, of individual as opposed to collectively grounded claims, pervade this thick network of forced solidarities, which is simultaneously a highly differentiated field of closely knit feelings of belonging. But also, very salient is the tension within the self: between competing responsibilities and the differential evaluation of family and friendship affective moralities.

## Life Histories and Regional Social Differentiation

Carmen, a woman in her late fifties, had worked as a homeworker covering heels of shoes for a distributor who is also a close neighbor and the husband of an old friend of hers. She can no longer work because she has Parkinson's disease. Her husband, a mason, is now unemployed. Her son, now married, used to work as a leather cutter in a local shoe factory but with other specialized workers he demanded higher wages and was fired. He had to find work elsewhere, in a different town. Her daughter is an *aparadora* (she sews shoe uppers). She has worked alternatively in small workshops or as a homeworker. When she worked at home Carmen used to help her with the *trabajo de mano* (handwork) organizing batches, cutting threads, and so on. But she recalls that, when her own aging father got sick and she had to take care of him, "I became very nervous because I couldn't help my daughter. Then, even my husband was helping her. The *trabajo de mano* is not paid at home. In the workshop she works alone, has a break for lunch and she ends her day at 8pm. Here we all worked and in the end we earned the same thing. And we stayed up until midnight or 1am. working everyday."

In the workshop, a worker who gets paid for it does the trabajo de mano. What we can see very clearly in this case is that the pressure for higher productivity brought by the piecework rates paid in *aparado* (the sewing of shoe uppers) generally, does not affect equally homeworkers and workshop workers. The trabajo de mano and the organization and ordering of batches in the proper way is a key aspect for increasing productivity at work that gets accounted for in one case and not in the other. But, even more important, in the workshops, tensions that arise around the proper realization of this handwork are set in the context of coworkers or worker–owner labor relations, and bring into trial exclusively the labor process, even when most of the workers are close kin relations. At home things are quite different, and the tensions that arise are densely woven with family responsibilities and affects.

Pilar is in her late forties. She works at one of the big shoewear factories in town in the quality control and packaging department (*envasa*). She has only recently acquired this job. Before, she worked in a smaller factory where she was also in the *envasa*. This job she got through a friend of hers, Eulalia, who was the wife of a small factory owner and managed the envasa there. Pilar worked there for ten years, but she finally quit (or was fired) because tensions rose between the two old friends. Pilar seems to have strongly resented the authoritarian boss in her old friend: "[S]he wanted to be the boss and to have everybody know she was the boss" but she was also (or had been for a long time) grateful to Eulalia for giving her a job when she needed one. Pilar and her husband have three sons, one in university, two still at school. They are members of a local Catholic base group and are active participants in local folkloric festivals, such as the Moros y Cristianos, which require large personal investment in terms of money and time.

Marta is the wife of Roberto, one of the main local distributors of homework. Marta started doing homework herself (covering shoe heels) but eventually, as the network of homeworkers and the volume of production expanded, she took on the work of quality control and fixing defects. She also helped her husband organize the batches at home, a task that is done before distribution to homeworkers. Marta recalls being really depressed when her parents got very old and she had to take care of them continuously, while she also wanted to keep on helping her husband with the business. However, her parents' old-age pension was, in turn, used to cover the cash flow needs in order to pay homeworkers their weekly salaries.

Recently, other tensions have risen. Marta and Roberto's daughter, Montse, still in high school, is now in charge of organizing and pairing the pieces in the batches before distribution, a monotonous and time-consuming task. She does this work after school and gets paid a weekly set amount of pocket money, which is not explicitly conceived as a salary by her parents although she seems to perceive it as such and resents its meagerness. She also resents that her older brother is not pressed to work for the family business as she is, and hardly helps at all. Violence between mother and daughter is constant because Marta, in addition to her work for the business, wants Montse to help with the household chores. Says Montse: "On the one hand my father wants me to help him and if I don't he punishes me by forbidding me to go out with my friends on Saturday. On the other hand my mother is always on my back asking me to help her with household chores"; and Marta retorts, "[W]ell, I have to teach you something useful for the future" (meaning her future responsibility as a housewife). Immediately after we witnessed this conflict, Marta began showing us in detail the marriage chest she was preparing for Montse while stressing "[S]he doesn't value it. She is ungrateful, we are giving her all this."

Dolores is in her late sixties and a widow. Her husband worked in construction until he got cancer and until he died, he received an invalidity pension. Her two sons were still in high school and she wanted them to keep on studying because, coming from a day-laborer family and herself a day laborer until she began to take homework covering shoe heels, she highly valued education as a way out of a miserable life. She said: "My children are going to study . . . my children even if I have to drag my tongue on the dirt they are going to study, even if it is only to learn where their right hand is . . . because him who doesn't know won't find anything and him who knows will always find (*porque el que no sabe no encontrará nada y el que sabe siempre encontrará*)."

Dolores recalls long days of work until midnight, and the help of her two sons when they got back from school and even of her ailing husband.

She knows that the glue she uses is highly toxic and flammable and that's why she sits in the middle of a corridor in order to get the air draft. The skin on her hands is peeling off because of the contact with the glue, but the doctor only tells her to stop doing this work, but she needs the money to get her kids through university.

What these few vignettes clearly show, I think, is how deep tensions are generated or aggravated by present-day embeddedness of production relations in the social fabric of the community, the family, and the self. These tensions arise from conflicting loyalties toward those who are part of people's sense of belonging, those around which personal and collective identities are constructed and security against uncertainty is intimately built. Conflicting loyalties are experienced as part of the same "morality of affects," although with clearly differentiated objectives— interest/care—that render decisions about prioritization of particular work tasks emotionally stressful.

But there is more to it: the aggravation of in-family tensions reveals the transfers of conflict-laden relationships from the market and the state into this split morality of affects and the realities of making a living. The more "economic" responsibilities are loaded with the transferred tensions induced in social relations of production by the larger context of market competition within the shoewear sector and the local and global strategies of capital. While on the other hand, the more "filial" responsibilities are loaded with the transferred tensions of an uncompromising or retracting public care service deficiently provided by the state, with the result of over-burdening particular members of households, namely, middle-aged and older women. In every case, to work for a member of the family or of the friendship network, although motivated by a general morality of affects, is generally overdetermined by very distinct contexts of material and moral pressures that we may summarize as the interest/care and market/reciprocity polarities, of which agents are acutely aware. Moreover, through the observation of this particular regional economy, we can see the permanent articulation of these split responsibilities within a more general morality of affects. Social reproduction of these extremely flexible and dynamic regional economies seems to be based on the parasitic instrumentalization of affective relationships for market-oriented business objectives, and this is part of a historical experience of labor/capital relations as they have developed locally. But also, reproduction of social identities is increasingly linked to the reproduction of work opportunities and in general to the access of economic resources through affective networks. We see young people trying to construct their individual identities through consumption, while collective identities are tied to participation in festivals, such as the Moros y Cristianos, which are also dependent on consumption capabilities. We see marriage chests, that is, alliance opportunities, being produced through unwaged work in the family business. We see mothers working as homeworkers in very harsh conditions in order to give higher education to their kids, while these same kids help them with the handwork. We see adult daughters caring for their aging parents and cashing in their pensions in order to keep the business going. It is this very messy reality, fraught with tensions that express ongoing processes of social differentiation, that social scientists and policymakers hide behind the economistic—and therefore rational and nonemotional—concept of social capital.

The ethnography, however, enables us to perceive that these tensions do not affect in the same way people in this regional economy. In general terms, what we can observe is that the more access to capital (material and "social" in Bourdieu's sense, that is, connections, prestige, and so forth), the less tensions from the use of affective relations seem to arise. Clearly, the closer to the capital side of the labor/capital divide are the economic agents, the more explicit is their instrumentalization of affective relationships. But also, the higher are the potential benefits for all those involved, although these will be shared from within a distributive justice pattern overlaid by an economic idea of fair returns for capital invested.

The case of Juan Tarres's family firm is a good example of this. This middle-aged man in his early sixties owns a factory manufacturing cork and wooden soles for sandals. The son of a carpenter he had the skill to work wood when he went to Elche in 1964 as a young man to look for work in the shoe industry. He found work there in a plant manufacturing cork soles where he worked for over ten years. When the general crisis hit the industry in 1976, he decided to go back home and open his own firm. He associated with his brother-in-law Miguel and another specialized worker in the trade, a colleague from the Elche factory. His wife Eulalia and her sister Sonia, Miguel's wife, all work in the firm. Recently, Juan and Eulalia's son and his girlfriend have begun working in the firm as well. In addition to family labor, the firm hires five male workers in the manufacturing department and some ten women in the packaging department during the production season. The firm produces 80 percent for export and the rest for national shoe manufacturers such as Castañer, a high-fashion firm. Management and control of production is in the hands of the family. Juan is the boss: "[W]e've never had any problems because everyone knows I am the boss." Miguel takes care of relations with purveyors and marketing. Eulalia manages the packaging and quality control department; Sonia is in charge of the finances; Juan's son does research on design trends and designs, while his son's girlfriend

works as the secretary. Juan has two other brothers whom he helped organize an auxiliary industry that recycles the sawdust they produce and
turns it into agglomerate that can be reused for cheaper-quality sole manufacture, or other industrial uses in furniture firms. Juan says he sold his
part of this auxiliary firm to his brothers because they were having lots of
problems between them because they both wanted to be in control and
that could not work: "[O]ne has to be the boss."

When described in this way, the family firm seems a truly cooperative endeavor where different members pool their social and human capital in an entrepreneurial manner. However, it is clear that not everyone
has access to the same capital. Particularly, gender differences crystal-
lized in formal job opportunities in the Elche years, and were therefore
incorporated in human capital in a gender-specific mode. There are
crucial differentiating processes within the family firm. In this case, we
might say that Juan is the one who becomes the entrepreneur instru-
mentalizing all the different "capitals" he can claim through his kin and
friendship networks. He is the boss, he decides on investments and production and commercial strategies. But he says, "All of this, the business,
the work, I have done it in order to 'subsist,' not in order to make money
but in order to 'subsist.' But then, if we have made some money, one always is glad that it works well." The "reproductive" argument or logic is
ideologically a very strong component of the small family firm, and we
could be tempted to interpret these production units as petty commodity production. However, the entrepreneurial, capitalist dimension is
overwhelmingly present and social relations in the family, among brothers, sisters, brothers-in-law, are contingent on the firm's expanding needs
and management requirements and not the other way around.

## Social Capital in the Vega Baja

Social capital in the Vega Baja should not be conceived as a homogeneously distributed "atmosphere" in a region to be used by any entrepreneurial spirit, in much the same way as any other resource is not
naturally and equally available to all local residents, either. Social capital,
or the ability to turn particular nonmarket relations into capital, depends on a concrete social structure in which individuals and families are
positioned in very different ways in regard to their capacity to access and
claim local "social" resources through personalized networks. Moreover,
we should again recall here the history of the region.

First, at the turn of the twentieth century, there was a tension between different experiences of exploitive relations of production, the one

supporting collective strategies in order to push forward claims, the other based on personalized politics. After the Civil War, a violent politically repressive regime was in power that excluded those who were vanquished in the war, the "reds"—precisely those who had supported collective public politics—while imposing a corporatist framework for labor relations, one that relied strongly on networks of personal relations and patronage. Finally, the experience of the 1970s of the industrial factory work and labor organization was interpreted in an ambivalent fashion by local historical subjects. It did empower workers, but the results were perceived as fatal for the industrial structure in the long run. In Spain, the effects of the 1973 oil crisis, which coincided with the demise of the Francoist regime, were interpreted as caused by the pressures of labor unions over employers, forcing them to close their big factories and decentralize and "diffuse" production. Jaime Andreu, who at the time was working in an Elche shoe factory and was shop steward for the communist union Comisiones Obreras and is now the owner of the second largest shoewear firm in Spain, located in the Vega Baja, describes those years: "These were the transition years. Unions were legalized. There was a historical movement and factories started to fear the unions. That's when factories start to dismember. Because of fear." This interpretation was supported and expressed by the hegemonic discourse on the rigidities of the labor market and the need for flexibility all over the Western world. It was also backed by the memories of the Francoist discourse (and practice) when labor struggle was equal to social anomie and extremely dangerous for the social body. Therefore in Spain, in the context of almost forty years of a corporatist regime that outlawed and repressed all types of collective expressions of dissent, particularly labor unions, this interpretation was charged with political consequences. People returned quickly to the use of well-proven personalized networks, and away from the new, democratic public space of civil society, unions, regulation, and the state.

On the other hand, it is important not to confuse social relations that are extremely different in their intent. The term *capital* does so as it expands by this means the "entrepreneurial" capacity even to homeworkers having to use their children's labor in order to make a living. The fact of having to put to use affective, nonmarket relationships in production processes does not mean that everyone is pressed into it for the same reasons, everyone has the same objectives, everyone has the same type of social resources, everyone can put them to the same uses, and everyone will benefit in the same way. Thus, Juan is in a very different position from Dolores, and it would seem a cruel misrepresentation to speak of Dolores's use of her family's labor as anything close to capital. Roberto's use of homeworkers and their families' labor through his neighbor and friendship acquaintances might be closer to capital, but, in turn, the use of his own wife and daughter's labor is fraught with ambivalence. His own entrepreneurial activity is always on the verge of collapse, and his use of affective networks benefits mostly the commercial firms upstream. Juan's position is very different and his entrepreneurial use of affective relations can be thought of as social capital. Thus, access to social capital is not evenly distributed in a region as the community integration discourse would have it. It is not evenly distributed among members of the same family either. Access to nonmarket, reciprocal, affective resources, as happens with market resources, is unevenly distributed following a differentiation process that is rooted in history (past local social relations of production) and tends to reproduce itself. The uneven access to these other social resources will depend on many factors, among others: a history of the family's position in the socioeconomic structure of the region, the position of individual members within the family structure, gender and the reproduction of gendered ideologies and practices, education opportunities, professional life histories, and the affective claims on other people's resources. Some groups are consistently unable to use a region's social capital, not because they lack entrepreneurship, but because they lack resources and the power to mobilize them. As with the commons in general, those who have more private resources are able to better make use of the commons and profit from them. Here, the commons, the regional social capital or local "atmosphere" or "culture," is hardly a shared reality.

## Toward a Corporatist Model

The Vega Baja history and ethnographic present show an unromantic vision of social relations of production and a profound differentiation in economic and political agency for most people living there. Why, then, does the model of social capital gloss them under idyllic "community" relations?

The concept of social capital, indeed, seems to have a very strong corporatist ring although with an economistic (less moral? or can we speak of a new moral of economy—not moral economy) turn to it. Apparently the concept stands for the collapse of economic determinism when the social becomes the fabric—the support—of labor/capital relations, in production, distribution, and consumption. Economic relationships are described in this model as the natural development of social and cultural interaction, but also, the social is there for the economic. This is a different angle to Polanyi's insight of the social as embedded in the economic, that is, of the economistic co-option of all social relations and institutions by a market-based hegemony. Moreover, the model is based on an organic and nonconflictive interpretation of the social, and on the separation of social and economic realms of reality, in the sense that the social would be there before (*ex ante*). The model thus supports a perspective of nondifferentiation within the social through the use of community and culture as homogenizing metaphors.

The similarity with a paternalist, Catholic, and corporatist view of society and social relations of production common in the early twentieth century in Europe is striking. One might ask if the models themselves and the reality they describe are in some way connected with the history of the consolidation of particular corporatist regimes at the turn of the century in Italy and Spain. When speaking about the political subculture that supported the establishment of the *economia diffusa* in the northern Italian regions, for example, Bagnasco (1994) tries to explain how these regions with a "typically communist political culture" were particularly fertile to the development of an industrial district:

> It has been a play between a particular ideological evolution, to-
> gether with the values and practices of autonomy of the artisans and
> peasants, that has resulted in the cultural definition of the develop-
> ment based on the "economia diffusa" as a collective endeavor.
> *Rather than with the socialism of daylaborers'* (braccianti) *associations,*
> *this ideology is related to the municipal socialism of the artisans, the small*
> *merchants and the peasants.* Interpreted in this way, the political sub-
> culture appears then also as a resource for local development and
> the source of motivation of economic action. (40; emphasis added)

The corporatist interpretation of a so-called communist political regional culture is salient. However, the regions in northern Italy where the economia diffusa has developed (Emilia-Romagna, Veneto, Friuli-Venezia Giulia) have a conflicting history of political practices. These included wide support to the fascist movement during the 1920s and 1930s, as well as strong union movements in towns that were centers of class struggle, and strong employers organizations that co-opted the state during the First World War and during Mussolini's regime (Meriggi 1996, 79–115). This often very violent history, fraught with social differentiation and with the use of diverse and conflicting political spaces in order to further claims, is completely obscured by Bagnasco (and the other apologists of the Third Italy model). In fact, the conflation of a communist political culture with a corporatist selective reality contributes to the socially at-tractive face of the economia diffusa (i.e., if communists support it, it must be good for workers). In the best tradition of corporatist ideology the conflation of social intent, hierarchical authority, and organic differentiation are all present in Bagnasco's (1994) pseudohistorical model: "Consensus did not derive, in fact, generically from a traditional culture, incapable of defining the differences between social classes, rather (it derived) *from an implicit pact of institutional composition of these differences*" (41; emphasis added).

In the case of Spain, it is certainly impossible to avoid referring to the corporatist politics of the state during the dictatorship of General Primo de Rivera (1923–1929), the long Francoist regime (1939–1975), and the recurrent violent repression of collective class struggles when trying to understand the economic region of the Vega Baja and the process by which present-day social relations have acquired their personalized character. Thus, although the Italian theorists of the industrial district use the reference to history to justify the existence of a particularly fertile ground for the development of a successful economia diffusa, it is indeed a very selective history, one that underlines the more corporatist aspects of the region's relations of production and highlights an organic interpretation of local society, while obscuring other relationships, struggles, and repressive practices.

We have observed that the confusion of the social spaces where labor/capital relations take place with those where reciprocal/affective relations take place generate strong tensions that displace conflicts (about access to resources, distributive claims, and so on) from the ground of public politics to the ground of private personal conflict (the self and the family). But also, in a dialectical mode, the reverse is also true: new social relations of production (decentralization, economia diffusa, informal economy, illegal labor migration) produce a closure of the public space where citizenship rights can be claimed, and drive people toward personalized and organic forms of politics. Conservative governmental policies retracting from public-shared responsibility for citizens' well-being and from universal regulation of the limits to labor exploitation and basic universal rights for workers,[5] effect a de facto closure of the public space. Moreover, European Union redistributive policies targeting "regions" enhance the appeal of voicing claims in terms of community in regional models of political action. What I have tried to confront through the ethnography is summed up in the following questions: What about differential access to a region's social capital? How is it historically constructed through processes of differentiation grounded in social relations of production and in power relations in the family, the community, the family farm or firm, conditioning individual positions and leverage within the social fabric? How does the construction of a particular form of state and public institutions affect local processes of differentiation?

## Conclusion:  From Model to Hegemony

One might ask, then, What is new in this regional economy of the dynamic industrial districts of Europe as compared with the classical cases of petty commodity production described as "transitional" to "real" capitalism? I think that the main difference relates to what Polanyi described as "the society being embedded in the economy." Karl Marx also addressed this problem through the concept of alienation. In capitalism we seem to observe an extreme mode of alienation in which the human person is alienated from the objective conditions needed to reproduce life. In an extreme mode in today's realities, the human person is particularly alienated from the social conditions that reproduce her or his "subjective social being" (something close to our concept of identity). Now, to paraphrase Marx (1970, 705–706), the objectification of affective relations, their embodiment and materialization in production relations appears as a loss of reality of the person and a loss of these affective relations themselves. The more the affective relations are objectified in production, the less they belong to her or him, being absorbed into the realm of capitalist growth. I do not wish to push this analogy further. However, what I want to stress in this last part of the chapter is the way in which capitalism needs "externalities" (nature, nonmarket-mediated social relations, and so forth) in order to reduce costs (transaction costs, production costs, and so forth), and is permanently locked in a dialectical tension between consuming them and, in the process, "internalizing" them and reproducing them as externalities. This is a similar observation to what Polanyi pointed to in *The Great Transformation* (1966) when speaking of the fictive commodities—nature and human life (he added money)—and how the social system had to generate protective devices (such as labor laws) in order to reproduce them as fictive commodities. Following this insight, I would suggest that the social reproduction of these necessary externalities takes place through the generation of particular hegemonies (Williams 1989, 145).

Moreover, in order for a hegemony to reproduce itself as such, it must obliterate the possibility for a counterhegemony to emerge, it must try to effect a cultural and political closure in which no space for experiencing or imagining different realities is allowed. This, I contend, is best realized by organic models of society, models that are based on concepts of equity as opposed to concepts of equality. I am here not speaking of reality itself, where equity and equality are not easily separable for they seem to be part of a dialectics of justice. Rather, I am highlighting the salience of particular models of society. It is also realized through the institutionalized use of violence and repression.

At the end of the nineteenth century in Europe, an organic version of society based on the model of the family as a hierarchical, authoritarian, yet consensual, organization was confronted as a political option to the liberal model of a state of equal citizens (Tönnies 1979). This was not only, or even mainly, a survival of ancien régime institutions or ideologies. These were bourgeois policies trying to produce a new organic hegemonic social space (different from the Traditionalist order) precisely when industrialization and class struggle are creating conditions for a restructuring of society in other terms, supported by the opening of the political public space by the liberal policies of the anti-Absolutists central governments (Narotzky 1997, 177–189). This organic ideology was produced in the explicit attempt by the local bourgeois class to put an end to the social problem (that is, class struggle) in the context of unstable or powerless central states. It is expressed politically by the consolidation of nationalist ideologies and in economic policies by the attempt to push forward the paternalist social recommendations of Catholic doctrine (Leo XIII 1959).

The analogy with the social capital model is striking. Here also, sharing ideas, sentiments, and affection in an organic mode is crucial for progress, while economic and social well-being seem to be one and the same thing and fairly distributed among all members of a region. Differentiation within the region is tied to individual entrepreneurial ability—autonomy—to put to good use the region's relational potentialities—embeddedness. Naturalization and essentialism are also present in the model through the idea of a homogeneously shared system of values and thought (Becattini 1994, 41), a regional culture. Thus, affects and spatial proximity are seen to contribute to a dynamic and flexible economy and lead to social progress. However, in the present model; the organic and cultural dimension is entirely integrated into the economic model; it does not require the mediation of a structured political body such as was the case in the nationalist bourgeois programs. As a result, the closure of the public politics space is even greater; public space appears as a residual form that does not concern the reproduction of regional economies.

In the actual process of construction of the political and economic agenda of the European Union, the notion of "subsidiarity" plays an important role in the discourse of political decentralization. Likewise, the spatial designation of particular regions as recipients of European subsidies through the structural and social cohesion funds. One can perceive a trend, I think, toward an increasingly organic conception of political bodies and of economic processes, and this seems to require the delimitation and homogenization of the space of social interaction through the reference to a shared reality of regional scope. The fact that this happens while capital (and labor) is increasingly mobile and delocalized, and assets such as information are increasingly ubiquitous, seems to point to an apparent paradox in the way capital accumulation is developing worldwide. It would seem that as capitalists in regard to their reproductive strategies (including most of the institutions that regulate their global movements) seem to be acting increasingly as a transnational class (and this includes the instrumental use of locality to access resources), labor is increasingly pushed to address their claims in terms of particular identities defined in cultural or local terms, or both. Although the fact of addressing claims on the basis of cultural membership or on those of citizenship participation will depend on the historically produced opportunities to do so in either terms (Smith 1999, 195–227), it seems increasingly apparent that the power-holders' hegemonic project, while opening the political space for capital, is trying to close the political space for labor (Bologna 1997). And I think that the concepts of economic embeddedness and social capital are important instruments in this political economic process.

## Notes

This chapter is the fruit of work funded by research project PB98-1238 "La reciprocidad como recurso humano" (Reciprocity as Human Resource) in the Programa Sectorial de Promoción General del Conocimiento, Ministerio de Educación y Cultura, Spain.

1. The fieldwork was done in collaboration with Gavin Smith in 1995. Previously, Smith had done fieldwork in the same area in 1978–1979. Funding was provided by the Social Science and Humanities Research Council of Canada, Grant No. 410-93-0683. Many of the problems raised in this chapter are the result of many years of intellectual debate with Smith although I am totally responsible for their present development.

2. This is different from Pierre Bourdieu's (1980) concept, which is part of his definition of the interaction of various types of "capital"—economic, symbolic, cultural, and social—in the social reproduction of a society, through the structuring of the habitus.

3. For a critique of the industrial district model, see Amin and Robins (1994); Gertler (1992); Hadjimichalis and Papamichos (1990); Smith (1999).

4. This mobility of the factories makes it possible to reproduce permanently local pools of "reserve army" labor, and generates a strong feeling of labor market insecurity and personal expendability and exchangeability on the part of the workers. This is the impersonal face of the industrial district of the Vega Baja.

5. For example, the recently approved Ley de Extranjería denies basic civil rights such as the right of reunion and association to irregular immigrants in Spain.

# References

Amin, A., and K. Robins. 1994. El retorno de las economías regionales. Geografía mítica de la acumulación flexible. In *Las regiones que ganan*, edited by G. Benko and A. Lipietz. Valencia, Spain: Alfons el Magnanim.

Bagnasco, A. 1988. *La costruzione sociale del mercato: studi sullo sviluppo di piccola impresa in Italia.* Bologna: Il Mulino.

———. 1994. *Fatti sociali formati nello spazio. Cinque lezioni di sociologia urbana e regionale.* Milan: Franco Angeli.

Becattini, G. 1994. El districto marshalliano: una noción socioeconómica. In *Las regiones que ganan*, edited by G. Benko and A. Lipietz. Valencia, Spain: Alfons el Magnanim.

Bellandi, M. 1989. The industrial district in Marshall. In *Small firms and industrial districts in Italy*, edited by E. Goodman, J. Bamford, and P. Saymor. London: Routledge.

Bernabé, J. M. 1975. *Indústria i subdesenvolupament al País Valencià.* Mallorca, Spain: Editorial Moll.

Bologna, S. 1997. Dieci tesi per la definizione di uno statuto del lavoro autonomo. In *Il lavoro autonomo di seconda generazione*, edited by S. Bologna and A. Fumagilli. Milan: Feltrinelli.

Bourdieu, P. 1980. *Le sens pratique.* Paris: Les Editions de Minuit.

Fine, B. 1999. The developmental state is dead—Long live social capital? *Development and Change* 30(1): 1–19.

Gertler, M. 1992. Flexibility revisited: Districts, nation-states, and the forces of production. *Transactions: Institute of British Geographers* 17.

Granovetter, M. S. 1985. Economic action and social structure: The problem of embeddedness. *American Journal of Sociology* 91(3): 481–510.

Hadjmichalis, C., and N. Papamichos. 1990. "Local" development in southern Europe: Towards a new mythology. *Antipode* 22(3): 181–210.

Harrison, B. 1992. Industrial districts: Old wine in new bottles? *Regional Studies* 26(5): 469–483.

Harvey, D. 1989. *The condition of postmodernity.* Oxford: Blackwell.

Leo XIII. 1959. Rerum novarum. In *Doctrina pontificia. Documentos sociales,* edited by F. Rodriguez. 1891. Reprint, Madrid: BAC.

Marshall, A. 1964. *Elements of economics of industry.* 1892. Reprint. London: MacMillan.

Marx, K. 1970. *Manuscritos: Economí y Filosofía.* Madrid: Alianza Editorial.

Meriggi, M. 1996. *Breve storia dell'Italia settentrionale dall'Ottocento a oggi.* Rome: Donzelli Editore.

Moreno Saez, F. 1987. *El movimiento obrero en Elche (1890–1931).* Alicante, Spain: Instituto de Estudios Juan Gil-Albert.

Narotzky, S. 1997. *New directions in economic anthropology.* London: Pluto.

Piore, M. J., and C. F. Sabel. 1984. *The second industrial divide.* New York: Basic Books.

Polanyi, K. 1957. The economy as instituted process. In *Trade and market in the early empires: Economies in history and theory,* edited by K. Polanyi, C. Arensberg, and H. Pearson. New York: Free Press.

———. 1971. *The Great Transformation.* 1944. Reprint, Boston: Beacon Press.

Richards, M. 1998. *A time of silence: Civil war and the culture of repression in Franco's Spain, 1936–1945.* Cambridge: Cambridge University Press.

Sabel, C. 1989. Flexible specialization and the re-emergence of regional economies. In *Reversing Industrial Decline?* edited by P. Hirst and J. Zeitlin. Oxford: Berg.

Smith, G. 1991. Writing for real: Capitalist constructions and constructions of capitalism. *Critique of Anthropology* 11(3): 213–232.

———. 1999. *Confronting the present: Towards a politically engaged anthropology.* Oxford: Berg.

Tönnies, F. 1979. *Comunidad y asociación.* 1887. Reprint, Barcelona: Ediciones Península.

Williams, R. 1989. *Keywords: A vocabulary of culture and society.* London: Fontana Paperbacks.

Woolcock, M. 1998. Social capital and economic development: Toward a theoretical synthesis and policy framework. *Theory and Society* 27: 151–208.

Ybarra, J. A. 1991. *Industrial districts and the Valencian community.* International Institute for Labour Studies, Discussion Paper No.44. Geneva: International Labor Organziation.

# Part II
# Liminality and the Narrative of Survival

# 4

# Manufacturing the New Man

*Professional Training in France—Life Stories and the Reshaping of Identities*

Angela Procoli

At a time when workers are supposed to be competent, mobil, and multiskilled, training, that is to say, the implementation of means to increase the individual professional skills, is turned into a strategic tool to adapt the individual to changing techniques and working conditions. These are the terms in which it is described by the European Commission (EC; 2001): "In looking to future job creation we need to recognize the change taking place in the nature of work. The old concept of a job for life, based on an initial training, is rapidly disappearing." Today's economy calls for flexibility." This means that Europe needs a multiskilled workforce that is capable of being rapidly retrained to work in new situations, and workers who are open to the concept of lifelong learning. Some experts have said that the average worker or professional will have three "careers" in his working life. "This means the educational and training systems need to ensure that people learn, and continue to be equipped with, the appropriate skills" (European Commission 2001).

The EC's discourse on the topic, steeped as it is in ideology, in which the recurrent necessity to adapt is presented as a positive development, throws a thin veil on an often very hurtful human reality. As one goes to where the action takes place and investigates matters in a professional training center in Paris, the sufferings brought about by a volatile work market are fully revealed and the all-encompassing nature, both professional and personal, of training becomes clear. Paradoxically enough, training appears both as the place where institutional violence is directed against the worker to cast him into the mold of modern economy and a protective haven within which he or she can reconstruct his or her identity.[1]

## Training the European Worker

Professional training nowadays is a core element of the employment policy of the EC, the self-proclaimed objective of which is to see to it that workers are mobile, a purpose served by validating professional qualifications as between different countries. Since Europe is no longer considered an area where goods and capital have a free run and an area for exchange and economic activity, "worker mobility" is no longer merely the right of individuals to move in freedom, but becomes one of the building blocks of economic and community development (Merle 1993, 44). The all-encompassing greater European market must go side by side with worker mobility even though the workers concerned generally belong to the category of skilled manpower (Marsden 1993). Training is "a strategic investment of vital importance for the firm's future success" as stated in the report "Education and Skills en Europe" published in January 1989 by the European Round Table (ERT).[2] A full-fledged program for professional training was consequently launched in 1994 to implement the EC policy in the field of professional training, promoting "lifelong training" and "the development of new forms of apprenticeship" (Sélys 1998).[3] In 1995, another ERT report insists yet again on "the necessity of many-sided training . . . an inducement to learn throughout one's life." I will discuss later that the notion of training "throughout one's life" did not spring up in an office in Brussels but follows a clearly marked pedagogical tradition, that of the Enlightenment, inspiring as it did the innovations of the First Republic (1792–1804), the purpose of which was to train an "enlightened" citizen. The novelty lies in the fact that training and education alike are clearly identified as subservient to economic considerations. This is understandable when taken in the context of mass unemployment where priority must be given to matters of urgency. Such subservience, however, is sometimes criticized (Petrella 1991). Training is also considered in a European context as a tool to requalify and obviate the risk of downright exclusion from the employment market. Throughout the 1980s, as unemployment grew in Europe,[4] training was given a new role to see to it that the workforce threatened with exclusion was redeployed elsewhere. This in varying degrees in the different countries where the future of training is in the hands of public authorities or the unions. Thus, in Italy there is no established tradition for vocational training; in the United Kingdom, it has been deregulated step by step by the conservative government early in the 1980s (the trade unions, much weakened, and the state have a very small share in the training activities of firms). Training thus becomes a deliberate choice left to the free initiative of entrepreneurs and individuals alike (Rainbird 1994).

Contrary to this, training is regulated under trade union control—this is the case in Belgium and Germany, where training-cum-reconversion programs to implement projects for collective redeployment in new firms—or by public authorities. In the latter case, training activities are strongly institutionalized at the highest level: this is the case in Spain and, above all, in France where the state takes a hand in situations of mass repatterning and encourages training to reconvert as a means to avoid wholesale exclusion from the work market (Villeval 1993). In political-cum-media language, training looms very large: to the extent that exclusion from work is a consequence of inadequacy, in social terms, of those who cannot assimilate the "logic of competence," training would bring about the worker's acceptance of the newfangled rational productivity, resting on the principles of flexibility and adaptability to the needs of the firm (Dubar 1996).

This discourse has a strong ideological twist and gives rise to a question: How can training, at one and the same time, be a tool to roll back professional exclusion and help high performers along the way?— by this I mean that the very concept of competitiveness bears the notion of discrimination within itself. Professional training schemes of one kind or another have been scrutinized and appear in the end as a tool for discrimination, inasmuch as they have been conceived of as directed to technicians and engineers, ruling out "the less skilled" (Roustang 1974). European policy, as it appears, seems to be directed, to a great extent, to highly skilled workers called on to circulate in networks where mobility is prevalent (Marsden 1993).

The community's discourse, overriden by economic considerations, makes no mention whatsoever of the deep-seated changes in identity brought about by a period of training, long or short. While training nowadays is a professional institution, the changes in identity that it involves, as I will show, may well go beyond the professional sphere and be thoroughly unsettling. The case of France becomes particularly interesting since training there was considered a tool for the worker to improve his professional knowledge and skills so as to become a "good citizen."

# The Institution Is Revolutionary in Origin

In France the concept of professional training originates in the revolutionary pedagogical trend of the late eighteenth century,[5] which aimed for making the right to knowledge more democratic and establishing the control of the Republican state on the transmission of knowledge, a privilege hitherto held by an elite of priests and the nobility. Condorcet,[6] who was a key figure among the intellectuals of the French Revolution, formulated the theory of an all-encompassing project for national education to train the citizen of the new Republic through self-improvement and lifelong learning (Condorcet 1989).

Two centuries later, the revolutionary ideas are at the root of the law on lifelong education that grants every worker, for the first time, the right to apply for leave with training.[7] This law (No. 71-575) on professional training, promulgated on July 16, 1971 (*Journal officiel*, July 17, 1971) after a decade of deep-seated economic and social change, attempts to include the necessity for training in a more extensive plan that goes far beyond mere professional training. To quote article 1 of the law in two different places: (i) "lifelong professional training makes it possible for workers to adapt to changing techniques and working conditions, to enhance their position in society by providing access to various levels of culture and professional skills and favors their contribution to economic, social, and cultural development"; (ii) the training institution "has as its purpose to see to the training and development of man at all stages of his life, to make it possible for him to acquire the knowledge and all of the intellectual or manual skills necessary for his fulfilment and for cultural, economic, and social progress." As Jacques Delors, the driving spirit behind this law, said, as he evoked Condorcet's ideas, training must provide for the individual's "personal fullfilment," it must set mankind "free" and, "capable of autonomy," protect it against the risk of alienation necessarily involved in "progress" where the ascendancy of techostructures, complex rules, splintered human activities, and the pervasiveness and aggressivity of the media are permanent features (Delors 1974).[8]

Delors considered training a means of saving man from "breaking into a million pieces" (alienation). A few years later, under the pressure of escalating unemployment, Delors took the lead in a "change of course" so that training became part of an emergency call to act on the spot and produce solutions for the short term. Conceived as such, it became a defensive weapon to obviate the risks of an out-and-out exclusion of the employment market or, as he stated in the press, "means to emerge from a situation that is materially and psychologically difficult"

(*Le Monde*, 10 January 1980, p. 33). It is true that even today the notion of emergency has become so pressing that workers undertake training for fear of becoming redundant. But it is precisely as one analyzes the trainee's speech and experience that it becomes clear that the "emergency call" is now well behind us and the very value of this institution is considered in an entirely new light. Beyond the pronouncement of officialdom, training becomes a vantage point to observe precariousness as part of a situation in society that amounts to upheaval and where the quest for survival in a world where social equilibria are uncertain takes the path of the repatterning of "identities." This is an aspect that is made clear in the ethnographic study that I carried out from 1992 to 1998 in the oldest French institution for professional training, the Conservatoire National des Arts et Métiers (CNAM) in Paris.

The CNAM was founded at the end of the eighteenth century (at the time of the French Revolution). It was intended to be a kind of university for any worker (worker, technician, or engineer) who attended in the evening, at the end of his or her workday, to keep abreast of new technologies and to be educated in the most recent techniques applying the tools of his or her trade. Today, the CNAM looks for a compromise between loyalty to the revolutionary idea that everyone has the right to have an education (*omnes docet*) and the necessity to be adaptable to the rules of the market. Thus, in the 1970s, the Conservatoire, where today people still traditionally train after work hours (from 6 P.M. to 10 P.M.), adopted a new training program exclusively for executives with a long working experience, while traditional evening courses were open to technical personnel or the unemployed, or even to young people who did not have any professional experience. From the point of view of the institution, traditional training is separated from the new mode of training. This introduces for the first time in Conservatoire the notion of "selection." While evening courses are almost free, day classes are particularly expensive and employers cover the expenses. The arrangement is known as "leave with pay for training"; the law establishing this right for the first time in France was promulgated in July 1971. While evening courses are open not only to employed people (workers and technicians) but also to the unemployed, day classes are strictly reserved for those who have a job. Middle or senior executives (they are 35–45 years old) attending the day classes come to the CNAM intending to prepare for a new job or a promotion. To them, daytime training has a good brand image; they are monitored at close range by those responsible for training. Competence is guaranteed by "switching" (between workplace and training institution; Rosanvallon 1992). This is supposed to give trainees the opportunity to adapt the theoretical learning acquired at the CNAM to the firm's practical needs.

For the first time, recent courses allot a substantial role to the management of human resources over the long term. This form of training is earmarked for groups of forty trainees as a maximum and lasts two years. This is conceived of as a cycle to indicate the perennial nature of the training. Trainees come and go as twice a year a new group is introduced and another one emerges. The course develops at three different levels: beginners, middle course, and leavers.

The CNAM continuing-education course in which I carried out my study is quite heterogenous from the standpoint of the sociological profiles involved. There is a mixture of actors from a wide variety of social backgrounds and professional paths. The child of immigrant origin sits next to the scion of a long line of aristocrats, social or hospital workers study with executives from ministries or private firms. The forty- or fifty-year-old manager who, having started out as a skilled worker, has built his career on night-school diplomas rubs elbows with the young engineer straight out of a "Grande Ecole" who has jumped directly to the top of the professional hierarchy. One even encounters former trade union activists hoping to retrain as company managers. Above all, the trainees' relationship with the job market is extremely varied: the program mixes without distinction securely integrated executives, workers unsure of keeping their job, and even the unemployed (despite the fact that they are not targeted by the day classes).

The ethnographic study that I have carried out in groups training in human resources management shows how, as the time of training goes by, actors from such different horizons come to form a genuine "group" inscribed in a well-defined space and time (those of the training program). The group constitutes itself through the leveling of this sociological mixture and through subscription to the same retraining project. Analysis of the retraining method will enable us to understand this process better.

## The Principle of Deconstruction/ Reconstruction of Identity

The focal point of the teaching method is self-evaluation and then evaluation of the other. "To manage the other, you first have to know how to manage yourself," the instructor would repeat time and again. Knowing how to evaluate (oneself) supposes a distancing process. That is why trainees must step back from their professional and family involvements, even if this may affect their personal stability. Although, for the instructor, the ultimate goal of this process is purely professional (to become a manager), we will see that, in reappropriating his methods, the trainees took their professional goal to come second. Their viewpoint is comforting, at all events, for the changes they undergo in their professional lives do not always coincide with what they had envisaged when they enrolled in the program. For instance, destabilization, as a consequence of distancing, is not necessarily followed by new professional stability, notwithstanding the instructor's assurances. Every destabilization (which occur in reality at every level during the training period) must be analyzed in a more global perspective, in which what is truly at stake for the trainees is a transformation of their identity (Broda 1990).

The training method draws on two principles: "deconstruction" of one's life path and its "reconstruction." The aim of the method is to produce new person (the manager), for, following a logic of initiation, it is only by learning to change oneself that one will be able to change (manage) others and thus integrate them into the company's future. The entire program has been organized to compel trainees to invest to a maximum, while giving them the impression of operating almost independently of the instructor (Procoli 2001a,b). Trainees practice management techniques through simulation and role play. Beginning with a real company, they break down the profile of a (fictional) individual into his or her various functions and select those worth developing. In effect, after deconstructing the old, something new must be constructed. Trainees are supposed to elaborate their career plan. The deconstruction/reconstruction method is no longer being applied to a fictional person here, but to a flesh-and-blood human being, oneself. It is no longer a matter of evaluating an abstract person, but of learning to evaluate oneself. In learning to look at one's life history from a distance, trainees are invited to step back from everything outside their program (family and work). They expose their life history (at all levels: family, job, and so on) to their fellow trainees to show how their professional life came about. They do not hesitate to explain their motivations, their hopes and fears for the role the program will play in their professional future. Those listening are then invited to deconstruct the individual's past so as to select the elements they themselves, based on their own experience, judge to be useful for constructing a career plan. The individual's own image, reflected by the others, introduces a greater degree of complexity into his or her initial career plan, which expands to a general reflection on the program and on life itself. Through the feedback received from fellow trainees, the individual learns to look at his or her path from a distance, as if it belonged to someone else.

As conceived by the head instructor, this method constantly encourages trainees to go beyond their family and professional stabilities, to deconstruct the specificity of their own life path. All must subscribe to the same objective: find new sources of stability. As a rule, trainees enroll in the program in the framework of a *congé-formation*, or training leave: their employer allows them temporarily to leave their post in order to acquire the professional skills necessary to the company's evolution. It is therefore not unusual for the subject of the final memoir to be chosen in consultation with the employer: in this case, trainees are led to apply the instructor's method to questions felt to be urgent in their own professional setting. The principle of alternation allows them to put the new work methods into practice on the job and to discuss their validity with their colleagues and their employer. But it is this very return to the job that becomes a critical moment when the trainees discover they are "out of step" with their colleagues, who do not understand their objective and their new working methods. Tension arises as well between them and their hierarchical superiors, who do not appreciate their subordinate taking an analytical-critical view of the way their department is run. Yet even when these tensions build up, it is unusual for a trainee to drop out of the program, even if this may lead to his or her dismissal.[9] Why then do they allow themselves to be destabilized by a program that, paradoxically, is supposed to be beneficial to their company and to themselves? To answer this, one needs to understand how the group reappropriates the training method and elaborates a symbolic discourse on retraining in which the professional objective no longer appears as a priority.

## From Individual Narrative to Collective Narrative

Narratives can be "a potent force in mediating disruption," writes Gay Becker (1997) in her book dealing with the ways in which people make sense of life crises and the impaired identities thereby acquired. I agree with Becker on the importance of narratives when they serve to overcome a crisis, but, contrary to her views, I do not believe that everything is resolved at the level of the individual. Indeed, the case of the CNAM goes to show that identity repatterning can be carried out in a working group—and only there, as the "individual discourse," based on the notion of "disrupted lives," and encouraged by the training method itself (Dominicé 1994)—merges into the "collective discourse" centering on the notion of a repatterned life course.

The individual narrative, encouraged during the training sessions, took on a more informal note during the breaks. The trainees tended to "tell their story," to recount the incidents in their lives. At the individual level, the actor evoked his or her suffering at the loss of a loved one, or when he or she was made redundant after many years with the same company, or finally when he or she dropped the ideology underpinning his or her union activism to choose a career in management. At the collective level, the lost object was fuzzier. For instance, confusion arose between losing and the risk of losing a job, between death and separation (divorce). The weakening of the social bond, the professional or family disorder, visible in certain individual narratives, became the object of a "shared" discourse in which the trainees imagined the "death" of the ties outside the program and their reconstruction inside the course. Even those who had not lost their job and who would not lose it, at least not during the program, spoke and acted as though they had already been made redundant. The program became the place where they "learned to accept the loss of their job" or talked about their "professional death" (these are expressions used by the trainees themselves).[10] In an analogous way, the slightest sign of trouble in the couple became the object of a narrative on the breaking of family ties. Furthermore, in keeping with the logic of the program, where all former forms of stability must be abandoned, "sterility" of the couple was highly appreciated. It was an unspoken rule not to have a child during the training period. When a couple did procreate, its fecundity also went unspoken. By this silence, the person who has a child behaves as though he or she had none. If he or she happens to be found out, the "transgressor" becomes the butt of jokes by means of which the group seeks to "devaluate" biological parenthood and to replace it by symbolic parenthood. Thus all the trainees declare themselves the child's godparents (Procoli 2001).

Typical, too, of the collective narrative is the foundation of a new order. First, it is important to realize the distance the actors have put between themselves and their family and professional universe. In the framework of a method that encourages distancing, the training program symbolically becomes the "inner" space where the trainees crystallize into a group. Whereas "outside" is used constantly, the concept of "inside" appears in a more indirect fashion: in the trainees' discourse, the program is represented as a closed space in which the variety of sociological backgrounds is transcended and the social body becomes symbolically unified. It is important to emphasize just how much this representation runs counter to the official discourse on the program proffered by the faculty. For them, the day program is a high-level course reserved for those working in the world. Above all, it must not be confused with the evening classes, open to all comers (even to those who are no longer exercising a profession). This discourse is sometimes carried to the extreme by the leaders of the daytime courses, who consider that the continuing education program is reserved for genuine "professionals," while the evening classes are the dumping ground for the unemployed or for young people with no work experience. And yet, the facts show that the distinction between daytime "high performers" and the evening school "nonperformers" is not all that clear-cut. The division between the two programs is called into question by the trainees themselves, who, in practice, mix the two. Some enroll in the continuing-education program after having taken evening classes for many long years. Others continue their daytime training by attending the evening classes. By training on a full-time basis, they succeed first in getting a truly "continuing" education and, second, in translating into concrete terms the "ethic of sacrifice" which, for all actors at the CNAM (instructors and students alike), is one of the basic tenets of the institution (Grignon 1976). *"Pour bien se former, il faut tout sacrifier"* (to succeed in one's education, one must sacrifice everything) is a saying frequently heard at the CNAM. Finally, in these continuing-education courses, one also encounters people without the expected profile for a specialized program. They are unemployed, or women wanting to go back to work ten or even twenty years after having stopped their formal education. They are attracted by the public image of this kind of program that, with its principle of alternation, appears to offer them a precious link with the professional world from which they have been excluded. For the latter, to enroll in a program means a genuine financial sacrifice, for they pay the whole, or at any rate the greater part, of the tuition fees. These fees are significantly higher than the enrollment fees for evening classes.[11] The presence of a mixed public clearly indicates a transcendence of sociological roles as defined in the outside world (worker/nonworker, parent/nonparent) and their redefinition within the program. Subscription to the same retraining plan is synonymous with a single description of the past where, regardless of each person's own experience, there reigns a general identity crisis. Overcoming this crisis becomes the objective of the course, the goal "narrated" by the group.

## All-Encompassing Change

In the training space, where the trainees progressively distance themselves from their outside sources of stability, the retraining loses its professional meaning. In this global transformation, two new forms of stability need to be affirmed. To achieve this, stress must be laid on the value of sacrificing the memory of the past: reconfiguration of one's identity begins to resonate profoundly with the training method, which constantly invites the trainees to sacrifice their professional and family past in view of a "higher good"—the acquisition of a skill, that of managing.

Some of the things that happened in the course can be interpreted as staged events, the only goal of which was to neutralize the old alliances within the group. These events can be caricatures, like the "weddings" which, within the space of the program, celebrate new liaisons that will replace the old ones. It does not matter much that these ties are limited to the time and the space of the program (they usually do not last beyond the end of the course). "Pure products" of the program, they clearly show that, in the group's symbolic system, the program is a space where a new family can take shape. The family solidarities "played" out in the program sometimes find an extended life in the foundation of new forms of stability after the program. There is a correspondence between the destabilization acted out "inside" the program and the reproduction of a new social order on the "outside." Thus, for a certain number of trainees, the end of the program coincides with a change in family or professional circumstances. The acquisition of a new professional stability is, of course, the fervent wish of the instructor, who wants the trainees' new career to take the direction set out in the project formulated at the beginning of the course. "These courses," he says with pride, "are the only training program I know of that produces such great changes in the professional path." But what makes the most vivid impression on the trainees are the new forms of family and affective stabilities set in place after the end of the program. "The CNAM," they joke, "is the house of divorces and remarriage." Of course the instructor is not unaware that his program may prompt changes at the personal level, but for him, everything is secondary to the professional goal. Alternatively, the professional objective is no longer the priority in the collective narrative. What counts for the group is that the program ultimately "bring forth a new being." This reconfigured identity is, I stress, a collective product, in the true sense of the term, for it can come about only in the group setting. Over the two-year program, it is rare to see a trainee who has not been more or less destabilized at some level or other. The program brings about real changes in the actors' lives, positive for some and negative for others. For instance, some—in difficulty when they enrolled—find a new stability upon leaving the CNAM. Others, who have followed apparently more linear paths, find themselves in precarious situations. All of this would be in the nature of a paradox if the collective narrative were not taken into account. It is by the group that the quest for stability is set in place and not by the simple individual. It is also at the level of the collective (mythic) narrative that a connection is made between the "destabilization of the stable"—an expression I have borrowed from Robert Castel (1995)—and the "stabilization of the unstable."

The correspondence (causal link) between the destabilization of some and the stabilization of others can be seen in spectacular events worthy of the stage, but which really do change the trainees' lives. This was the case of one "fragile being" (she came to the CNAM from a precarious professional and family situation) and another "high-performance" cadre (he had built himself a remarkable career thanks to a great number of training courses), who saw their respective roles reversed. Even before the end of the course, he was suddenly destabilized at the professional level (he was made redundant in a wholly unexpected manner whereas he expected to become his company's regional director), while, she, at last, found stability (she took over the job her companion had lost) (Procoli 2001, 2000).

This role reversal, which calls into question the official division between high performers and nonperformers (the first being enrolled in the day program, the second attending evening classes), is an exemplary illustration not only of the sacrifice of the memory of the past, but also of the sacrifice necessary for the reproduction of the social relations within the group. This is the sacrifice of the renouncer: the member of the program regarded as the model of "professional and family performance" (to which everyone aspires) renounces all he or she possesses so that others may succeed in their training and find stability.

## Constructing a "Mythic Past" in Order to Legitimize an Uncertain Future

Sacrificing one's memory of the past is not the only modality for reconfiguring an identity. I would like to pause here over a singular reappropriation of the training method. This method today encourages the trainee to deconstruct the past so as to become a manager in the future. The concept of deconstruction remains ambiguous. If deconstruction makes it possible to go beyond the old forms of stability, it also selects certain elements from the past for incorporation into the career plan of the future. The past is genuinely "recycled."[12]

In the collective narrative, the past, purged of all its negative elements, is transformed into a mythic past, which will serve as a basis for legitimizing an until-now uncertain future. The discourse is less abstract than it first seems. I will briefly summarize the analysis of two "scenes" that I have analyzed in detail elsewhere (Procoli 2001). In these scenes, the trainees acted out their revenge on a past, in which, they said, they were wronged. One of these was acted out in the management techniques sessions, where the trainee learns to be a "competent" manager, in other words capable of assessing the capacities of the fictional candidate so as to decide on his professional future. In the reappropriation of this scene at the collective (mythic) level, those who, in the past, had been victims of the violence of the world of work (through redundancy or the threat of redundancy) would inflict the same violence on the fictional Other (the condemned/the accused becomes the judge/the executioner).

The other scene is not taken from a role-playing session proposed by the institution. It was a spontaneous creation by the trainees themselves, and is the mirror image of the preceding scene. The trainees designated a "scapegoat," who was to be charged with all the "sins" of management and sent out into the desert. For the manager's greatest sin is exercising his right to mete out justice over the Other. It is no accident that the director and principal actor of this scene was the former union activist. Although they represented a minority of the trainees, ex-union members were very active in the course.[13] They were going through a difficult transition between their former state as union members and their future status as company managers. Their conversion is highly problematical: they must gain acceptance in a world (that of company managers) where they have always been viewed as enemies, they are leaving a world that openly accuses them of being traitors. Better than all the other trainees, the former activists expressed the need to reformulate a past that, if left intact, would be incompatible with their plans for becoming company managers. In particular, to avoid this infamous accusation of treason, they energetically maintained that certain noble values from their activist past (altruism) would guide their future action (in their capacity as a manager).

However, this redefinition by former activists of the manager glosses over all the negative aspects of the job. In effect, it is highly likely that they will be led to formulate restructuring plans. Moreover, their training teaches them to identify "jobs at risk," a euphemism for "jobs to be eliminated." But this dark side of management is generally a taboo subject. It emerged in role-playing sessions in which the manager learns to become competent and, explosively so, in the enactment of driving out evil, which was at the same time a witch-hunt, since the former union activists deflected the accusation of betrayal onto a small group of "young" women.

The "witches" were five young women termed "little careerists" and "young women without a past" (all were under forty and were never activists). They embodied everything the ex-activists said they had left behind: ambition and career plans. As a consequence, they did everything they should not: for example, used the program "to get ahead." They were described as aggressive and incapable of altruism. They undermined the cohesiveness of the group by violating the obligation for all group members to help each other: they were aggressive toward the program members who were the most fragile in terms of family or job. In the eyes of the majority, these borderline figures concentrated everything that was negative for the group. It hardly mattered that this was a carica-ture and did not always correspond to reality as it showed through in the individual narratives. For example, the leader of this little clan admitted to the anthropologist that she did not think this course could really help her get a career. Alternatively, her most vindictive accuser was a former activist on her way up the professional ladder. For her, the program had always been a means of making up for her extremely humble origins. This training course would even bring about a dazzling promotion within her company.[14] By designating the traitors—those who go on a course solely to advance their career—the former militants deflected the accu-sation of ideological betrayal of which they themselves were the target. But this reenactment above all permitted them to neutralize the danger of "bad management" and to proclaim the truth of the program: to manage is to give to the Other. That is why this reenactment, which re-sembled a ritual of atonement, was much more than a settling of per-sonal accounts. The former union activists were defining what "good management" meant. This definition was effected through an elimina-tion of evil (the failure of society to recognize and be grateful for militant action) and through a recycling of good (the militant ethos). The mem-ory of the past was not destroyed as it was in the sacrifice of stability, it was instead recast in mythic terms. The very fact that the great majority of the trainees subscribed to the ex-unionists' point of view and supported them is proof of the mythic and collective character of this redefinition.

## Against the Ideology of Flexibility

In the two preceding examples, it is by giving up any notion of high per-formance that identity is reshaped; or again, by expelling evil from the area of training—and stigmatizing "climbers." Clearly, the very meaning of management as understood by the CNAM is strongly distorted: opposition to the prevailing philosophy, enhancing as it does individual performance (it is the high-level athlete in the media), becomes manifest, of all places, in an institution that trains managers (Watson and Harris 1999). Equally, the whole machinery of professional flexibility is criticized. As he follows the course, the trainee learns to break down and evaluate the others' past and to rebuild it into the firm's future. He is even compelled to apply these techniques to his own situation. However, there are views vindicating ancient know-hows and denying that such steps have any validity.

　　　Neither has the concept of a worker moving unattached across, at least, Europe become rooted (in the minds of those concerned). Witness the semantic diversion of the very object of management: human resources. Appropriating the term, the trainees retained only the word *source* and developed a discourse of renewing oneself at the source (*ressourcement*). Paradoxically, it was the high-performance cadre, victim of the spectacular destabilization mentioned earlier, who best formulated a plan for recentering his life. His new training would enable him to return to the land of his ancestors, at last to put down roots after a particularly mobile professional career (he had spent over two-thirds of his life abroad). It was perhaps in view of this plan that he was willing to carry the logic of retraining to the extreme by his sacrifice renunciation. Such a logic may seem aberrant at the individual level, whereas it is consistent at the group level.

As a criticism of individualism, flexibility, and mobility, this collective discourse builds itself up in opposition to the philosophy of officialdom, as it is echoed in the various rungs of the French educational ladder, such as the CNAM which by virtue of its historical tradition is in a somewhat ambiguous position in relation to the emerging pattern. The permanent process of deconstruction and recomposition as economic necessity prevails (flexibility/mobility) is what is most sharply criticized by the trainees. While the latter, by virtue of the method of training, do indeed undergo a phase of the breaking down of Self ("man in a million pieces"), the groups' internal dynamics, cut free from the trainers' influence, are such that during the recomposition phase, the professional objective is further and further removed while greater stability is being sought. One is entitled to see this as a strategy for survival in a situation that is markedly precarious.

# Notes

This research work (1992–1999) was funded by the "Fondation Delhaim" du Collège de France and the Centre National des Lettres Paris. Many thanks to Françoise Héritier, Jacques Perriault, Marc Augé, Dominique Méda, Robert Castel, and Monique Selim for their helpful comments.

1. Identity is to be considered in this context as embracing all society-related components, which make up individuality. This chapter will show that identity is not taken for granted, as fully formed and fixed, but it must be renegotiated time and again (Bruner 1984). This is particularly true of contemporary society where precarious social equilibria of necessity involve a repatterning of identity.

2. The ERT in Brussels is a powerful employers lobby.

3. This program, spanning six years, has been given a new lease on life in a new form (Leonardo da Vinci II) to be concluded in 2006. As presented by the EC,

its purpose is to enhance the quality, novelty, and European dimension of the program and practices of professional training through transnational cooperation. Its purpose is also to help young people find their feet, socially and professionally, to broaden and develop access to skills, to shore up the process of a return to work. Activities tend to foster physical mobility, virtual mobility, transnational projects, European training networks, and the development language of skills.

4. In November 2002, unemployment remained high in the European Union, at 7.7 percent (8.4 percent in the Euro-zone), while the U.S. unemployment rate was 5.9 percent, and the Japanese rate was 5.3 percent. Unemployment affects certain groups more than others: the unemployment rate for young people (under twenty-five) was 15.1 percent (16.2 percent in the Euro-zone); the female unemployment rate stood at 8.6 percent (9.8 percent in the Euro-zone), higher than that of males, that is, 7 percent (7.4 percent in the Euro-zone). All statistics are from http: www.europa.eu.int/comm/eurostat.

5. This is at the time of the French Revolution, which abolished the monarchy and installed the First Republic.

6. Philosopher, mathematician, and politician (1743–1794). He wrote articles of political economy for Denis Diderot's *Encyclopédie.* As a deputy to the 1792 National Convention, he tabled a reform aiming at a reform of the educational system. Arrested and imprisoned during the Terror, he was sentenced to death. He took poison rather than go to the guillotine.

7. Under the law, a worker who has been granted leave for training follows the course free of charge, and, while it lasts, keeps his salary and insurances, with contributions from the state and the firms. The firms, on the other hand, are under an obligation to pay a special tax toward professional training (2 percent of the overall mass of salaries).

8. Delors, with a left-wing Catholic background, held various posts in the socialist party, culminating n the post of prime minister, during the Mitterand presidency. At the end of the 1960s, his militancy was invested in the building of a "New Society" and he was at the origin of the "contracts for progress" as the cornerstone of the policy based on contracts—and the moving spirit behind the laws on professional training.

9. Out of forty-three trainees in this course, only two, highly destabilized at the professional (and the personal) level, did not complete the program. One dropped out after a year, when he suddenly lost his job (I will return to this later); the other, just as unexpectedly, interrupted her training just before she finished (she refused to write the memoir for the course, whereas, out of work, she had made a financial sacrifice to go on the course, which, she said, was supposed to help her find a new job).

10. The collective narrative and the dynamic that grew up within the group are an indication of how far beyond the training method the trainees actually go. For instance, when they were working through their loss, they carried

to an extreme this more distant perspective (on their family, their work) the instructor would have liked them to acquire. The influence of the training method on beginning to accept their loss must of course be taken into account, but the fact that the instructor lost control of the events quite quickly shows that the work of mourning went beyond the official goal of a temporary distancing. It was no longer a matter of giving oneself the room to achieve a professional goal. In reality, the distancing allows a trainee to acquire a new identity. Contrary to the instructor's intention, the job plan was quickly left behind and all, whatever their initial objective, undertook to work through their bereavement.

11. The cost of such a course (F50,000)—which can represent a considerable amount, especially if not reimbursed, or only partly, by the ASSEDIC (the French unemployment benefits department)—may be far higher than enrollment in evening classes.

12. As Elizabeth Tonkin (1992) reminds us, memory never fully recollects the past but reconstructs it and brings it constantly up to date. "Memory makes us, we make memory." It is true that memory is one of the building blocks of identity; identity will in turn display some characteristics that will encourage the individual "to retain" some specific aspects of the past, to select memories.

13. The former activists (all from the same age group, between forty and forty-five), enrolled in the program because they wanted to leave (if they had not already done so) their union activities and embrace a career in management.

14. This shows how the trainees' roles or respective qualities are reversed when going from the individual narrative to the collective vision.

# References

Becker, G. 1997. *Disrupted lives.* Berkeley and Los Angeles: University of California Press.

Boyer, R. 1988. *The search for labour market flexibility.* Oxford: Clarendon.

Broda, J. 1990. Formation et remaniements identitaires. *Formation emploi* 32: 37–50.

Bruner, E. M. 1988. *Text, play, and story.* Long Grove, Ill.: Waveland.

Castel, R. 1995. *Les Métamorphoses de la question sociale.* Paris: Fayard.

Condorcet. 1989. *Écrits sur l'instruction publique.* Paris: Edilig.

Delors, J. 1974. Une stratégie pour le progrès. *Projet* 82: 167–176.

Dominicé, P. 1994. *L'histoire de vie comme processus de formation.* Paris: l'Harmattan.

Dubar, C. 1996. Socialisation et processus. In *L'Exclusion, l'état des savoirs,* edited by S. Paugam. Paris: La Découverte.

European Commission. 2001. *Employment, growth, competitiveness, and solidarity.* Available: http://europa.eu.int/en/comm/dg10/build/en/empl.htm.

Grignon, C. 1976. L'art et le métier. École parallèle et petite bourgeoisie. *Actes de la recherche en Sciences sociales* 4: 21–46.

Marsden, D. 1993. Existera-t-il un grand marché européen du travail. *Formation emploi* 43: 5–13.

Merle, V., with O. Bertrand. 1993. Comparabilité et reconnaissance des qualifications en Europe. Instruments et enjeux. *Formation emploi* 43: 41–56.

Petrella, R. 1991. L'évangile de la compétitivité. *Le Monde diplomatique* (September): 32.

Procoli, A. 2001. *Anthropologie d'une formation au Cnam. La fabrique de la compétence.* Paris: l'Harmattan.

———. 2000. The myth of "anti-management" or how managers-to-be express their resistance to the new forms of work. *Anthropology of Work Review* (winter): 11–15.

Rainbird, H. 1994. La formation continue en Grande-Bretagne. *Formation emploi* 48: 65–79.

Rosanvallon, A. 1992. La formation continue des ingénieurs pour de nouvelles organisations du travail. *Formation emploi* 38: 29–42.

Roustang, G. 1974. A-t-on besoin de gens formés? *Esprit* (October): 380–390.

Sélys, G. de. 1998. L'école, grand marché du XXI$^e$ siècle. *Le Monde diplomatique* (June): 14–15.

Tonkin, E. 1992. *Narrating our pasts: The social construction of our history.* Cambridge: Cambridge University Press.

Villeval, M.-C. 1993. Gestion des sur-effectifs et politiques de formation de reconversion en Europe. *Formation emploi* 43: 25–39.

Watson, T., and P. Harris. 1999. *The emergent manager.* London: Sage.

# 5

# Passages to No-Man's-Land

*Connecting Work, Community, and Masculinity in the South Wales Coalfield*

RICHARD-MICHAEL DIEDRICH

In this chapter I will focus on the articulation of work and gendered identities in a context of radical economic restructuring in the former coalfield of the South Wales valleys in Britain. In the 1990s, work continued to be an extremely important moment of identification in spite of—and, perhaps to some extent, because of—the lack of paid employment. However, the connectedness of work and identity makes the loss of paid employment particularly difficult for men. In the working-class context of a former mining community in the South Wales coalfield the dominant meaning of work is inextricably connected with the construction of male identities (Dunk 1994; Willis 1988).

To show the connections between the discourses of work and gendered identities, I will begin with a discussion of the meaning of work and its articulation with masculinity in a Welsh working-class context and continue with a discussion of the problem that unemployment poses for the maintenance of male identities. These aspects are linked by the double-edged reality created by the articulation of work and masculinity. For men the experience of work, in a capitalist economy, can be both the experience of a subaltern position constituted by the relationship between employer and employee and the experience of moments of positive individual and collective (self-)identification in terms of gendered difference.

The dominant meaning of work is not fundamentally undermined by unemployment. On the contrary, unemployment, particularly long-term unemployment, highlights the primacy of work as a key element for the construction of male working-class identities. I will draw on the concept of liminality—the state of being betwixt and between as Victor Turner (1991, 97) has called it—to show that not only the everyday temporal and spatial structure of life is suspended by unemployment but that liminality extends toward the identification of men in terms of gender. Prolonged liminality imposed by long-term unemployment paves the way for an extreme challenge to the self.

For most men unemployment can only be imagined as a liminal period. However, the radical economic restructuring in the South Wales coalfield has transformed the experience of unemployment. In the case of long-term unemployment many men can no longer make sense of the experience of being without work in terms of a liminal period leading to the reaffirmation of their masculinity by taking up new paid employment. For them the feeling of being betwixt and between appears to be never-ending. The longer they remain suspended in-between, the more difficult it becomes for them to identify themselves—or to be identified by others—as "real" men. However, the dominant meanings of work and masculinity seem to survive relatively unscathed while unemployed men sink deeper and deeper into a state of prolonged liminality that tends to silence them permanently. The concept of work that enabled working-class men to construct positive male identities in a situation characterized by exploitation ultimately inscribes negative identities when work "disappears." Thus, I will show that the discourse of "work" is not losing its powerful hold over the discursive constitution of everyday reality.

## (Re)producing Miners' Counterculture

Before industrialization set its mark on the upland valleys of South Wales, they were a thinly populated agricultural area. Only a few hill farms lay scattered in the densely wooded valleys. Industrialization changed the face of Wales more radically than anything before and turned the country into a significant player in the global economy. The ever-increasing need for coal transformed the remote rural valleys into an urban industrial landscape. The abundant opportunities for work brought people from all over the United Kingdom, and even other parts of Europe, to the South Wales valleys. Throughout the nineteenth and early twentieth centuries the privately owned coal industry thrived in the coalfield. In the Cynon Valley alone 12,300 men were working in the pits in 1921. The lives of these men, and their families, were characterized by hard physical labor, exploitation, and poverty.

Ruthless exploitation, the hardship of poverty, the antagonism of miners and capitalist employers, and the development of political movements among the working class paved the way for the political organization of the working class in South Wales at the turn of the nineteenth century. The South Wales Miners' Federation—known as "the Fed"—was to become one of the most influential unions in Britain's labor movement and had a profound effect on the development of South Walian society.[1]

However, in the early 1920s the tide turned for the coal industry. Economic depression and the decreasing importance of coal as industrial fuel marked the beginning of the long decline of the coal industry. As a result, the boomtowns of the coalfield were transformed into a depressed area where unemployment was the norm and work the exception. In 1987, only 1,783 men were still working in the last two collieries in the Cynon Valley. At the time of my fieldwork in the area, in 1995, only 242 men were employed in the last remaining deep mine, Tower Colliery, in South Wales. The decline of the coal industry and the lack of other employment opportunities in the South Wales valleys did not only turn unemployment into a persistent everyday reality for many people in the area it also initiated profound changes in what had once been a "vibrant" coalfield society (Smith 1993, 5).

"There's a hell of a change down here. It's all mixed up now." That is how an unemployed man described to me the situation on a council estate in the former coalfield of South Wales.[2] For him the changes he perceived in the social life of the community were symptoms of a severe crisis. The background to this crisis was the eradication of the coal industry from the face of the South Wales valleys by Conservative governments under Margaret Thatcher between the mid-1980s and the mid-1990s. The communities in the South Wales valleys had been totally dependent on the coal industry for well over a century and its decline threatened individual self-identifications as well as the whole fabric of mining-community culture. However, the postwar decline and the Conservative crusade against the miners' trade union in the 1980s was not the first severe crisis the people in the South Wales coalfield had to face. Total dependence on the coal industry for employment and the struggle for political dominance between employers and the trade unions produced not only a distinctive mining-community culture but also a number of crises throughout the history of the South Wales coalfield.

However, the closure of every colliery in the coalfield was by far the most severe threat experienced by the people in the mining communities. As a result of this radical economic restructuring of the coalfield, mass unemployment, insecurity, and poverty returned to the valleys. Insecurity and poverty had always been part of the everyday reality of employment in the coal industry before the industry was nationalized shortly after the Second World War. The men were always in danger of being sacked and the experience of long-term mass unemployment and poverty in the 1930s burned itself into the collective memory of the people in the coalfield. Between 1920 and 1936, employment in the coal industry was cut by over 50 percent—from 271,161 men to only 126,233 men (Francis and Smith 1980, 33). In 1929, 45.6 percent of the miners in South Wales were unemployed and in some valleys well over 80 percent of those formerly employed in coal mining were on the dole (Baber and Thomas 1980, 525, 537–538).

Although large-scale, long-term unemployment threatened the power of the miners' trade union, it was, nevertheless, able to establish itself as the dominant political power in the coalfield in the 1920s and 1930s. It did not only establish a firm hold over the miners at work in the collieries. The influence of the union extended to all aspects of life in the mining communities. Hywel Francis and David Smith (1980, 66) argued that the unions were the driving force behind the creation of an "alternative culture" in the South Wales coalfield. This alternative or counterculture developed in the context of the struggle for political dominance between the miners' trade union and the capitalist employers in the coal industry and produced persuasive narratives for making sense of the persistent reality of poverty and unemployment. The ability to survive the adverse condition of pit work as well as the hardship of poverty and unemployment became an important characteristic of working-class identities in the mining communities. A crucial factor for the understanding of how the people in the coalfield survived these adverse conditions of perpetual crisis is an ongoing dominant narrative: the discourse of survival, which constituted a pervasive concept of equality in poverty. Through the discourse of survival the experience of poverty was integrated with the more abstract concept of the working class, and the values of loyalty and solidarity experienced at work and in the community became entangled with the ideology of workers' unity. Mining-community culture was constituted by a political discourse of the working class that linked categories of distinction—expressed in terms of class differences as "them" and "us"—with concepts of work, community, and gendered difference. The powerful hold of miners and their trade union on the everyday practices of constructing and negotiating meaning at work and at home was almost completely encompassing. Thus, the miners' counterculture achieved hegemony in the South Wales valleys. Even the decline and final destruction of the coal industry did not cause a radical reimagination of working-class identities that were still constituted through the persuasive and pervasive hegemonic discourse of the miners' counterculture.

To gain insight into the reasons for continuing persuasiveness of the concept of work in working-class contexts suffering from mass unemployment, I will now follow the connections between work and the construction of community as well as gendered difference.

## A Man's Land: Connecting Work, Community, and Identity

The fieldwork on which this analysis is based was not done in a "traditional" mining community but rather on a council estate in the Cynon Valley, South Wales, in 1995. The people living on the estate were severely affected by economic restructuring. When the estate was built between the 1940s and the 1960s the majority of the male population was still employed in the coal industry. In 1995, however, according to official figures (Cynon Valley Borough Council 1993), almost one-third of the population was unemployed. In spite of the fact that only three men were still employed in the coal industry, most inhabitants had, in the past, either worked in the industry themselves or grew up in a miners' family.

The council estate was built to provide adequate accommodation for families from the slums created by the industrial revolution. As a result, people from all over the valley were allocated new houses on the estate—the local authorities simply "chucked them all together," as Arthur, who grew up on the estate, put it. In contrast to a "traditional" mining community where social networks were established over an extended period of time and identification with the community was closely connected with overlapping networks of work and nonwork relationships (Bulmer 1978, 35), the population of a council estate was more fragmented and social networks had to be created anew. The initial feeling of being "chucked together" was difficult to overcome. However, many people on the estate perceived it as a "community." They explained the development of community in this "artificial" environment, created by the allocation practices of the local authorities, as the outcome of their awareness of their structural position as miners, working-class people, and council tenants, which distinguished them from the rest of society. Equally relevant was the discourse of survival produced by as well as producing the shared experience of poverty—an experience connected with low wages and large families, and the subsequent dependence on social welfare in the form of comparatively cheap council housing. But how were they able to create a meaningful collective most people could identify with?

When the first families moved into their new houses on the estate the majority of the men were still employed in the coal industry. Even today, although construction workers are the largest occupational group among employed men, only a minority of people on the estate could not construct a personal relationship to the coal industry through family and/or friends. Furthermore, severe crises provided the opportunity to (re-)create the emotionally charged bond between miners and nonminers in the communities and reaffirm the dominance of the miners' counterhegemonic political project. Even in the 1980s, when only a minority of the population in the South Wales coalfield was still employed in the coal industry, the attempt of the Conservative government to close most of the remaining collieries in South Wales and destroy the powerful National Union of Mineworkers was met with overwhelming support for the miners' cause in most of their communities. The one-year strike during 1984–1985 was more than "just" a miners' strike. It became a symbol for the struggle of working-class people against the ideological identification of their identities as an obstacle to the neoliberal definition of progress. Furthermore, the experience of hardship and solidarity during the strike temporarily revitalized the persuasiveness of the discourse of survival. During the strike the importance of unity and solidarity for the survival of the community were stressed and provided an opportunity to mask the fragmentation produced by changes in the occupational structure, unemployment, emigration, and—in the case of council estates—the council's allocation practices. The fact that the men who were on strike were not working and would have to face long-term unemployment if the strike was lost highlighted the importance of work for the construction of male identities.

In addition to that, the individual as well as collective identification with the distinctive working-class culture of the mining communities that invested work with particular meanings were crucial elements for the imagination of the estate as a community. The articulation of class, respectability, work, and masculinity provided the basis for powerful narratives that constituted mining-community culture. "I mean—see, when you work—in a community like [this] then, everybody is in the same boat then, you know" (Peter).

Phrases like "everybody is in the same boat," "we're all the same here, we're all working class!" (Peter), or "there's no difference between anybody, really" (Arthur) were frequently used symbolic expressions of equality and unity, of identification with the collective, in the face of a power differential that placed them in a powerless position in the hierarchy constructed by ideological discourses that were dominant in capitalist society. The expression of equality and unity was historically rooted in the shared experience of work and a strong trade unionism in the coal industry.

The rhetoric of Peter, a retired miner and chairman of the local workingmen's club, reveals an extremely important connection: those who work are considered to be in the same boat. To be identified as belonging to "the community" a man had to be in employment, had to identify with the dominant meaning of work, and had to be identified as doing so by others—not just any kind of work, but rather paid employment involving hard physical labor.[3] Especially the extreme conditions at work experienced in the coal industry were regarded as "making" a real man. The hegemonic discourses of class and respectability in capitalist society that prescribed an attitude to work based on thrift, honesty, reliability, and a willingness to work were central in producing working-class subject positions. The continuing "adherence [of men] to the discourse of work and employment with its morally sanctioned ideal of the hardworking man as opposed to the irresponsible man who is not willing to work, led to a perpetuation of the discourse of respectability and its individualistic idea of deservingness that divided the community and consequently the working class" (Diedrich 1999, 40).

As a symbol of difference and similarity, which was crucial for (self-) identification, the idea of the working class was inherently contradictory because "working class people would not earn a living if they did not enter into some sort of dependent and exploitative relation with capital" (Narotzky 1997, 218). The identification with the dominant concept of work produced a contradiction between the perception of work as a positive moment of self-identification and the reproduction of the subordinate position of the worker in relation to the employer. While hegemonic masculinity was perceived as a practice of resisting exploitation and powerlessness, it also constituted men as exploitable, subordinate subjects. The discourse of work provided a connection between gendered (self-)identifications with the community and the working class as meaningful collectives. It was a crucial factor in the construction of male identities and (a male-dominated) community.

The workplace was an extremely important space for the construction of gendered difference and men who no longer worked were excluded from a prominent arena for the negotiation of male identities. Emrys had worked as a miner at Tower Colliery for twenty years when the pit was closed in 1994. However, he had not started his working life in the coal industry. He had worked in a factory for eight years until he was made redundant. He did not try to find another factory job but convinced his father, a miner at the local colliery, to get him a job at the pit. One night in the local workingmen's club I was talking with him and Arthur, with whom he had worked underground for a number of years, and he stressed that he would never go back to factory work. He liked the work in the pit, the comradeship, and the fun they had underground. Arthur made it quite clear why he regarded work underground as a manly task: "[I]t's physical," he said, and "although we got all the machinery today, it's still physical and requires even more skills." However, the work of miners does not only entail hard physical labor and construction of close social relationships, it is also an exclusively male world.

Working together with women was regarded as being detrimental to one's masculinity and Emrys emphasized that he "couldn't get used to working with women." Arthur, who had been a miner all his life, made it quite clear that while factory workers may be used to working with women, he would never work with them: "We're not male chauvinist pigs, as some might say, we've been brought up this way. We're not used to working with women." While the workplace was the most important space for the negotiation of male identities and the construction of gendered difference, everyday practices in the communities were also geared toward establishing male dominance. In addition to showing the "right" attitude toward work, surviving the hardship of poverty and the ability to act in solidarity was a practice that was regarded as necessary to attain the status of a real and respectable man.[4] Although women could contribute to the survival of the community by assisting their men, survival was ensured by acts of loyalty, solidarity, honesty, and, last but not least, the demonstration of the willingness to work; all of these were regarded as core elements of masculinity.

Women were generally categorized as subordinate and were almost totally excluded from the public and political arena. Apparently, the discourse of survival was inextricably connected with the hegemonic masculinity. This generated a contradiction because despite its emphasis on equality and unity, hegemonic masculinity was very exclusive. Other occupational identities, constructed outside the coal mining industry, were categorized as less masculine and men who had never worked in the coal industry had to prove that they could be regarded as real men (see Diedrich 1999, 195–197). Thus, by privileging hard physical labor in the coal industry as an essential category for identifying real men women were assigned a subordinate position and subordinate masculinities were created.

If the discourses of work and masculinity were geared toward the dominance of men working in the coal industry, how could they survive the destruction of the industry, the return of mass long-term unemployment, and the stereotyping of poor and unemployed people as "scroungers" by the dominant political discourse?

## Passages to No-Man's-Land: (Re)Connecting Work, Community, and Identity

Let me return to the connection that Peter has made between work and identification with/by a meaningful collective: "when you work" you are "in the same boat" with us, you are part of the "community." But what happened to those men who were unemployed and not working?

For the (former) miners on the council estate, the closure of a colliery, the fact that they were made redundant and had to join the dole line, was an emotionally disturbing experience. It was the beginning of a passage producing fear, anger, and desperation. For a miner the passage led from operating the cutter at the coal face to operating the television's remote control in his living room. Furthermore, in a region already suffering from mass unemployment it would be a passage to no-man's-land for many of them. Thus, when the last pit, Tower Colliery, was closed in the South Wales coalfield after a long struggle with British Coal in 1994 (Tower Colliery Lodge NUM 1994)[5] the men were totally desperate: "I've worked twenty years underground and they said now, so long, we don't want you here at all. And down the road I'd to go and that was the saddest day in my life" (Emrys).

> Well, in my own experience I said because Jim had always been in work it was very hard and . . . the first three weeks were . . . you know, the first week is a novelty but as the third week was coming, I mean, we were starting to get on each others nerves. And again, . . . I think Jim felt it . . . maybe it was gettin' to him because he wasn't in work. and it wasn't his fault. And he was very upset about losing his job. It, he took it very, very badly. He was very, very bitter. Jim was bitter about the pit closing. . . . And he was very angry with a lot of men who voted to close the pit. In fact to the point of being very aggressive about it. Because he felt that he was coming to fifty, fifteen years to work, knowing that he wasn't gonna get another job. (Susan, Jim's wife)

For Emrys and Jim their worst fear never came true because they were part of a group of miners who managed to buy their pit from British Coal and started to work again eight months later. For both of them unemployment was but a temporary phase. However, at the time when the colliery was closed they were afraid that they would not be able to find employment, no matter how hard they tried, and, thus, be more or less confined to a domestic existence.

As John Hayes and Peter Nutman (1981, 44) pointed out, for working-class men, work is virtually synonymous with activity and being without work is perceived as boredom. On the council estate many men used the expression "sitting round the house," which showed their fear and/or experience of immobilization not only in a psychological sense but in a physical sense as well. Sitting round the house, not knowing what to do, and not being able to do something that conformed to the dominant practices of work, was the worst-case scenario for most men in the community. It could end in a process of (self-)identification as somebody "not willing to work" or, even worse, a "scrounger." In his ethnography of unemployment in Northern Ireland, Leo Howe (1990) argued that "[f]or many of the long-term unemployed . . . the loss of work appears to entail more than the narrowing of their previous life-styles. Many aspects of their existence are brutally circumscribed, and the time which was spent in work is replaced by individualistic activities in the home. Many admit to feelings of impotence, shame and isolation" (11–12). Howe's study of unemployed men in Belfast as well as Daniel Wight's (1993) study of unemployment in the Scottish village of Cauldmoss show that unemployed men tend to withdraw from the public sphere because they cannot afford—financially and socially—to participate in the social activities and rituals of social drinking favored by workingmen. It becomes more and more difficult to communicate with those men who are working and keep up the image of "deserving" unemployment benefit. As a result, many men are forced to stay at home all day, in a space regarded as the domain of women. They are confined to their own no-man's-land, acutely aware of what they have lost and hope to regain. "Unemployed men are squeezed out of the public realm—but their retreat into the private realm becomes public business" (McKee and Bell 1986, 147).

In many ways the transition from employment to unemployment resembles the experience of a rite of passage. Like unemployed men the subjects of rites of passage are transferred to a no-man's-land in-between and are removed from the public eye. They are confined to a liminal phase. The notion of liminality describes "the blurriness of transformation and the acute consciousness of status on either side of it" (Cohen 1994, 127). During the "liminal period" people become "structurally, if not physically, 'invisible'" (Turner 1991, 95). The anxiety involved in passing from the status of a workingman to that of an unemployed man is directly associated with the acute consciousness of the importance

placed on work for the (self-)identification of men. When an unemployed man is "squeezed out of the public realm" he becomes physically
and socially invisible because he is no longer taking part in the publicly
visible routines of work, and those who work expect him to show restraint in his leisure activities. After losing a job the former employee is
cast into a space where temporal and spatial structure of the worker is
no longer part of his daily routine. Moreover, the morally required removal of unemployed men from the public eye makes them even more
visible because it draws attention to the fact that some members of the
community should not indulge in the usual public social activities of
men if they want to be identified as respectable and responsible. Their
invisibility has become public business and their activities are subject to
moral scrutiny. An important aspect of this heightened public awareness
of these individuals is the fact that they are transitional beings who are
betwixt and between and, therefore, expected to return to the world of
working men.

   Anthony Cohen (1994) argues that the difficulties of passing from
one status to another status "seem curiously understated" in ethnographic accounts "as if such adjustments were as unambiguous, even if
more troublesome, than crossing a national frontier" (127–128). The
confusion of liminality, the blurriness of being in a social equivalent of
no-man's-land, is not as easily manageable as the concept of a clear-cut
reintegration into society after a temporary (spatial as well as temporal)
suspension suggests. For Cohen it is "hardly plausible" that the individual
who went through the ordeal of a radical questioning or negation of
himself or herself remains unscathed and is simply content with being
"loaded with new rights and obligations" (128). In much of the anthropological literature on initiation rituals that transform boys into men, the
radical imposition of a new (gender) identity is masked by the use of the
metaphor of rebirth (Gilmore 1990). However, as Maurice Godelier
(1986) has shown in his account of initiation rituals of the Baruya in the
highlands of Papua New Guinea, during initiation rituals the self-identity
of the boys is radically devalued to the point of almost complete negation, which causes extreme emotional stress for the participants who are
cast into a state of liminality. In the process of transformation to adult-
hood the boys are radically regendered. Rites of passage are not just passages from one culturally accepted state of existence to another and
liminality can often turn out to be a forced crisis of the self. The transformation of status requires a process of adjustment, a fundamental reformulation of the self, and this reformulation, which can be perceived
as a total negation of one's identity by others, can be an extremely traumatic experience. Thus, to make the almost complete reconstitution of

one's self manageable, the process of transformation has to offer new avenues for constituting one's self.

Unemployed men are likewise cast into a state of liminality. However, liminal periods are not meant to last indefinitely. They are transitional periods, passages to new forms of identifying oneself—of being identified by others—as belonging to a collective. However, for a growing number of men unemployment turned from a temporary state of existence, a liminal phase between two jobs, into a never-ending ordeal. Did the process of transformation from workingman to unemployed man offer any new avenues for reconstituting the self in a positive way when the period of unemployment was extended indefinitely and the unemployed man was not able to find new employment?

The answer to that question is a complex one because some men survived long-term unemployment relatively unscathed. They were able to maintain (self-)identifications of real and respectable men. For other men, however, the loss of employment ended in an almost total negation of their former selves by others. Although a growing number of long-term unemployed men in the community lacked access to the world of hard physical labor, which made the (self-)identification as real men increasingly difficult, some managed to remain real men. The key to their success in maintaining a male identity conforming to the prescription of hegemonic masculinity was their membership in informal groups of workmates. These groups were the key to the survival of working-class mining-community culture and were crucial for the maintenance of hegemonic masculinity because they kept the connections between work, respectability, community, and gendered identity alive. They were at the center of the local networks of power and were able to provide a safety net for those men whose (self-)identifications as real men were threatened by long-term unemployment because they continued to provided the arena for the negotiation of masculinity. An important factor for the re-creation of a man's identification as a real man was the discussion of past work experiences with men of the informal group over a pint in the local workingmen's club. These exchanges between unemployed miners and the few working miners reaffirmed the status of the unemployed as belonging to the locally dominant male collective. The identification with and by a collective made the psychological problems, the lack of shared work experience, the individualization, and the shame of being without work more bearable. Those unemployed men who were still supported by their informal groups were no longer suspended in a liminal state of existence and, although they were required to show some restraint, were legitimately taking part in the social activities of men—they remained visible. In their case, showing a willingness to work by doing odd jobs was considered to be a sufficient demonstration of their compliance with the moral norms of hegemonic masculinity. The chairman of the local workingmen's club expressed the problem quite pointedly:

> Not only the job they're taking their dignity of them. They're taking their pride. You take a man's dignity and his pride of him, what's he left with? He's left with nothing. No man wants to be on the bloody dole. They talk about scroungers, the social security and God knows what now, right. There's nobody there—likes to go down to them bloody people's office, man. They want work, they want to provide for their family. (Peter)

Men, who were part of these dominant informal groups of men, were not in danger of being categorized as "scroungers"—a stereotypical identification of unemployed people as exploiting the welfare state imposed by the dominant Conservative ideology of individualism. The fact that they were unemployed was explained as the outcome of structural factors that were beyond their control. They were identified as "deserving" unemployed (Howe 1990, 191–192).

While the identification of unemployed working-class people in general as scroungers was rejected by the men, they were also engaged in reproducing its legitimacy. By identifying some men, who were regarded as possessing subordinate masculinities, as scroungers who "have never worked in their life," they were not only engaged in keeping the dominant meaning of work alive but were also reproducing a discourse that inscribed their subordinate position. This process of deflecting stereotypical identification to even more powerless men could also facilitate the perpetuation of the dominant discourse and, at the same time, the fragmentation of the community. The discursive strategies of men in employment and without employment "cannot unambiguously be defined as forms of resistance because they are equally forms [of] co-operation and complicity. Images of the scrounger are not in any simple sense resisted, rejected or even re-interpreted by unemployed men. Rather, they are deflected away from themselves and directed at others" (Howe 1990, 543). The process of deflection implies the reaffirmation of the dominant meaning by deflection to the even more disadvantaged subjects.[6]

The contradictions inherent in the process of deflection become visible when imposed stereotypes are strategically used in the negotiation of power between men. The case of Tom shows that the deflection of the scrounger stereotype onto him and the disidentification of him in terms of the hegemonic discourse of masculinity were closely connected. The strategies employed in disidentifying Tom as a man also indicates that the liminal state of being betwixt and between, imposed by the transition to unemployment, can be strategically used in negotiation of power between men to legitimate exclusion in terms of gendered difference.

Tom was a long-term unemployed former miner who was chairman of the local community center. He had to leave the coal industry as a young man because of an accident in 1965 and has lived on a pension and invalidity benefit ever since. His life was dominated by the so-called system—the welfare state bureaucracy—that was regarded as denigrating and, the longer a man was subject to its influence, as detrimental to one's masculinity. "After I had interviewed Tom, some of the men felt that they had to give me their opinion of him so that I could see his comments in the 'proper' light. Mike told me not to take Tom seriously because 'he's a liar, he takes advantage of the system,' and Phil added that 'he invented the cowin' [damn] system.' Finally, Mike said, 'he hasn't worked since he was seventeen'" (my field notes).

Tom is said to have lived quite comfortably despite the fact that he is long-term unemployed and, thus, was regarded as threatening the persuasiveness of connection between hegemonic masculinity and work. On an individual level Tom believed that it was fortunate that he could work as the chairman of the community center, which helped him to preserve his self-esteem: "So I'm not sitting round the house all day, you know" (Tom). Although the access to some kind of work kept him occupied, the fact that he was not working, in the sense of being in paid employment, left its mark. The fact that he was not forced to sit at home but took part in public activities did not contribute to the identification of him as a respectable man. He lacked access to the collective experience of work—and could not even rely on past experience—that was regarded as an essential element for the confirmation of masculinity.

The strategies employed to exclude him show that unemployed men are always in danger of being identified as possessing a liminal gender identity. The disidentification of Tom as a man was evident in Mike's rather generalized characterization of him as "a liar," which categorized him as someone disregarding the moral values of honesty and loyalty that were regarded as essential for manliness. Phil's remark that Tom had "invented the . . . system" categorizes him, along the lines of the dominant discourse, as a scrounger who is working the welfare state to his own advantage.

> He's got a bad back, you see. He was in the mining industry, he's on a pension, he's havin' his coal and he's done that when he's about nineteen, twenty. And there's nothing wrong with him. So, I mean,

and he's always been in these little jobs and that and he'd have a couple of bob for his beer. He always—and some of the decisions he made as the vice chairman of the club— He put people out the club for silly, stupid little things, childish. He's got—a sexist remark again is coming to me—he's got a brain like a woman. That's what used to be said in here, right. Sexism there, right. But that's the way, that's the way I think and he's not very well liked as such to a certain degree by a lot of people. (Arthur)

Arthur, a powerful trade union leader, questioned Tom's masculinity quite openly along the same lines by calling him a "selfish man" because he is living on benefit despite the fact that "there's nothing wrong with him." Arthur systematically dismantled Tom's masculinity and respectability. He accused him of having abused the power he had been given by the men. After Arthur had recollected a number of events that he considered to be examples of Tom's unmanly behavior, he came to the conclusion that Tom could not think like a real man but rather thought and acted like a woman: the ultimate disidentification of him as a man. Childishness and silliness, the lack of rationality, and the inability to act responsibly in a position requiring integrity, disqualified him in a way usually reserved for the stereotypical legitimation of male dominance over women.

By disidentifying him as a real man and identifying him as possessing negative attributes ascribed to women, such as irrationality and powerlessness, a liminal gender identity was inscribed in Tom. He was categorized as "not really one of us," and, even worse, neither man nor woman. This strategy of identification in terms of liminal gender identities highlights the fragility of working-class male identities in the process of transformation from unemployment to the prolonged liminality of long-term unemployment. For long-term unemployment the question is How long can they cope with the awareness of being betwixt and between? The Baruya boys are offered a way out, but unemployed men are hardly able to see an end to their suspension in a liminal state of being. They have to live with the fact that their masculinity is always in danger of being negated by dominant men. Thus, identifying men in term of liminal gender identities is a strategy aimed at securing relationships of power and dominance, and, ultimately, hegemonic masculinity. For those men who lost their jobs, and remained on the dole for longer periods of time, the hegemonic ideal of masculinity, to which they themselves subscribed, could turn into an "inescapable torment" (Howe 1990, 46). The exclusion of Tom highlights the contradictions inherent in a strategy for survival that is based on the persuasiveness of hegemonic masculinity articulated through discourses of work, respectability, class, and community. It was a strategy geared toward securing relationships of power and dominance, created as part of the attempt to counteract the hegemonic project of capitalism and to safeguard the survival of the working-class community. However, the hegemonic discourse of masculinity could not only confine unemployed men to a liminal state of "inescapable torment," it also sustained the salience of the dominant discourse that assured their subordination.

## Conclusion

In British working-class contexts, work continues to be a crucial moment of identification despite the fact that it has either virtually disappeared (e.g., the coal industry) or has been transformed by insecure, temporary employment and odd jobs in the informal economy. The articulation of the dominant discourse of work, that constituted the thrifty, honest, responsible worker as a subordinate subject that was exploitable, with gender, class, and community, produced a double-edged reality. On the one hand, the morally sanctioned ideal of the hardworking man constituted working-class people as exploitable subjects. On the other hand, the articulation of these discourses created a space in which positive moments of identification were possible. They made the alienating conditions at work and in life more bearable and opened up avenues for undermining and resisting domination.

The discourse of masculinity that achieved hegemony in the context of coal mining communities in the South Wales valleys was part and parcel of this highly political process of articulation. When the mining and other heavy industries declined and work became a scarce resource in the coalfields, hegemonic masculinity, nevertheless, continued to a exert a powerful hold over working-class men. The persistence of hegemonic masculinity was largely due to the influence of informal groups of men that formed the centers of power in their communities.

For some unemployed men, these groups were the most important space for the negotiation and affirmation of their gendered identities. For those unemployed men who were already categorized as possessing a subordinate masculinity, these powerful groups could be the reason for their exclusion. As Jacob Torfing (1999) pointed out, hegemonic articulations are acts of exclusion that involve the negation of alternative meanings and of the people who identify themselves with these meanings. Viewed from the perspective of those whose identity is negated it may lead "to either self-blame or self-denial ('it is our own fault, we are simply not good enough!'), or to a resigned and traumatic incorporation of a lack ('It is really a shame, but I have to live with it as I can do nothing about it!')" (120). Unemployment highlights the problem of exclusion and negation not only of those people who identify with alternative meanings. The case presented here demonstrates that even people who identify with dominant meanings may be excluded because their self-identification is not accepted by those who possess the power to define what is acceptable.

Furthermore, processes of exclusion and negation are related to the transformation that is set in motion after the loss of work. I argue that the transition from work to unemployment can be understood as a kind of passage and that unemployed men are transferred to a liminal space. The anthropological concept of liminality provides a useful way for gaining insight into the experience of unemployment. When the liminal phase of unemployment was but a transitional period between two jobs, the problems involved in being suspended in-between were quite manageable. For most people reintegration and the reaffirmation of their status as respectable men was only a question of time.

Today, however, unemployment is no longer characterized by a temporary removal from the world of the working. Long-term unemployment transforms the temporary crisis of self-identity into a prolonged ordeal that is slowly but steadily dissolving what the individual had believed to be the stable core of his or her identity. Unemployed men are acutely aware of the fragility of their self-identities when they lose the basis for imagining themselves as complete and possessing stable identities (especially occupational and gender identities). It becomes increasingly difficult to identify, not only with what they imagined to be their selves, but also with others engaged in identifying them. In the context of a Welsh mining community, hegemonic masculinity contributes to this crisis produced by the awareness of fragmentation and/or negation of the self. The re-production of the dominant discourse of work as a key element for defining a man—intended to maintain its persuasiveness and the power of those men who are its key producers—is undermining hegemonic masculinity because it keeps a growing number of men suspended in a liminal no-man's-land and provokes either despair or resistance. Thus, the strategies of survival geared toward the preservation of male dominance in working-class culture produce contradictions that are intensifying the effects of crises for those excluded and are, ultimately, furthering fragmentation, individualization, and subordination of working-class people in capitalist society.

# Notes

1. With the foundation of the National Union of Mineworkers in 1945 the South Wales Miners Federation became the South Wales Area of the National Union of Mineworkers.

2. Council housing was a form of public housing provided by local authorities (councils) in the United Kingdom.

3. For a discussion of the mental/manual dichotomy in working-class culture, see Dunk (1994) and Willis (1988).

4. For an extensive discussion of the concept of respectability in working-class culture and for an in-depth analysis of the development of this counterculture as part of a hegemonic political project of the miners' trade union and its contradictions and connections with dominant discourses in capitalist British society, see Diedrich 1999, chaps. 2 and 3.

5. It was bought by the workforce and reopened in 1995.

6. However, the process of deflection implies a twofold "othering": the othering of those who dominate through a symbolic reversal subverting the dominant meaning as well as the othering of even more disadvantaged. Thus, it can, simultaneously, represent a practice of resistance and of domination (see Diedrich 1999, 37–40).

# References

Baber, C., and D. Thomas. 1980. *The Glamorgan economy, 1914–1945: Glamorgan County history.* Vol. 5 of *Industrial Glamorgan from 1700 to 1970.* Cardiff: Glamorgan County History Trust.

Bulmer, M. 1978. Social structure and social change in the twentieth century. In *Mining and social change: Durham County in the twentieth century,* edited by Bulmer. London: Croom Helm.

Cohen, A. P. 1994. *Self-Consciousness.* London: Routledge.

Cynon Valley Borough Council. 1993. *1991 census information.* Aberdare, Wales: Cynon Valley Borough Council.

Diedrich, R.-M. 1999. You can't beat us! Class, work, and gender on a council estate in the South Wales coalfield. Hamburg, Ger.: Staats- und Universitätsbibliothek. Available http://www.sub.uni-hamburg.de/disse/878/dissertation.pdf.

Dunk, T. W. 1994. *It's a working man's town: Male working-class culture.* Montreal: McGill-Queen's University Press.

Francis, H., and D. Smith. 1980. *The fed: A history of the South Wales miners in the twentieth century.* London: Lawrence and Wishart.

Gilmore, D. D. 1990. *Manhood in the making: Cultural concepts of masculinity.* New Haven: Yale University Press.

Godelier, M. 1986. *The making of great men.* Cambridge: Cambridge University Press.

Hayes, J., and P. Nutman. 1981. *Understanding the unemployed: The psychological effects of unemployment.* London: Tavistock.

Howe, L. 1990. *Being unemployed in Northern Ireland: An ethnographic study.* Cambridge: Cambridge University Press.

McKee, L., and C. Bell. 1986. His unemployment, her problem: The domestic and marital consequences of male unemployment. In *The experience of unemployment,* edited by S. Allen, A. Waton, K. Purcell, and S. Wood. London: Macmillan.

Narotzky, S. 1997. *New directions in economic anthropology.* London: Pluto.

Smith, D. 1993. *Aneurin bevan and the world of South Wales.* Cardiff: University of Wales Press.

Torfing, J. 1999. *New theories of discourse: Laclau, Mouffe, and Žižek.* Oxford: Blackwell.

Tower Colliery Lodge NUM. 1994. *14 days that shook Britain.* Hirwaun, Wales: Tower Colliery Lodge NUM.

Turner, V. 1991. *The forest of symbols: Aspects of Ndembu ritual.* Ithaca: Cornell University Press.

Wight, D. 1993. *Workers not wasters: Masculine respectability, consumption, and unemployment in central Scotland.* Edinburgh: Edinburgh University Press.

Willis, P. 1988. *Learning to labour: How working class kids get working class jobs.* Aldershot, Eng.: Ashgate.

# 6

# Unemployed and Hard Workers

*Entrepreneurial Moralities between*
*"Shadow" and "Sunlight" in Naples*

ITALO PARDO

As it has often happened in recent history, today's Italy exemplifies important processes in the Western version of democratic life. Understanding what is going on there, particularly in the south, may help to clarify similar processes elsewhere in Europe. Over the years, Naples, as a major center of Western urban life, has proved to be a fruitful context in which to look for empirical material on phenomena that are politically and economically central. The problematic relationship of real people to superimposed models has emerged as an important topic.

Since 1978, I have carried out extended field research in Naples among the *popolino* (literally, populace), the bourgeois, and the elite.[1] Research on key elite domains, which is continuing, started in 1991 and has involved long-term fieldwork, as well as periodical short visits.[2] It has helped to penetrate crucial dynamics of power and to construct a detailed account of issues of responsibility, trust, and legitimacy that affect the relationships among different elite groups and between them and the rest of society (Pardo 2000e); in particular, I have gained insights into the attitude, and resulting policies, of the dominant political and intellectual elite toward those who do not conform to, or defy, their ideology and interests (Pardo 2001).

In the 1990s, while engaged in my research on the elite, I started a comparative project with other colleagues, involving the southern Italian regions of Campania (the Naples region), Apulia, and Sicily. We focused

on development policies, conducting an in-depth study of how these policies are implemented at the microlevel and of the effects the different
approaches of the ruling elite have in these regions.

In this chapter, I draw on my research to study the ethnography of
work and entrepreneurship in a social and economic context that, as is
widely known, is characterized by a historically weak industrial development, the presence of organized crime in various sectors of the market,
and high official unemployment. Thus far, the numerous governments
of the center and the center–left that have ruled Italy since the Second
World War have implemented development schemes in the south ineffi-
ciently and mostly through the politics of clientelism and corruption.
Public funds have been systematically used for assistance, as opposed to
investment. Industrialization has been fragmented and insufficient, leading to a situation in which nonindustrial and postindustrial values are
prominent. The approach of the left-wing local governments that have
ruled in most of the south, and particularly in Naples, over the past
twenty-five years have made things even worse (Pardo 2001, chap. 5).
They have rhetorically condemned assistance and clientelism, while prac-
ticing both, and have implemented weak policies of proletarianization
mixed with selective development and the staunch support of mass
culture. More recently, these leftist administrators have become over-
committed to their flattering, though quite untruthful, media image; a
gloss that fools no one.

Things are made more difficult by objective financial and political restrictions that bring into question the interpretations of responsibility, and
the legitimacy of rulers and of important institutional domains. Linking
my Naples material to the broader picture in the south and in Italy as a
whole, I shall examine how ordinary people construct their choices and
careers under such restrictions. More specifically, I shall look at their culture of work and at the moral and practical choices that inform their entrepreneurship and their negotiations of aspects of the laws of market
capitalism in a social setting that, as I have mentioned, has become postindustrial without having ever been fully industrial. The discussion builds
toward an analysis of the weakened legitimacy of government in south Italy
and of the radical changes that need to be implemented in legislation and
in financial and economic policies.

## Management of Existence

Categorical assumptions about human behaviour (Wilk 1996, 36–39) are
of little help to the anthropologist faced with the variety and complexity

of life on the ground. As I have explained at length in a recent mono-graph largely based on the Naples ethnography (Pardo 1996), the empirical analysis of formal and informal aspects of work and entrepre-neurship, as they link to the interplay among morality, norms, and prac-tical choice, offers formidable insights into the complexity of individuals' management of their existence and their role in society. There, I set dominant theories in social anthropology[3] against the argument that we cannot assume that moral themes are basically an opportune veneer for instrumental motives. I agreed with Jonathan Parry (1989) that inten-tional and purposeful action concerns much more than the formal laws of maximization of profit. I also accepted that an interaction exists between the moral aspect and the monetary aspect (Parry and Bloch 1989, chap. 1); and that nonmaterial resources, such as contacts, information, time, and identity (Wallman 1984) are important. However, I also suggested that we should take a step further in our analysis. People's construction of identity and choice, I have found, is strongly based on a strong continu-ous interaction between material and nonmaterial (religious, symbolic, moral, and spiritual) aspects, between the symbolism of personal identity and the ethics of entrepreneurial management of existence firmly set in the culture of well-being (Pardo 1996, chap. 1). This key concept of strong continuous interaction underpins the general argument that the "rationality" of actors' actions and choices in the pursuit of fulfillment in the broad sense is informed by negotiated choices that involve various spheres of their lives, it is not determined absolutely—or explained solely—by material values and social belonging, or by their formal position in terms of production and consumption.

In the present discussion, I focus on ordinary people's work prac-tices. I set detailed case material in the broader economic, financial, and political context that is significant to the southern Italian situation to ex-amine the negotiated relationship, as opposed to a dichotomy, between morality and interest that informs ordinary people's culture of money and monetary gain.[4]

The ordinary Neapolitans I have met over the years are bearers of a strong entrepreneurial culture that is firmly based in the morality and ramifications, in practical life, of the aforementioned strong continuous interaction between the material and the nonmaterial. I shall expand later on the morality that underlies such a culture. For the moment, it will suffice to say that such entrepreneurialism is widespread, affecting all aspects of their lives. Its economic expressions are perhaps best embod-ied by a variety of small-scale businesses often, though not exclusively, rooted in what is called the "informal sector," but generally addressing the market as a whole. I suggest that these people's modes of exchange, entrepreneurialism, and other economic activities may not always be strictly legal and they may not always agree with the "laws" of market capitalism, but not for this should they be misread as evidence of marginality—cultural, economic, political, and moral. On the contrary, far from being caught in a culture of short-term moves and immediate goals, even people with a disadvantaged background are actively engaged in negotiating the redefinition of their lives and of their place in society. Such negotiation is informed by cultural values that are best understood in the context of an intricate relationship between short-term and medium- to long-term exchanges.[5] Their rulers' repeated failure to trust and to come to terms with their approach has thus far contributed to frustrate the potentially positive contribution that such an approach could give to providing answers to the problems of postindustrial society in the south.

## Work and Entrepreneurship in the Southern Italian Context

According to an established stereotype, southerners are bogged down by amoral "familism" (after Banfield 1958), mutual distrust (Gambetta 1988) and lack of civic culture and sense of society (Putnam 1993).[6] Several writers have endorsed the cultural determinism underlying such a stereotype.[7] In much of the relevant literature, southerners are described as people who lack any sense of cooperation and who are prone to clientelism and corruption. It is, therefore, concluded that they cannot be trusted. Having dismissed most of their work activities as *arte di arrangiarsi* (art of living by one's wits; Allum 1973)[8] most commentators have long settled for the view that southern Italian, and particularly Naples, society is irreparably undermined by unemployment and worklessness, and by a cultural sympathy with criminality. Contentiously (D'Antonio 1995), and running roughshod over the complexities of a varied situation (Miller 1985),[9] it has also been argued that the south is characterized by a peculiar deep-rooted and widespread willingness of the official financial world to allow dirty money in legitimate business (Arlacchi 1987, 88). Unemployment has been widely argued to provide a breeding ground for criminal enterprise.

As I have said, industrial development in south Italy has been weak and patchy, and for a long time life here has been marred by clientelism and corruption. It is also well known that in Italy, and particularly in its southern regions, an interplay exists among political, economic, and criminal interests, to the obvious disadvantage of the majority of the population, who run their lives without becoming involved in such an interplay.[10] The view that I have just outlined remains, however, highly contentious. Reminding us of similar processes going on in comparable areas elsewhere in Europe, it has also caused remarkable damage, for it has interlinked with political interests and ideology justifying devastating processes of exclusion (Pardo 2000b, 2001), the protracted absence of efficient investment and the failure to develop necessary infrastructures.

Let me be more precise. In some cases, business may well draw on cooperation with criminals and criminal enterprise to gain unfair advantage, through intimidation and money laundering, in overt conflict with legitimate market competition (Pardo 1996, chap. 2). However, it would be inexcusably simplistic to say that such cases account for the general situation. Anthropological research has brought to light serious flaws in such a standard interpretation, pointing to a highly graded situation that underlies official employment, including all forms of work that can be performed legally. Such a complexity, with which most anthropologists would be familiar in their research (see, e.g., Smith 1989), transcends a straightforward distinction between "employment," including all types of formal and paid labor, and "work." It must be understood in the light of three major considerations that can be usefully summarized at this stage.

First, there exists, in real life, a blurring of the boundaries between such categories of the modern organization of labor and many people make a living drawing on the interaction between the formal and the informal;[11] between, that is, activities performed *nell'ombra* (in the shadow), at the margins of the law, and activities performed fully legally, *alla luce del sole* (in the sunlight). Second, even the more pessimistic estimates concede that the socially diversified people involved in crime-related activities account for a tiny minority of the population. There is indeed no plausible justification for the claim that the thousands of officially unemployed either starve or become employed by organized criminals, the Camorristi (members of the criminal organization called Camorra). This leads us to the third consideration that, here, the relationships among the domains of the legal, the semilegal, and the illegal appear to be problematic and flexible, not necessarily ascribed and self-perpetuating.

Of course, it would be superficial to maintain that such a situation, found throughout Italy and especially prominent in the south, is evidence of valuelessness. The lives of ordinary Neapolitans are profoundly informed by a moral framework that combines material interest with generosity and the culture of helping each other. It is within such a framework that key principles play a crucial role in the entrepreneurialism that marks their management of existence. More precisely, Neapolitans say *"Ajutat' ca Dio t'ajut"* (God helps those who help themselves). Equally important, they also say *"Nun voglio sta' suggett' a nisciun"* (I don't want to be subject to anyone) and *"Chi pecora s' fa 'o lupo s'a magna"* (If you behave like a sheep, you'll become a wolf's meal). These principles are highly significant throughout the south and are expressed in the various southern dialects in equally graphic terms. They underpin my informants' pursuit of goals in direct conjunction with the culture of *sapé fa* (cleverness), pooling personal resources of all kinds and using what is there or can be set up within the law or at its margins in the pursuit of material or nonmaterial goals. They play a crucial role in their work strategies and in their careers more generally, with an emphasis on establishing independent enterprise.

The restrictions I have described are, thus, continuously negotiated in real life through a combination of entrepreneurialism and management of monetary and nonmonetary resources that tends to exclude predatory practices. The moral legitimacy of such negotiations (established in the terms of moral, spiritual, and material well-being) is widely recognized by the peers, of some significance, of those who undertake them.[12] It is according to these moral and ethical imperatives that ordinary people draw the line between activities that are not strictly legal but enjoy an aura of legitimacy and activities that are unequivocally criminal and illegitimate. A clear distinction is established in real life between actions that are illegal or semilegal and acceptable (in various degrees), and actions that are criminal (and condemned and unacceptable). Here, professional criminals belong to the *abbiente* (the "environment"), a social, cultural, and economic domain different and separated from ordinary life and from the moral order people recognize and contribute to establish. The abbiente is characterized by values and activities with which ordinary people do not identify.

In Italy, the rate of unemployment is 11 percent. In the South, it is 21 percent, compared to 8.3 percent in the center and 9.2 percent in the north. In Campania, 52.9 percent of those between the ages of fifteen and twenty-nine are without a job. In Naples, the officially unemployed are 23.7 percent of the active population.[13] Nevertheless, it is widely accepted that only a small part of the Neapolitans registered as unemployed are actually out of work; many work hard to improve their lives, and it is not simply a question of them being constrained in their choices. Drawing on empirical experience, I would totally agree with such an assessment of the situation. A sizable minority of these men and women have joined the various so-called cooperatives of the unemployed, officially fighting for the right to a formal job. Periodically, their protest makes the headlines. As such protest often happens to contribute significantly to making or breaking local government and ministerial appointments, it is the opinion of most observers that it is instrumental to political competition.

There are other major considerations that need to be made. In obvious conflict with what some have chosen to believe (Pinnarò and Pugliese 1985), most of the officially unemployed reject their "proletarianization." In spite of lack of guarantees and insurance, they tolerate dependent work for informal workshops (mostly done at home) as a "necessary evil," because it allows flexible timetables and the hope to gain the necessary experience and contacts to develop personal enterprise. At the same time, they generally shun industrial work in the formal sector, describing it as unhealthy and alienating in terms of work procedures and control over their time and production. On the contrary, free enterprise—when possible, in cooperation with others—is desirable, for it is seen as meritorious and morally and financially rewarding.

Many of the officially unemployed aspire to a secure public-sector job, as it is widely believed that such employment is comparably less demanding and allows free time to pursue rewarding, if illegal, "side activities" that, as I have indicated, usually take the form of various kinds of individual or joint enterprises. However, the ethnographer soon realizes that, whether they are successful or not in achieving such an aspiration, these people often cope with the messiness of managing existence by operating in what is appropriately described as a gray area. This is an apparently ever-expanding semilegal shadowy interstice—officially nonexistent but factually significant—between "legality" and "illegality" (Pardo 1999, 2000c). It would be easy, and unhelpful (Smith 1989), to dismiss what happens in this gray area by straightforwardly associating it with crime. People's actions in this interstitial domain, as opposed to operating strictly legally, point to complex forms of control over the relationship between transgression (of formal law) and order—an order that is compatible with their shared morality and ethics of management of existence. Underlying such an approach is the cultural imperative that they should not become involved in criminality and should be able to consider themselves, and to be seen, as "honest" people; a strong motivation that leaves morally and socially isolated those who engage systematically in blackmail, extortion, drug dealing, and so on (Pardo 1995; 1996, chaps. 2, 3, 4).

Thus, many people, officially unemployed or employed, perform work and other activities that fall outside the strictly defined boundaries of the law. Bringing to mind a classical theme in economic anthropology (Smith 1989, 309ff), they say that they do so because overregulation and high costs prevent them from operating legally, which, they say, they would prefer because operating illegally is costly in terms of worry, money, and time. These "informal" activities are diversified across society, ranging from workshops to various activities in the tertiary sector (especially services). But they also include trading with or without a license, home labor, and a variety of tax-dodging enterprises, which in many cases are run in conjunction with, and in support of, fully legal business. Among these enterprises are tradesmanship; small- and medium-scale moneylending;[14] selling merchandise (usually linen, household appliances, and jewelery) at shop price door to door, on credit and charging interest (5–10 percent per month) on the installments; dealing in clandestine lotteries; obtaining documents on other people's behalf; selling smuggled cigarettes, pirated cassettes, videos, and so forth; petty organizing and management of gambling; provision of unlicensed private medical assistance and other social services; colorful but monetarily rewarding activities such as selling goods and cleaning windshields at traffic lights; working as unauthorized parking attendants; and so on. Of course, organized crime controls some, though by no means all, of these activities. But such a control is not always felt or recognized at the microlevel. On the basis of the evidence available, it would be inaccurate to say that those who operate at the low level in areas in which organized crime has an interest (such as, say, petty selling of smuggled cigarettes or clandestine lotteries) are inevitably and directly in the employment of criminals.

Apart from the aforementioned informal sources of income, the household budgets of the majority of my informants not only do benefit from do-it-yourself and household jobs done free of charge by friends and relatives, as part of delayed and often generalized exchanges, the significance of which reaches well beyond this domain of activity. They also benefit from "savings" derived from tax evasion and manipulation of meters. Some also work in unlicensed workshops, earning more than in legitimate industry, for they and their employers do not pay taxes. Many use their contacts to gain access to the unemployment lists, in the hope of obtaining welfare benefits (assistance, housing, and the like).

This complexity raises the crucial point that compliance with the law is not an absolute condition of the obligations of citizenship (Dahrendorf 1996, 33). It also brings new light to ordinary people's relations with their rulers—present and past—and also to fundamental questions of legitimacy in the drafting and implementation of legislation and policy (Pardo 2000d). Later, I shall consider in detail how this point is emphasized by the serious restrictions, imposed by overregulation and adverse financial policies, that mar this situation.

In the next section, I discuss the cases of Paolo, Giovanni, Peppino, and Lello, self-made entrepreneurs of popolino origins for whom crime and criminals are nonoptions, and for whom the monetary promises of criminal action hold no aura of desirability. I have chosen these cases because they exemplify different versions of the kind of entrepreneurialism that I outlined earlier. They also exemplify significant gradations of choices between "shadow" and "sunlight," between the domain of the illegal and that of the legal, accounting for the great role played by modes of action that fall in the large, negotiated domain in-between, the domain of the semilegal. For lack of space, here I can only summarize these case studies. In a monograph I have provided a more complete descriptive analysis of these men and of their culture and social and economic connections (Pardo 1996). Here, a brief outline will help one grasp aspects of the situation on the ground that are central to the arguments of this chapter. I shall, then, proceed to set such material in a broader framework, taking into account the issues raised by other small and medium entrepreneurs, who manage their businesses in a more orthodox fashion.

My aim is to see how ill-thought-out or ideologically slanted policies contribute to frustrate both the development of individual initiative and enterprise and their beneficial implications in terms of closer links. This will be the subject of the closing part of my discussion, in which I shall look briefly at how the powerful elite that has governed Naples in recent history has failed, or has appeared to be deliberately unwilling, to understand these crucial aspects of life among ordinary people. Its rhetoric and policies have been informed either by a drive to exploit a situation of economic weakness through corrupt practices or by a determination to eradicate a culture that it regards as subaltern and to replace it with values and practices that ordinary people resent as alien and illegitimate.

## Work and the Morality of Sapé Fa

I have indicated that among ordinary Neapolitans, and southerners more generally, the listed principles God helps those who help themselves, I don't want to be subject to anyone, and If you behave like a sheep, you'll become a wolf's meal form a significant context in which the concept of sapé fa holds the status of a moral imperative. It is in line with such a moral imperative that people construct their careers. Accordingly, the fundamental distinction is established here between those who choose crime as an "easy option" and those who pool their resources (time, contacts, and money, as well as spiritual resources) to achieve their and their families' material and nonmaterial betterment. I do not mean to imply that in their work activities people always strictly abide by the culture of sapé fa. I would say, however, that it is within such a cultural framework that people sharply distinguish between *lavoro* (work) and *fatica* (toil), and behave accordingly. The concept of work accounts for activities that are morally and monetarily rewarding and are promising for the future. Toil is a word used for work activities that are unrewarding and leave one without prospects. Let us see how this works in a number of cases, and what implications there are in terms of people's economic strategies and moral choices.

In the mid-1980s, Paolo was an unlicensed stall holder in a workshop, who was described by his local peers as an example of poverty and failure; a man bogged down by toil and lack of contacts (Pardo 1996, chap. 2). By the early 1990s, he and his wife had established a fashionable and remunerative shop, and they are now thinking of opening a second shop in which to employ two of their children. The story of this couple highlights aspects of the lives of the disadvantaged in Naples.

Paolo used to run an unlicensed workshop in cooperation with others, producing leather goods, which they were forced to close due, in Paolo's own words, "to misfortune and lack of capital." When I met him, Paolo had recently set up a new stall, owing to the "good heart," as he put it, of a local woman to whom several local stall holders were obliged for favors received from her in the past. This woman's intercession happened at a particularly harrowing time for Paolo and his family. His previous unlicensed stall had been definitely closed down by the police, so he found himself deprived also of that meager source of income. Moved by his predicament, this woman persuaded two licensed stall holders to make room for Paolo to set his stall for a fee. The income from the stall was supplemented by that from Paolo's other work as a door-to-door salesman in the evenings, the sale of garments made by his wife, and the weekly income their older son earned as a delivery boy in his free time from school. In spite of this, the family just managed to survive. Lack of money, in turn, affected Paolo's business, for he could not borrow money even from local moneylenders. Moreover he was in constant fear of being fined and shut down again by the police because he had repeatedly failed to get a trading license and did not have the right contacts to solve the problem. This last point was explained by Paolo's refusal to engage in what he regarded as "corrupt actions" to obtain benefits "to which you have no legal right." This apparent contradiction in Paolo's life is explained by the fact that while he regarded his illicit trading as a necessity, dealing in bribery was an option he did not wish to take, quite regardless of whether he was in a position to do so. Paolo's way of coming to terms with such a moral dilemma was emphasized by other aspects of his approach.

When discussing the abuse to which he was constantly subjected by local people, Paolo mentioned that, had he wanted, he could have put an end to all that by asking the protection of a criminal who was in debt to him. Years earlier, Paolo had saved this man from a severe beating and on that occasion the man had sworn to help him, should the need arise. However, Paolo made it emphatically clear to me that he would never use such a resource because he wanted nothing to do with criminals. He stressed that he and his wife came "from humble but straight families and want[ed] to live honestly." He added, in line with what I had been told by many of his peers, that criminals are not so omnipotent as they seek to appear and that "things can often be obtained otherwise." Paolo's attitude was underlined by the conviction, also in this case widely shared among the popolino, that asking for their help is an implicit admission of failure.

By the end of the 1990s, Paolo had expanded his (still unlicensed) stall business. Having no access whatsoever (direct, that is, or indirect, through a figurehead) to formal credit, he borrowed money from relatives. However, he now had material assets that were locally recognized (therefore, recognized by the local sellers of money) to have some value. As the capital he had raised was still insufficient to make his trade profitable, and he was desperate to achieve such a goal, Paolo felt forced to take this option and successfully obtained a small loan from a local moneylender. Soon after, Paolo again made of necessity virtue. Following one of the periodic council campaigns against unlicensed street trades in central Naples, he was forced to close the stall. He sold out and used the money and, again, a loan from a relative to open a small shop in partnership with his brother-in-law, who worked as an assistant in a similar shop and provided the necessary experience and trading network. By now, Paolo was set on compromising his own moral values and "doing what everybody else [was] doing." So, this time, he obtained a license with the help of a policeman in exchange for a small fee and discounts on merchandise in the shop. Thus, he eventually indulged in what to an outsider is bribery, but was described by him as a lesser evil than starving. This, in his view, was a way to survive without too seriously violating his values; a compromise that typically allows him to steer clear of "true crime."

Gradations of the kind of morally and practically negotiated choices that I have just described mark an entrepreneurial approach that allows people to manage their existence often at the margins of the strictly defined boundaries of the law without stepping into what is to them the morally unacceptable realm of true crime. Important aspects of this issue are further illustrated by the case study of Giovanni.

When I met Giovanni in the early 1980s, during my fieldwork among the popolino of Naples, he was a young man strongly motivated to improve his condition through hard entrepreneurial work (Pardo 1996, esp. chap. 3). This was reflected in his behavior and aspirations.

While admitting he was handicapped by his popolino origins, he was
fully engaged in building a good local reputation as someone who is
clever and good-hearted.

Having given up on school, in which he did not believe, early in his
life Giovanni started working for cash. Only later, encouraged by his girlfriend, a university student, did he resume his studies. He obtained a
diploma through a combination of studying and "cooking-up" his marks.
Through his contacts he found tutors but also mobilized, and in some
cases bribed, people who helped him pass his exams. Over the years, he
has successfully invested money and other resources in deferred (but
also direct) exchanges and in materially rewarding activities in the legal
and semilegal arenas. Now steadily (and formally) employed, he has
been a reluctant "black laborer," working as a shop and workshop assistant, delivery boy, sign erector for political parties, and so on. In his late
teens, Giovanni briefly became involved in selling various goods door to
door without a license and on installments (on which his customers paid
what he and they described as "reasonable interest") and in smuggling
cigarettes and watches.

Such low-level illegal dealings exemplify the ethnographic imperative that ordinary people's relationships with organized crime are always
problematic and marked by strong motivations to stay away from criminals. Giovanni's attitude reflects that of most of his peers, who are similarly involved in selling smuggled goods or in dealing in clandestine
lotteries (which in many cases are controlled, at a high level, by organized criminals). He was at once aware and wary of the indirect links with
organized crime. He knew that at higher levels organized criminals were
often involved in the smuggling business and he deliberately kept his activities low key and, therefore, away from such problematic people. Giovanni felt that, unlike what went on at those higher levels, what he was
doing was perhaps outside the strictly defined boundaries of the law, but
it was certainly not criminal. He managed to keep a "clean sheet," and
gave up these illegal activities when he realized that he could not for long
avoid "becoming compromised with the law." Instead, he started a "legitimate" trade in which he profitably evaded taxes. His family operated similarly, the household's income included profits from his mother's
unlicensed trade, rent from a local flat, and his father's pension; Giovanni's brothers, who also lived with their parents, contributed with part
of their earnings from formal and informal jobs and trading activities.
Giovanni repeatedly used his contacts in the police department to avoid
paying or to negotiate the fines for tax evasion in his trade. In some cases,
he used direct bribery as an extreme resource. Like most popolino and
bourgeois whom I have met in Naples over the years, Giovanni at once

recognized the usefulness of such contacts and dismissed them as dishonest busybodies whose behavior is understandable only because they are paid miserably.

Typically, for Giovanni, dealing in the semilegal arena did not mean that he was dishonest, or, like many other formally unemployed, did he consider it dishonest to register as unemployed and benefit from (very limited) social security. Giovanni was similarly in line with many of his peers in that although he knew he could easily find employment in the criminal market, he dismissed the idea outright. He said, "I'm from an honest family . . . and I'm not interested in such easy money making. I couldn't hurt or abuse anyone, or steal anything. You don't have to become a criminal to earn a decent living. It's a matter of pride, you know; it's the rubbish of the neighborhood who become Camorristi." Consistent with his commitment to feeling part of a network of relatives as resources whom he can mobilize to achieve moral and material goals, he added, "I'm too concerned with my family's respect, which I'd lose."

In my ethnography, these themes of despising easy money making and spurning the advantage that the exercise of violence offers in market competition interlock strongly with the moral sanction of Camorristi as social, economic, and moral polluters of local life through their drug pushing. They are deemed responsible for the drug addiction of local youth and the consequent injection of a ruthlessness in economic and social life that is alien to the local culture of "good heart," "helping each other," and "sapé fa," and is absolutely contrary to ordinary people's way of life.

When he gave up dealing at the margins of the law, Giovanni first tried to obtain a steady job through his link with a politician and then started working as an assistant in an office managed by a local contact of his family. He established, through a relative, a relationship with a local politician who had an interest in the many cooperatives of unemployed youth operating in Naples, and Giovanni persuaded his equally unemployed friends to join him in forming a cooperative. Their hope was to obtain contracts for various types of council-related work. They, however, continued to pursue their strategies independently. Some, like Giovanni, found the politician's ways too corrupt and demanding (he expected them to behave as old-fashioned clients) and looked for work elsewhere, while remaining members of the cooperative; some were actually helped by the politician; most refused to campaign for him but did vote for him at the local elections.

While leading the cooperative, Giovanni met Andrea through another relative. Andrea was a middle-rank clerk, locally described as a clever entrepreneur who worked in the social services while operating a small business based in a local office but spanning the city. He had established a useful network among lawyers, accountants, and other professionals through which he was able to help people, usually for a price, in dealing with the bureaucracy and, sometimes, in finding jobs. His ability to bestow favors and his contacts were locally regarded as additional assets, of which Giovanni was aware.

Soon after Giovanni began to work in Andrea's business, Andrea experienced a crisis in his life and was considering closing the office. Giovanni and his mother pressured their relative into persuading Andrea to turn the office over to Giovanni. Andrea saw the opportunity to convert a total loss into a partial gain. Expecting Giovanni to be under an obligation to him in the future, Andrea invested time in training him and turning the business over to him without charge. Thus, a grateful Giovanni took up a business that required ability, was recognizably above average, and, especially, had been entrusted to him by "a man of the caliber of Andrea." Soon Giovanni began to benefit from the business in terms of money, as well as self-esteem, prestige, and contacts. Andrea later helped Giovanni to expand, finding new premises and giving him advice on how to raise funds "informally." Repeating the experience of many other informants, Giovanni had tried and failed to borrow money from banks. Part of the business was run informally, avoiding taxes, and he did not have assets. Therefore, on Andrea's advice, he asked his formally employed brother to apply for a bank loan and borrowed additional sums from other members of his family. This problem of obtaining credit from official institutions raises issues that I shall summarize later to clarify the general situation in which people like Giovanni are forced to operate. Giovanni registered the office business in his fiancée Lucia's name, thus leaving open other options for himself. He continued his door-to-door selling and occasional work for private firms, working only part time in the office. His fiancée helped in the business, while continuing her university studies and doing some home tailoring in the evening with her mother for a fashion firm. At that stage, Giovanni's continuing involvement in the cooperative was explained less by his interest in obtaining employment through it than by hope that the politician's gratitude might induce the latter to help him and Lucia in their pursuit of nonmanual formal employment. At the same time, operating according to the culture that informs the actions of many popolino, he refused to depend exclusively on that politician and invested time and energies in establishing other contacts among professionals.

Eventually, Giovanni's investments were rewarded as he obtained one of the state jobs for which he had applied. Lucia found employment as a teacher. They retained an interest in the business, but formally turned it over to Giovanni's younger brother and to a friend, who for many years now have run it in a legitimate fashion, keeping records in order and paying taxes. They have achieved some expansion through indirect borrowing.[15] But they have found it difficult to raise the larger funds necessary to expand further. Because they have no extra assets and cannot provide the guarantees demanded by the banks in the south (I will discuss this later), they have repeatedly failed to borrow from banks as entrepreneurs, and have found government schemes too obscure and cumbersome to be of any use. Thus, they have not yet been able to make the business a viable source of income to sustain their families.

The career and choices of an informant whom I shall call Peppino (Pardo 2000b, 64–69) illustrate entrepreneurship that moves further from shadow and beyond self-employment. Peppino started his business while he was still a formally unemployed trader in leather goods produced by an "informal" workshop. His wife and daughter worked at home for this and other similar workshops using machinery they had bought on installments. Peppino sold some of these goods door to door and in an improvised unlicensed stall. Having obtained a steady job in the public sector, Peppino mortgaged his salary to borrow money from a bank, which he added to savings to start his own unlicensed business. Peppino's wife and daughter and a neighbor and her daughter-in-law produced leather objects that Peppino's son delivered to stalls and shops throughout Naples and the province. The enterprise has enjoyed a remarkable success that is explained only in part by the financial advantage it draws from tax evasion (which makes it easier for his customers also to avoid tax) and freedom from the strings and the costs that choke many formal businesses. Peppino's trade is made highly competitive because of low prices, a flexible organization, and high productivity.

Recently, Peppino has begun to diversify the production and expand his custom, hoping that he would thus contribute to ensuring a better future for his children. Providing a further example (see, e.g., the cases of Paolo and Giovanni) of the degree of trust to be observed in the relationship prevalent in south Italy (Gambetta 1988), he is operating in partnership with his brother-in-law and a formally unemployed friend. They have raised the necessary capital in tellingly diversified ways. Peppino has invested his profits in the purchase of new machinery, raw material, and a second van. Peppino's brother-in-law has raised money by mortgaging his and his wife's salaries. The friend has converted a property to accommodate the larger workshop and has borrowed money from a moneylender. He and Peppino's brother-in-law contribute to the distribution, one full time, the other part time. The workforce now includes their wives and children, and a number of friends and neighbors.

One of the children of Peppino's friend works as an accountant, a role made necessary by the new size and complexity of the business. The other contributes his experience in marketing.

So far, Peppino and his associates have failed to "make most of the business legal," and certainly not for want of trying. They have also failed to expand further,[16] because, like Giovanni's brother and his friend, they have found it impossible to raise the necessary capital. As I have said, I shall expand on this issue of credit later. For now, let us focus on the difficulty of making business legal. Peppino and his associates echo the experience of the great majority of the Neapolitan, Sicilian, and Apulian entrepreneurs running established legal businesses to whom I have spoken when they say that they feel frustrated by the existing laws and regulations. Typically, they say that they are so overcomplicated and demanding that even those who can afford to employ professionals— clerks, accountants, and lawyers—run the risk of unwittingly breaking some rule at some point.[17] These are not wealthy businessmen. Like a very large number of informants, small traders, and entrepreneurs who operate in the legal and illegal sectors of the market, they point out that should they try to comply fully with the law (safety and health, taxation, and the like), they would go bust in a very short time. These objections— partly grounded in reality, partly myth—help explain the objective difficulty of running a legal business in Italy. They also serve the purpose of morally expanding the domain of the permissible. Thus, many entrepreneurs run their businesses just outside the strictly defined boundaries of formal law. In doing so, they embody a negotiated version of the approach of people like Paolo, Giovanni, and Peppino. They preserve a recognized moral legitimacy for they carefully avoid crossing the line between what is not legal but tolerable and what is unequivocally criminal. After all, in their eyes and in the eyes of those significant to them, they are doing no more than coping as best they can with the absurd system in which they are forced to operate.

The business of Lello, a man now in his fifties, is definitely set in the sunlight, although some, lucrative, activities do draw on shadowy aspects of production and the market. The business is fully licensed and in large part accountable. It is the result of choices that over twenty years have transformed Lello from a shop assistant to the owner of a large shop in Naples and a smaller one in a popular tourist resort in the province.

Lello had to leave school at the age of thirteen because his parents could not support him (his father was an occasional laborer and his mother was a housewife), and they needed an extra income. He found informal employment in a shop specializing in clothing. He worked there until he was twenty-two, when he became employed in one of a chain of large shops in Naples. He soon became an asset to the shop, establishing good relationships with suppliers. His entrepreneurial potential and drive to better himself were appreciated by the owners, who allowed him to take Mondays off work. Lello invested his savings in the purchase of a van and began to sell ever larger quantities of clothes produced in the Naples workshops (formal and, as he progressed, also informal) to shops and retailers throughout southern and central Italy. In part, he bought such merchandise, but in large part, he persuaded the owners of the workshops to entrust it to him, accepting payment after sale. Lello was in his thirties when he decided to use his savings and money borrowed from his parents to buy himself a quota in the Naples chain of shops. Within five years, he was financially sound enough to set up his own business. He started with a small shop in the center of the city selling inexpensive but good-quality clothes. His was the kind of shop in which fully legal workshops, as well as workshops like that run by Peppino, operating, in part, at the margins of the law, would place their products. Such an arrangement was profitable. Lello mainly ran his business legally, paying taxes on most of the merchandise, and was careful to keep the proportion of the clothes he bought from people like Peppino, which remained undeclared, sufficiently small to allow him to keep this side of his business undetected by the law. Such merchandise increased his profit significantly for, while being good quality, it was considerably cheaper. About ten years ago, Lello had saved enough to move to larger premises nearby. His wife became involved in the new shop and soon started managing it on her own, leaving Lello free to travel to sell to shops elsewhere in Italy.

Soon Lello realized that he was tired of traveling for such long periods of time, but also that he was now in a position to invest the profits from such double activity. He used existing capital to open a small shop on the coast catering to Italian and foreign tourists. After a trial period, he entrusted its management to his grown-up children who speak several languages and, he says, are quite good at keeping up with fashion. Lello and his wife now manage the shop in Naples. They feel, however, that the business could easily be run by one of them and that it would be much more profitable in terms of money and time to open a second shop in a wealthy area of the city, specializing in luxury clothes. To take such a step, they would need a fairly large sum of money. However, investment in the tourist shop has left them without capital, and they have been unable to borrow sufficient money from banks because, they have been told, their assets (the two shops) are not enough guarantee. Following a pattern that has emerged in our earlier discussion, the bank managers to whom they spoke said that an application for a loan would be considered if they owned property (which is not the case; they rent both the premises of the two shops and the house in which they live). Moreover, as Lello was particularly cross with a bank clerk who had suggested they approach a "friend" of his who lends money at interest informally—in other words, Lello pointed out to me, a loan shark. Having ruled out such a dangerous option, Lello remains, as he put it "stuck with the situation as it is, without prospect for expansion in the short-to-medium term."

## Individual Entrepreneurship and Access to Credit

The empirical examination of small-scale business initiative has shown that they are informed by an entrepreneurial culture that, underreported, frustrated in various ways, and subjected to the kind of misrepresentation I have mentioned earlier, plays a major role in the way people manage their existence beyond official employment and unemployment. Meeting the basic criteria set out by Michael E. Smith (1989, 294), the gradations of illegal or semilegal entrepreneurialism that I have examined at once open a path to community resources beyond official allocation and defy the attempt of the state to monitor, regulate, and extract revenue from the production, circulation, and consumption of goods. We have also seen that we are not faced, here, with a dual economy in which the informal is complementary to the formal, but rather with interlinked and interacting sectors of one economy. An important aspect of the informal entrepreneurialism that I have examined is that it develops in more or less strong connection with the formal sector of the market and interacts significantly with it.

I have outlined the moral set up that informs the choices of those involved in such enterprises and have determined that "dirty money" put into circulation by criminals is not regarded as an asset. People recognize the advantage such money may give in the expansion of business and in short-term competition. But they also are explicitly aware of the problematic and far-reaching implications in economic, social, moral, and legal terms of such a way of raising capital. Thus, when, as it often happens, formal sources of credit are unavailable, insufficient, or fraught with overcomplicated procedures, they may decide to purchase money from moneylenders. Such money comes at high interest and is used only for exceptional investment that is expected to yield sufficient dividends in a sufficiently short time to repay the loan before interest becomes crippling. Entrepreneurs who choose this course of action trust the solidity of their businesses, or have reason to feel secure because money is owed to them by "reliable customers," such as public institutions or large companies. I have said that the empirical reality of debt and repayment in the south is fraught with enormous difficulties that inform what appears to be a widening gap between the actual distribution of rights and access to them, and their ideal distribution and the attendant processes of inclusion and exclusion that determine factual membership of society. I have analyzed such difficulties in a recent work (Pardo 2000b). For the purpose of the present discussion, it will be useful to summarize the situation.

In Italy, banking services are very expensive (Stefanelli 1996). They are considerably more so in the south. The reports periodically published by the Bank of Italy and the bulletins produced by various professional bodies meet my empirical experience in pointing out that the financial situation in the south is traditionally made worse by two, interlinked processes. First, in the south, banks sell money at high rates (up to the periodically adjusted legal limit, beyond which interest is legally defined as usurious) that exceed by up to 5 percent those in the center and the north. They do so under considerably more restrictive conditions and lengthy and largely impenetrable banking procedures.[18] Moreover, accustomed to thinking of credit as a risk-free business,[19] we have seen that they demand guarantees—such as patrimonial assets, and especially mortgageable private property—that have nothing to do with the applicant's enterprise. Widely regarded by ordinary people as unjustifiably punishing, such restrictions combine with various kinds of hidden costs, particularly in the form of transaction and administrative fees.[20] Critically for the development of enterprise, for the accumulation of capital to invest, and ultimately for employment, such a combination of difficulties makes credit not only financially problematic but also exceedingly difficult to obtain.[21] According to the report published by the Associazione per lo Sviluppo dell'Industria nel Mezzogiorno (1998), this situation is even worse when it is individual and family enterprises seeking credit.

Second, there is widespread use of "alternative" ways to raise money, particularly through figureheads. Recourse to such alternative sources of credit is partly a consequence of the situation I have described, and partly due to the fact that so many who need to raise capital have no official assets to offer as guarantee. For reasons I have discussed earlier, money laundering and the use of moneylenders play a minor role in most legitimate and semilegitimate businesses. Here, it is worth stressing that while loan sharks are avoided on mainly economic considerations,[22] the involvement of criminals is widely ruled out not so much because it is illegal, but because it conflicts with ordinary people's culture of legitimate and fulfilling work and entrepreneurship, and because it involves consequences that are deeply subversive of the moral order they strive to establish and keep in their lives.

Further difficulties are injected in this situation by the fact that financial schemes put into place by national or local government, more recently increasingly in conjunction with the European Union, to help entrepreneurs through public money are made actually inaccessible by procedures that very few seem able to cope with. Observers and operators have repeatedly called for a clarification and simplification of such procedures, pointing out that only those who can afford highly qualified specialist staff benefit from such schemes. Sometimes, I have found, it is difficult even to gain access to the regulations and be informed in time of the exact procedures and deadlines. It is, again, small-scale enterprise that appears to be especially penalized. And yet, it is now being increasingly recognized that not only is this kind of entrepreneurialism important in the southern economy, but its development would substantially contribute to making the south stand on its own legs, financially and fiscally.[23] Such development appears to be frustrated by the distrust of ordinary people that informs some powerful political and financial elite's interpretation of responsibility, leading to unfair financial policies.

The need to respond to these difficulties is strongly felt. Recently, some young entrepreneurs of Campania have established a regional association on a voluntary basis. Their aim is to provide free help and assistance to people who wish to gain access to national government funds, in accordance with current legislation (Law 966/97, art. 15). Similar initiatives have been established elsewhere in the south and the idea of expanding their competence to European Union development schemes is under consideration. Of course, such initiatives are commendable and useful. It is, however, equally obvious that much more needs to be done and that, to begin to see results, the adverse ideology that has long inspired the state and its local agencies must be subjected to radical revision. It is imperative for the state to come to terms, well beyond prohibition and repression, with work and entrepreneurship that develops marginally or totally outside the law as it stands at the moment. Criminalization has largely proved to be counterproductive and ineffectual in terms of extracting tax returns (Pardo 2000d). Operative proposals have been drafted to encourage those who operate outside the law to bring their businesses "into the sunlight."[24] But this would be impossible in the absence of new, simplified legislation.[25] Moreover, it is equally imperative for political and financial institutions to develop an approach that is sophisticated and enlightened enough to match the sophistication and diversity of what goes on at the microlevel. This must happen quickly and effectively for both business and society as a whole to benefit fully.

## Conclusion

In this chapter I have examined empirical instances in which ordinary people who are bearers of a strong entrepreneurial attitude are forced to interact with a system biased by a deep-seated distrust of their culture, orientations, and lifestyles. Such distrust weakens the relationship between the individual and key public institutions. It engenders negative policies that make southerners feel treated as second-class citizens, and it seriously jeopardizes their hope of economic betterment. Such a distrust marks a situation in which what is impeccably legal is often identified in the wider society as unfair and unacceptable, and vice versa.

The failure of "the system" to link to real people in the south is emphasized by the working relationship observed in the center–north between financial and political institutions and entrepreneurs who operate in the informal, as well as the formal, sector.[26] Thus, it happens that in such an important field of economic activity as that of credit, as in others, a significant proportion of Italians end up dwelling in the gray area between legality and illegality. Deterred by the formal sector, people turn to the informal one taking options that are formally illegal, though not always identified in real life as immoral, unethical, or illegitimate. Thus, the reality of work and entrepreneurship becomes complicated by an interplay of choices and exchanges that raises crucial issues of political accountability and, ultimately, of legitimacy.

## Notes

1. My research has been funded at various stages by the British Academy, the Nuffield Foundation and the University of Kent at Canterbury. I am grateful to Dr. John Corbin and Dr. Giuliana B. Prato for their comments on an earlier draft of this chapter.

2. I have carried out research in the domains of politics, the judiciary, academia, business, the banking world, the media, and the church. Fieldwork has drawn on a combination of documentary research, participant observation, and open-ended interviews of key actors. I have published some of the findings (Pardo 1996, 2000b,d,e, 2001) and am preparing a book-length monograph for publication.

3. See Bailey (1969), Barth (1963, 1966), and Boissevain (1974). See also Wilk (1996) for an overview.

4. For an extended analysis of this issue and its broader sociological implications, see Pardo (1996). Wilk (1996, chap. 5) gives an account of the debate on cultural economics and the relationship between people's rationality and their economic choices.

5. Parry and Bloch (1989) have developed an interesting view of short-term and long-term cycles of exchange.

6. A precise evaluation of intellectual responsibilities in the development of stereotype on south Italy belongs to a separate discussion. Recently, I have examined aspects of this issue, also taking into account historical processes (Pardo 2001).

7. See, for example, Allum (1973), Altan (1986), Banfield (1958), Becchi-Collidà (1984), Belmonte (1989), Chubb (1981), Graziano (1980), *Micromega* (1990), and Pizzorno (1967).

8. This "art" would be characterized by individuals' commitment to cut-throat competition, to the ruthlessness of carpe diem, and to fatalism.

9. For historical-comparative aspects of such a situation, see Little and Posada-Carbò (1996).

10. For a contemporary assessment of such an interplay, see Miller (1999).

11. Keith Hart originally established this distinction "based essentially on that between wage-earning and self-employment" (1973, 68).

12. For a more complete discussion of the complexity of the relationship between morality and legitimacy, see Pardo (2000c) and the contributions in Pardo (2000c).

13. See the financial paper, *Il Denaro* (2001, g: p.1 and p.16).

14. Elsewhere (Pardo 2000b; see also Pardo 1996, chap. 5), I have developed an analysis of the culture of usury and moneylending, examining illegal sellers of money at various levels, and the moral and economic framework in which they operate. Here, it will be useful to mention that the illegal sale of money, involving usurious rates of interest and tax dodging, occurs on two distinct and internally differentiated, levels: usury and moneylending. This arbitrary distinction corresponds to that established, in this culture, between money sold at excessive interest and money sold at moderate interest. The illegal sellers of money are accordingly, and equally arbitrarily, differentiated between *strozzini* (sing. *strozzino*; literally, strangler) and "people who sell money at interest." An additional discriminatory factor is the use or threat of violence. Significantly, such categorization is set in the context of the complex interplay of ethical, economic, and social criteria to the important link that, in this culture, is established at the grassroots level between a person's morality and the use that that person makes of money. Not only does this link inform the definition of usury and moneylending, it also determines the degree of legitimacy attached to the exchanges that occur at each of these two levels.

15. This time, the money was raised by Giovanni and Lucia, now his wife, through a bank loan.

16. Although they have identified potentially receptive markets in foreign countries.

17. Mazzoni (2000) has given an enlightening descriptive analysis of this complex issue.

18. The banking world explains this policy with the higher risks to which credit is said to be subjected in the South. I have given elsewhere (Pardo 2000b) the details of their argument with particular reference to banks' complaint that credit is largely not repaid, and I have explained why it is rejected by leading economists and entrepreneurs, who point out that it is large and, in the past, state-funded businesses that are responsible for most of the unrepaid credit.

19. Such an attitude belongs to a bank culture that I have examined elsewhere (Pardo 2000b).

20. Through hidden costs, borrowers can be charged up to 48.5 percent per annum above the legal limit. Informants have repeatedly described as usurious the overall charges, which compound on high interest rates.

21. With reference to individual and family enterprises, a recent report by the Associazione per lo Sviluppo dell'Industria nel Mezzogiorno (1998) on the southern economy states that access to credit has increased in central and northern Italy (+5.4 percent), while it has decreased further in the south (−4.1 percent). See also Onado et al. (1990).

22. See note 14.

23. Elsewhere (Pardo 1999), I have examined political and economic initiatives that, taken at a local level in south Italy in cooperation with state agencies, are hoped to have a positive impact on the social, economic, and cultural environment.

24. See, for example, D'Amato (2000, 8–9).

25. Recently, calls for such legislation have been authoritatively expressed (see Pardo 2000d and the contributions in Pardo 2000a).

26. Banks in the north are often small, locally rooted, and linked to local enterprise through parallel growth and mutual dependence. On the profitable relationships between the formal sector and the informal sector in the center–north, see, for example, Brusco (1982).

# References

Allum, P. 1973. *Politics and society in post-war Naples.* Cambridge: Cambridge University Press.

Altan, T. 1986. *La nostra Italia.* Milan: Feltrinelli.

Arlacchi, P. 1987. Stato e mercati illegali. *La Voce della Campania* 1: 26–29.

Associazione per lo Sviluppo dell'Industria nel Mezzogiorno. 1998. *Informazioni SVIMEZ* (7): 11–12. Rome: Associazione per lo Sviluppo dell'Industria nel Mezzogiorno.

Bailey, F. G. 1969. *Stratagems and spoils.* Oxford: Blackwell.

Banfield, E. C. 1958. *The moral basis of a backward society.* Glencoe, Ill.: Free Press.

Barth, F. 1963. *The role of the entrepreneur in social change in northern Norway.* Oslo: Scandinavian University Books.

————. 1966. *Models of social organization.* Occasional Paper No. 23. London: Royal Anthropological Institute.

Becchi-Collidà, A., ed. 1984. *Napoli miliardaria: economia e lavoro dopo il terremoto.* Milan: Franco Angeli.

Belmonte, T. 1989. *The broken fountain.* 1979. Reprint, New York: Columbia University Press.

Boissevain, J. 1974. *Friends of friends: Networks, manipulators, and coalitions.* Oxford: Blackwell.

Brusco, S. 1982. The Emilian model: Productive decentralization and social integration. *Cambridge Journal of Economics* 2: 167–184.

Chubb, J. A. 1981. Naples under the left: The limits of social change. In *Political clientelism, patronage, and development,* edited by S. N. Eisenstadt and R. Lemarchard. London: Sage.

Dahrendorf, R. 1996. Citizenship and social class. In *Citizenship today: The contemporary relevance of T. H. Marshall,* edited by M. Bulmer and A. M. Rees. London: University College London Press.

D'Amato, A. 2000. Agenda 2000: Economia sommersa. *Il Denaro* (October): 25–48.

D'Antonio, M., M. Scarlato, and G. Zezza, eds. 1995. *Commercio Estero e sviluppo economico: Il mezzogiorno nel mercato internazionale.* Naples: Edizioni Scientifiche Italiane.

Gambetta, D., ed. 1988. *Trust: Making and breaking cooperative relations.* Oxford: Blackwell.

Graziano, L. 1980. *Clientelismo e sistema politico: Il caso dell'Italia.* Milan: Franco Angeli.

Hart, K. 1973. Informal income opportunities and urban development in Ghana. *Journal of Modern African Studies* 11(1): 61–89.

Little, W., and E. Posada-Carbò. 1996. *Political corruption in Europe and Latin America.* London: Macmillan.

Mazzoni, C. 2000. L'impresa tra rispetto della legge ed eccessi normativi: *la fiducia e* l'operativita' come deterrenti verso la corruzione. *Svilupp o Economico* 4(3): 89–102.

*Micromega.* 1990. *Le ragioni della sinistra* 1990. Napoli e Dintorni 4, p. 111.

Miller, A. 1985. Misure di prevenzione patrimoniale ed esercizio del credito. *Banca, Borsa e Titoli di Credito* 38(3): 399–407.

———. 1999. La corruzione e il "colpo d'ariete." *Il Denaro* 25: 9–10.

Onado, M., G. Salvo, and M. Villani. 1990. Flussi finanziari e allocazione del risparmio nel mezzogiorno. *Banca d'Italia*: 65–102.

Pardo, I. 1995. Morals of legitimacy in Naples: Streetwise about legality, semi-legality, and crime. *Archives Européennes de Sociologie* 36(1): 44–71.

———. 1996. *Managing existence in Naples: Morality, action, and structure.* Cambridge: Cambridge University Press.

———. 1999. Il crimine tra realtà e rappresentazione. *Il Denaro* 25: 2–6.

———, ed. 2000a. *Corruzione, Moralità, Legge.* Rome: Sviluppo Economico.

———. 2000b. Credit, entrepreneurship, and the repayment of debt: Mismatched conceptions of legitimacy in Italy. *Self, Agency and Society* 2(2): 51–87.

———, ed. 2000c. *Morals of legitimacy: Between agency and the system.* Oxford: Berghahn Books.

———. 2000d. Retorica e interessi di potere tra criminalità e criminalizzazioni. *Quaderni Radicali* 67–69: 195–209.

———. 2000e. When power lacks legitimacy: Relations of politics and law to society in Italy. In *Morals of legitimacy: Between agency and the system*, edited by I. Pardo. Oxford: Berghahn Books.

———. 2001. *Élite senza fiducia: Ideologie, Etiche di Potere, Legittimità.* Catanzaro, Italy: Rubbettino.

Parry, J. 1989. On the moral perils of exchange. In *Money and the morality of exchange*, edited by J. Parry and M. Bloch. Cambridge: Cambridge University Press.

Parry, J., and M. Bloch, eds. 1989. *Money and the morality of exchange.* Cambridge: Cambridge University Press.

Pinnarò, G., and E. Pugliese. 1985. Informalization and social resistance: The case of Naples. In *Beyond employment: Household, gender, and subsistence*, edited by N. Redclift and E. Mingione. Oxford: Blackwell.

Pizzorno, A. 1967. Familismo amorale e marginalità storica, ovvero perché non c'è niente da fare a Montegrano. *Quaderni di Sociologia* 27(3): 247–261.

Putnam, D. R. 1993. *Making democracy work: Civic traditions in modern Italy.* Princeton: Princeton University Press.

Smith, M. E. 1989. Informal economy. In *Economic anthropology*, edited by S. Plattner. Stanford: Stanford University Press.

Stefanelli, R. 1996. *Usura e banca. Un suicidio del mercato.* Rome: Liocorno.

Wallman, S. 1984. *Eight London households*. London: Tavistock.

Wilk, R. R. 1996. *Economies and cultures*. Oxford: Westview.

# PART III

# Continuity or Discontinuity with the Past?

# 7

# Productivity and the Person

*From Socialist Competition to*
*Capitalist Mission in Eastern Europe*

BIRGIT MÜLLER

The unpredictability and inertia of central planning made socialist enterprises heavily dependent on informal problem solving and on the skills of improvisation of its workforce. Workers spent long hours in the enterprises to make up for the irregularities of central planing. They also enjoyed spaces of liberty at the workplace, granted to them in exchange for their goodwill to make up for the shortcomings of centralized planning. It was therefore close to reality when workers were celebrated in official discourses as the pillars of the socialist state. The dark side of this ideological stylization, however, was that workers had to take part in the ideological and political celebration of the "workers state." They had to sacrifice part of their leisure and working time for political meetings and demonstrations, brigade diaries, and wall newspapers. The end of socialism was welcome by most of them as a liberation from chaotic work rhythms, scarcities, and ideological indoctrination. With the advent of market economy the shortcomings of socialist planning would be overcome and the potentials of their enterprises appreciated in the right measure, or so they thought. Their positive self-perception and optimism, however, was shaken when the factory regimes changed after 1989. When the multinational elevator company HOCHINAUF[1] acquired three enterprises in East Berlin, South Moravia, and Moscow, large portions of the workforce were made redundant. The multinational proceeded to transform the factories into low-cost enterprises, to change the organization of work, and to propose its corporate enterprise philosophy as an identificatory frame. The remaining workers

were expected to make the objectives of the firm their own. They were
confronted with production politics intending to extract a maximum
productivity from them at minimum cost.

*To increase productivity* was the catchphrase in this process. In the
planned economy "labor productivity" had been considered an objective
category, scientifically determined, with a strong moral base.[2] The increase of productivity was presented as a political act, as the contribution
of the workers to the well-being of socialist society, made possible by an
improvement in technology (Honecker 1984, 68). The requirements of
the multinational company went against this idea of productivity, that
most members of the personnel had shared under socialism. The workers ceased to be political or social persons. What counted now was the
financial contribution their work made to the enterprise.

With the takeover of their firms by the multinational enterprise,
workers exchanged a system of political paternalism against a system
of domination that required the internalization of the capitalist work
discipline and the subjection of the individual worker to the aims and
objectives of the multinational. From a system of protective domination they were thrown into a system of domination that exposed them
to an uncertain future. They experienced the transition from one factory regime to the other as a drastic loss in status and reacted with categories from their socialist past to the new management practices
and ideology.

The three socialist enterprises of my research—the elevator factory LiftVEB in East Berlin, the elevator factory TRANSA in Moravia,
and the spare-parts factory Vijshe in Moscow[3]—were variations of the
uniform model of communist organization of production.[4] Czechoslovakia and East Germany had already been industrialized countries
when they entered the planned economy at the end of the 1940s.
In the 1980s, the enterprises in East Germany and Czechoslovakia
were still operating in unreconstructed planned economies with a
strong commitment to central planning. Until 1989, they were under
the regime of the most rigid central planning mediated through the
strong intermediary level of *kombinate*.[5] The Soviet Union, on the contrary, industrialized itself under a socialist regime and had lost after
seventy years of real-existing socialism a large portion of its initial
ideological principles and effective centralized control. When the
Muscovite spare-parts factory was taken over by the multinational combine, it had already gone through the transformations linked to perestroika (Gorbachov 1987, 112), introducing performance incentives at
the level of production and a certain devolution of economic control
to the enterprise.

## Growth and Productivity

The two competing economic systems of the twentieth century were based on the assumption that they would be able to free humanity from oppression and need through perpetual technical progress and growth of material production. However, both systems have failed many of the expectations set in them. Plan and market economies have been equally foreign to the workers who produced the material wealth both societies rested on (Méda 1995, 161). However, the reasons for this failure differ decisively between socialism and capitalism. They are linked closely to the objectives both systems pursued at the place of work: In the socialist system the objective of producing the goods society needed was complemented and sometimes contradicted by the equally strong objective to root political power firmly at the point of production. Work was sanctified as the communion between the individual and the higher social good. According to the political ideology of socialism, the worker was to find his individual fulfillment in the collective organization of work and in the contribution he made toward the satisfaction of social needs. However, the assessment of what these needs really were lay outside the realm of influence of workers and consumers alike. Party authorities claimed that they were better able to assess and fill these needs. In keeping with socialist egalitarianism they had a very unadorned definition of the basic needs they claimed to satisfy: "As long as the food offered was edible or the clothes available covered you and kept you warm, that should be sufficient" (Verdery 1996, 28). The regime thus prevented people from consuming by not making goods available and claimed at the same time that the standard of living under socialism would constantly improve. This translated itself on the level of the factory by the moral claim laid on the workers to produce more goods in a shorter time and thus to contribute toward improving the well-being of all the members of society. In reverse, if they failed consistently to come to work, they placed themselves outside socialist society and became potentially "enemies of the people" who had to be reeducated through work under close surveillance.

In the capitalist system, maximum performance was required; political convictions were secondary. According to the rational of capitalism, individual gain is the primary mover. Human labor organized in a rational way is a "magic force" (Méda 1995, 62) capable of creating an increasing amount of wealth. A person hired to work for a salary has to achieve a level of productivity that allows the entrepreneur to accumulate individual profits. If he of she fails to fulfill expectations and works less, he or she breaks the contract he or she concluded as he or she sold his labor power. To detach work as a creative human activity from its subject

(Méda 1995, 72) is the means employed to fulfill the goal of creating wealth and of transforming nature to serve man. The enrichment of the successful entrepreneurs would—per the optimistic assumption—ultimately trickle down to all the members of society, including the most disfavored.

Inherent in the capitalist and socialist concept of productivity is the idea that a constant growth of production has to be elicited from the working individuals. All through the history of early industrialism the major problem entrepreneurs were facing was to make the workers they were employing work more than they actually wanted to or thought necessary. E. P. Thompson (1967) in his vivid account of factory work in the nineteenth century describes how workers would leave the factory after a few weeks of work to spend the money they had earned and only come back to work once they needed more. Inciting the workers to expend a continuous regular work effort was the big challenge of early industrial work organization. One of the devices used to achieve it was to reduce the salary to the absolute minimum of subsistence, which would oblige the worker to return to his or her place of work.

A task-oriented notation of time was prevalent in the preindustrial era (Thompson 1967, 60). Social intercourse and labor intermingled—the working day lenghtened or contracted according to the task. The introduction of industrial wage labor allowed the employer to determine how the labor time purchased was to be spent and to increasingly exclude from work time all social activities. Thompson (1967) quotes a factory owner at the beginning of the industrial era setting the rules for workers at the Crowley Iron Works: "This service must be calculated 'after all deductions for being in taverns, alehouses, coffee houses, breakfast, dinner, playing, sleeping, smoking, singing, reading of news history, quarreling, contention, disputes or anything foreign to my business, any way loitering'" (81).

As the workers refused to produce more in a shorter time without being paid more in proportion, it was primarily through planning, control, and timing that this resistance was to be broken. At the beginning of the twentieth century, the Taylorist enterprise became the prototype for a modernist organization of production. It reduced the complexity of workplace relations to its most simple expression: "to the absolute necessity for adequate management to dictate to the worker the precise manner in which work is to be performed" (cited in Braverman 1974, 90). Working time should be scientifically determined, the work process simplified, and the enterprise clearly hierarchically structured.

The skilled worker of Frederick W. Taylor's days performed a large variety of tasks and possessed the actual intellectual and practical knowledge necessary for production, which the manager did not. The radical alterations proposed by Taylor to gain control over the labor power were directed toward deskilling the worker. His first principle was to render the labor process independent of craft, tradition, and the workers' knowledge. The second was to remove all possible mental labor from the shop and center it in the planning or layout department. The third was to use this monopoly over knowledge to control each step of the labor process and its mode of executions (Braverman 1974, 113–119). Taylor's ideas of scientific management became attractive to both capitalism and socialism. They prevailed in the formal work organization of socialist enterprises until the end of the 1980s.

However, workers in both the East and the West jeopardized the efforts to get them under strict physical control, wherever they could: executing orders to the letter, going on sick leave, or producing low-quality products. The "human factor" systematically reduced the chances of increasing productivity in socialist and capitalist factories. Motivating the workforce, not only measuring their performance, became a science in both the East and the West. To convince the employees to work continuously, diligently, and at high speed, the ideologues of socialism and capitalism used the core concepts of their respective ideological systems. The socialist worker should work hard in order to defend the socialist system that was the achievement of the working class and, therefore, in its interest to maintain. The worker in market economy by fully developing his work capacities was supposed to realize himself or herself as an individual and become a winner in the competition for success and achievement.

"Work" was a central category in real-existing socialism that defined the worth of a person as a "worker" for society. Because man took part in the appropriation and transformation of nature, he became truly man as separate and superior to nature. Because man produced the goods needed by others, he became a true social being. The declared aim of economic activity was not the accumulation of profit but the fulfillment of needs. The communist regime idolized the centrally planned satisfaction of necessary or "rational" needs instead of considering individual or even collective consumer preferences. This voluntary ideological choice had the far-reaching consequence that it became the main goal to outline, standardize, and then meet what was centrally defined as necessary or rational needs (Vecernik 1997, 120). This was to be done through the central planning of all economic activities—production and consumption—by the state.

Since profit was not at issue, the whole point was precisely not to sell things. The center wanted to keep as much as possible under its control, because that was how it had redistributive power; and it wanted to give away the rest, because that was how it confirmed its legitimacy with the public" (Verdery 1996, 26) The distribution of goods and their consumption were loaded with political and moral principles that the Communist Party set as a guideline for the socialist consumer. The role of its ideologues, planners, and administrators was to distinguish between basic and dispensable needs (luxury): the first was to be supported, the second restrained (Vecernik 1997, 121).

Instead of fulfilling the needs of consumers and producers, central planning led to an economy of scarcity. As the priority of needs was established neither by those who produced the goods nor by those who consumed them, the planned production was detached from the actual demands in society. Political factors determined whether a production received priority by the central planning authorities. Enterprises with a high political importance, such as firms producing arms or electronic components, had relatively easy access to raw materials and spare parts, whereas consumer industries had to struggle with inadequate materials and faulty machinery. A mechanism of feedback between producers and consumers mediated through the state did not function, nor was it even seriously pursued.

Michal Mejstrik and Jiri Hlavacek (1993), wondering why the management of the centrally planned economy did not improve with the advent of computers, attribute it to "an aversion to objective information at the centre" (58). Decision makers at the center maximized their power when they made decisions based on arbitrary criteria, as producers and consumers had to compete for their favors. Verdery (1996, 26) attributes the preference given by the socialist state to heavy industry at the expense of consumer industry to the fact that the regime wanted to amass control over means of production. Central power was less served by giving things away than by producing things it could continue to control. However, these explanations in terms of the accumulation of power by the center do not give the full picture. The priority given to the production of means of production was primarily an attempt by the central planing agency to remedy the shortages in modern production machinery and to improve productivity of the national economy. The resources devoted to building up a strong heavy industry were withheld by the state from the enterprises producing consumer goods. Thus, the socialist consumer had to defer the immediate satisfaction of his or her needs. However, this sacrifice was, in reality, useless as the machines produced were distributed in such a way that they hardly ever reached the enterprise that needed them most. Enterprises became used to accumulating whatever machinery they could get their hands on, regardless of whether it served their purposes.

In official discourse the responsibility for this main contradiction of real-existing socialism was shifted from the level of central planning to the level of the enterprise. Shortages were to be remedied by the socialist workforce that was to increase productivity and support the choices of the center politically. The fulfillment of the plan was stipulated as a political act: to work well and to be a good socialist was in ideological terms the same thing. On the one hand, a work brigade that came close to fulfilling the monthly or yearly plan was eligible for the honorary title "collective of socialist labor." On the other hand, the reverse held true: showing strong socialist convictions could make up for the fact of not working well. In many socialist enterprises this had the unwelcome effect that lazy workers joined the Communist Party and that some of the best ones were most critical of official politics. The Communist Party, in order to stay in power, needed the political support of workers in whose name they claimed to rule and they had to convince the workforce to produce the goods on the distribution of which their legitimacy relied.

Many workers loathed the rituals of socialist factory life and tried to withhold their personal engagement without openly offending the political authorities. In a perverse twist of logic, however, the fact that their political statements were required and carefully monitored showed them that it was important what they thought and what they did even outside the workplace. It was, relatively speaking, almost as important as what they produced in the workplace. The political ideology of the socialist system confirmed the workers in their identity as indispensable and responsible for socialist society. Indeed, the management of the socialist firm depended on the collaboration of the workers in order to overcome the shortcomings of central planning: the irregular arrivals of materials and spare parts, which caused a monthly work rhythm in which periods of "storming" alternated with stretches of time when nothing could be done. As their voluntary cooperation was required in the moments of high production pressure, workers were able at other moments to carve out spaces of liberty and even controversy at the workplace.

When the multinational combine HOCHINAUF started to expand business into eastern Europe, it bought already-existing service centers and factories and restructured them. LiftVEB in East Berlin was bought in 1991, TRANSA in Moravia in 1993, and Vijshe in Moscow in 1992. The multinational company intended to profit from established service contracts, cheap and experienced labor, and a functioning infrastructure and to introduce manufacturing in flexible production cells. Its success worldwide was based on the flexible production of large series of elevators that can be adapted to a large variety of customers' specifications. In the previous twenty years, it had developed a network of production sites in 38 countries and maintained service centers in 220 countries. Growth, technological innovation, customer service, high product quality, productivity, and the recruitment of the most qualified personnel were part of the "strategic plan" that HOCHINAUF presented as its "vision for the future."

The expansion of the enterprise toward eastern Europe was supported by the conviction that came to the forefront in many conversations with managers: HOCHINAUF had to accomplish not only economic and commercial goals but a civilizing and cultural mission. Against what they saw as the irrationalities and the arbitrariness of the planned economy, the managers offered an image of economic man based on economic rationality, optimism, and individualism. As capitalism had come out the winner from the "competition between the economic systems," they now wanted "to help the losers" to make the big leap into market economy and to create the cultural, legal, and social frames for it.

To give all members of the enterprise the same chances was one of the principles of the enterprise philosophy. The business interests of HOCHINAUF, measured in balances and share prices, were the objective criteria with which to measure the contribution of the employees. HOCHINAUF understood itself as the precursor of the global civilization of the future based on economic rationality without prejudice. The discourse of pure economic rationality was complemented, however, by a contradictory discourse that appealed to feelings and that used noneconomic arguments. Managers spoke about the multinational combine often as "the HOCHINAUF family." The term alluded to emotional relationships of solidarity and the experience of community and reciprocal obligation. Workers and employees were to integrate into the HOCHINAUF family and internalize its objectives and constraints. As the pursuit of individual success at the expense of all the others was corrosive for the enterprise as a social organization, the enterprise philosophy thus created an imaginary space where other value had prevalence. It was paradoxically the word *family* with its affective connotations that evoked social relations without calculation, radically opposed to the principle of competition without limit that otherwise was omnipresent in the multinational. The public relations manager used the imagery of social harmony and pushed off the responsibility for social and moral disintegration inside the enterprise to the forces of the market. His argument was, "Those who cannot stand up to the market competition have to be excluded, so that they won't endanger and weaken the family all together."

## Time and Self in the Planned Economy

Expanding into eastern Europe, the multinational enterprise was confronted with the complex heritage of the planned economy and with workers who used to think about themselves as being tied to their enterprise by multiple links and motivations—political, social, and material—and of being indispensable for the running of the enterprise. The workers in East Berlin operating fragile old machines knew that no one else would know how to handle them and wanted to hold on to them. The material manager in Moscow with a wide network of providers with whom he had complex personal contacts was not ready to share those with any of his colleagues, as they constituted the basis for his influence in the firm. The managers of the Moravian factory left a heritage of hundreds of elevator cars, which they had continued to produce for months in 1990 and 1991 after the total breakdown of demand.

Among the three enterprises of my research, the workers in the LiftVEB, the biggest producer of elevators in the German Democratic Republic (GDR), had been under the closest ideological supervision. In socialist Germany, the work brigades in the enterprise competed in what was called "Socialist Competition." At the beginning of the year, they engaged themselves in a detailed written declaration of intent to "live, learn and work in a socialist" way:[5] they promised that they would recruit new members to the Communist Party group of the enterprise, that colleagues would attend the schools of Marxism–Leninism, that they would start work punctually in the morning, and so forth. The Socialist Competition thus was not only about evaluating the speed and skills with which brigades accomplished their tasks but also about their political activities, the social relations in the brigade, and their willingness to reproduce the teachings of the great socialist thinkers. The workers were expected to discuss official political topics without giving expression to the slightest deviation from the prescribed official interpretation. Discontent and disagreement should not come into the open, even if informal discussions at the workplace often took the form of critical anecdotes and political jokes. The nonproductive activities could take up a lot of the working time: brigade diaries had to be kept and all the social and political activities had to be diligently recorded, the wall newspapers had to be changed every month, and the decisions of the Central Committee were to be commented on approvingly. Workers were given time off to go to political meetings, to maneuvers of the enterprise militia, or to centrally organized demonstrations. Brigades that took part in the Socialist Competition more or less diligently could expect a yearly payment in bonuses of about 7 percent to 10 percent of their yearly salary.

It was impressive that the foremen who were not party members and who had a difficult position in the enterprise tried to organize the Socialist Competition of their brigade as perfectly as possible. The foreman of the machine section of the LiftVEB, for instance, the son of a "bourgeois" owner of a private bakery, had refused to join the party. To make up for that he put up an overdimensioned billboard of two meters long by two meters high next to the entrance of his workshop which he conscientiously decorated with red velvet, flags, and emblems and with the right political texts.

For the workers and employees, the political aspect of their work relations was ambiguous. On the one hand, most of them resented the Socialist Competition as an unwanted constraint, as a treatement of workers as children. They loathed the fact that their brigade diary was evaluated at the end of the year by the party secretary and the director to determine what place they deserved in the Socialist Competition. On the other hand, the Socialist Competition celebrated workers as the dominant political force in society.

As layoffs were near to impossible and other disciplinary measures counterproductive because workers would refuse to cooperate when it became necessary to obviate the shortcomings of central planning, the management of the LiftVEB resorted to carefully planning and monitoring each step of the manufacturing process. The workers received detailed construction drawings in which each welding line and each drilling were explained. This Taylorist organization of work with an elaborate hierarchy of responsibilities had, however, the adverse consequence that the workers refused to be accountable for the quality of the product outside the strictly determined parameters given to them. As one of the technicians pointed out, when controlling the quality of the finished products, he felt like one of the pigeons in the Grimms' fairy tale *Cinderella* that were sorting out lentils—putting the good ones in the pot and the bad ones down their throat (*Die Guten ins Töpfchen, die Schlechten ins Kröpfchen*). It was up to him to find the mistakes, not up to the workers to avoid them, as they could refer to the old machines, the lack of appropriate materials, and the late arrival of spare parts that made the perfect accomplishment of their tasks impossible.

The employees were well aware of the strength of their position and made use of it to negotiate with their superiors a rhythm at work that suited them. Work in these enterprises was characterized, therefore, by a subtle mixture of refusal and cooperation. It was this mixture that Ulrich Voskamp and Volker Wittke (1991) referred to as "the pact to accomplish the plan" (31). The consensual nature of the pact for the accomplishment of the plan made it difficult to impose complete discipline in GDR enterprises, although foremen have always assured me that they managed to maintain discipline in their workshops. The foreman of the machine section of the LiftVEB trained himself to become able to distinguish by the noise in the workshop which machines were running empty or at low speed. He monitored his workers with the help of a panopticum that resembled the one described by Michel Foucault (1975, 228). He had scratched a little hole in the white paint covering the windows of his foreman cabin so that he had an overview over the shop floor without being observed by his workers. He was thus able to intervene as soon as production slowed down. However, as a reaction, his workers practiced absenteeism. The section had the highest number of sick leave days of the enterprise.

Such a method of surveillance is reminiscent of a primitive model of a "disciplinary society" (Foucault 1986, 241) in which discipline has not yet become normal and interiorized: it still has to be continuously imposed by those in power. The workers, for their part, stressed that they did not have to show much respect for their foreman. The foreman could delegate disagreeable tasks or reduce the end-of-year bonus. In extreme cases he could write an unfavorable report when a worker wanted to travel to visit family in the West, but all in all, he could do little to force increased effort, as workers could not be laid off.

The organization of production in the planned economy provoked two typical reactions among the workers that were not incompatible. It encouraged workers to test the limits of their freedom, and work as little as possible, but at the same time they were encouraged to work on their own initiative, to find informal solutions to the shortcomings of socialist planning, and to be proud of their creativity. Production in the enterprise TRANSA, the biggest producer of elevators in Czechoslovakia, showed similar mechanisms as in East Germany. The enterprise was interested in a soft, therefore easy to fulfill, plan, that allowed it to establish a reserve from the difference between the real output required in the plan and the maximum output that would be attainable with a given input (Mejstrik and Hlavacek 1993, 56). This strategy was in the interest of all the members of the enterprise from the director to the worker, as it liberated the factory from some of its dependencies on central planning. Workers, employees, and their respective family members endorsed this strategy to such an extent that they volunteered to build a big storage hall in the center of the factory grounds in their spare time, called "the cathedral," for spare parts and material in reserve and finished elevators produced in advance of the plan requirements.

The organization of production based on brigades was, in the Czechoslovak enterprise, less systematic and less politically explicit than in the East German one. The brigade diaries looked like family albums in which the marriages and births of children among the members of the brigade were diligently recorded together with pages recalling the year-days of socialism—for example, May 1, March 8—and the achievements of the brigade in improving production. For the members of the enterprise who had a negative political record, joining a brigade and taking over responsibilities was a means of improving their relationships with the regime. The current head of the elevator mounting section, for instance, had openly protested again the Soviet invasion of Czechoslovakia and had taken part in the funeral of Jan Palach in 1969.[6] As a punishment for his act of dissidence, he lost his coordinating position in the enterprise and worked for years in an office job where he was isolated and deliberately cut off from the cooperation with other people. Joining a brigade at the end of the 1970s was a means for him to normalize his relationship with the regime so as not to compromise the future of his children and their chances to get permission to study at the University.

The control the socialist factory regime could exercise over the workers was far from complete with regard to the work effort that could be extracted from them, but it encroached on other more intimate aspects of their person: their ways to voice political convictions, to interrelate with colleagues, and to share aspects of their private lives with them. The regime by paying a salary to the workers was not only making inroads in their time by producing goods for the state but increasing their subservience to it (Verdery 1996, 45). By complying with the rituals of socialist competition at work, the workers contributed—willingly or not—to its ideological reproduction. Through the Socialist Competition, the regime attempted to extend its grip on social spaces otherwise jealously guarded from state control: the leisure activities, family relations, and ties of friendships at work. Attempting to control everything that moved and changed in socialist society, the regime seemed to have effectively slowed down time and immobilized the social order until the big upheavals took place at the end of the 1980s.

In the Soviet Union of the Gorbachov period between 1985 and 1991, production had lost much of its ideological justification. In the enterprise Vijshe, which was producing spare parts for elevators for the big central elevator maintenance company in Moscow, the Socialist Competition continued in the 1980s to regulate the distribution of bonuses for plan completion, innovations, work discipline, quality improvement, and cost reduction attributed to work groups and individuals, but political and social work was no longer required. Party membership, however, remained an important tool for gaining influence in the enterprise and for improving one's position.[7] The relationship between management and workers was more antagonistic in the enterprises in Russia and Romania than in the GDR and also in Czechoslovakia (Verdery 1996, 23). This might have been partly due to the fact that official planning and control mechanisms had been thoroughly undermined by bureaucrats and factory owners acting in the second, or black, economy. Workers experienced the relationship to the powerful enterprise nomenclatura as one of domination, as an antagonism between us and them.

In the years of Gorbachov's reforms, emphasis was put on the increase of production through the restructuring of work and power relations in the enterprise. As the former party secretary, a strong skillful worker in the machine section, pointed out, workers were encouraged in the 1980s to form work brigades and to take an active role in the running of the enterprise. The "glass roof" that had limited the wages that could be earned at a maximum was removed and workers were encouraged to produce more and earn more in proportion, however, not individually but collectively as a brigade. In the accounting of the firm a proportion of the value of each item produced was set aside for a wage fund. The brigade as a whole received money from this fund according to its performance and redistributed it among the members of the brigade according to the pieces produced by each worker and according to the income category he or she was in. A work group working twice as much in one day would earn twice the amount of its daily salary. The party secretary saw himself as a model for his coworkers. He put his pride into a Stakhanovistic tour de force operating six antiquated lathes simultaneously.[8] This had the consequence that the workers themselves became interested in eliminating the less-performing and undisciplined workers from the brigade.

Gorbachov's perestroika thus reversed the Soviet time definition. His rhetoric from the 1980s is full of words and phrases about time: the Soviet Union needs to "catch up," to "accelerate" its development, to shed its "sluggishness" and "inertia," and leave behind the "era of stagnation" (Verdery 1996, 36). Workers were effectively producing more in a shorter time. However, the idea of systematically increasing the surplus value to be extracted from the workforce had not yet taken hold in the enterprise. The socialist directors under perestroika did not invariably seek to maximize the profit margins of the state-owned enterprises by increasing the difference between the value created by the labor of the workers and the salary paid to remunerate their labor power. Not infrequently, though, they were successful in extracting money from the enterprise for their own private purposes.

# Profit and Personhood in the Multinational Company

A lot has been written about the low productivity in the enterprises of the planned economy by economists, business advisers, and politicians. The productivity of the workforce was a major concern for investors expanding their business into the former socialist countries. Leaving aside personal relations, passions, and political convictions, workers in the East European factories were reassessed in terms of how much they were able to produce in a given time. The concept of productivity lost in the process of transformation the moral dimension of increasing production in order to fulfill the "rational" needs in society. Instead, capitalism claimed neutrality with respect to the appetites of individual consumers and focused on the increase of profit that an increase of production and consumption might generate.

The managers of the multinational enterprise waged a struggle, in all three enterprises, to extract from the workforce maximum productivity without surrendering to its financial demands. Simultaneously, they conjured an irrational world of feelings, visions, and utopias. As it was not sufficient to control the workers through the imposition of bodily discipline that Foucault (1986) referred to as "a type of power which is constantly exercised by means of surveillance" (239), they wanted to train members of their staff to actively strive toward the proposed model of the winner. While obedience to the objectives of the firm was the norm, it should be embraced by animating the individual competitive spirit. The staff members should equate their measure of personal success with the contributions they made to the success of the enterprise. Their identity was to be merged with that of the firm. The member of the enterprise was, as such, no longer a person but an aggregate of parts of a person, that had his or her thinking reduced to the specific aims of the enterprise (Bateson 1996, 574). It was a supreme form of the normalization of discipline that was required—the active self-disciplination. Foucault (1987, 246) describes this mechanism of power as transforming individuals into subjects. The subject is subdued through control and dependency and at the same time he is tied to his identity through conscience and a specific interpretation of the self. This does not mean, however, that the impact of this mechanism of power is complete. It encounters opposition and is met with struggles for the status of the individual, for his identity, against the privileges of knowledge and the concrete tangible consequences of power (Bateson 1996, 574; Foucault 1987, 246).

As the glossy brochure distributed worldwide to all HOCHINAUF firms states, "[W]ell informed staff members who are encouraged to use their energy and initiative" should work together in "real teams" and should attempt to realize the HOCHINAUF visions for the future as if they were "independent entrepreneurs" ready to confront the competitors. The HOCHINAUF model not only set the aims for economic practices and management choices in the company, it is also expressed and specified, in a code of conduct, standards for the attitudes and behavior of the staff members.

To think and act in a positive, optimistic way was the norm that the enterprise set for its staff: the mental and psychological self-discipline required. A West German manager of the firm commented on these expectations:

> When you are sitting together in the circle of department chiefs and you say "We need productivity. We have to improve. You on the shop floor you have to contribute to it, now!" And then, if you get five or ten times the answer "But what is going to happen if we cannot do it?" and if you answer ten times "Then we close the shop" and if they don't understand this, then I don't know how often you want to tell them that. I always maintain that for me this is not an acceptable statement if someone says "This does not work! I cannot do that!" I don't accept that. I only accept, if somebody says "OK. The aim is clear. I will think about, how to get there." Then it is legitimate that he makes his claims.

The aims are given. The autonomy of the enterprise members does not consist in the fact of questioning them, but to think about the way how to achieve them. Also, the possibility of not reaching the aims should not even be considered. If they hesitate and have doubts as to the possibility of success, "then," as the Western manager commented, "something is wrong in their heads!" "People have to believe in success," was his philosophy and he was ready to "preach, preach, and preach" it all over again "this is the way and now do it! If you don't want, then its over!"

The goal-oriented conscience the members of the enterprise should develop does not allow for probing nor for thinking in larger contexts or systems. Bateson (1996, 559) would call it an unsystemic thinking, greedy and unwise. By excluding all other considerations from the strive for economic success, the ideologues of the enterprise even pretend to have found a category with which to evaluate objectively the members of the enterprise according to their merit. All other factors, such as gender, belief, ethnicity, and political convictions, should be irrelevant when the contribution members made to the enterprise is to be evaluated. Western managers called this part of the democratic mission of their enterprise in formerly totalitarian societies. The cultural model of the enterprise was on the one side a legitimizing ideology and on the other side a code of conduct. The legitimizing ideology explained why the enterprise in order to be competitive and to survive on the world market had to be tough and demanding toward the people inside. The HOCHINAUF family had to eliminate the nonperforming members because of the pressure of outside market forces. The code of discipline was geared toward social and economic practice. The modern enterprise requiring flexible and responsible members calls on them to discipline themselves. It was not so important what people thought and what their political convictions were, it was important how they behaved. The "winner" may doubt the rationality of market economy as long as he or she behaves like the winner. The cultural model sets a frame of parameters that cannot be ignored but to which the enterprise members resist or adapt.

The HOCHINAUF model provides a complete worldview, ready to fill the gap that the ideological model of real-existing socialism has left. In a moment of individual disorientation and social and economic upheaval, the ideological model of the enterprise pretends to give a "home" to the "homeless mind" (Marcus 1992, 313). It is the model of the self-made man transposed on the level of the firm that is giving the direction, advocating an unlimited belief in the strength of the individual will. As a Western manager strongly claimed: to have this belief was not a possibility, it was the only correct state of mind accepted in the firm.

Of course, this model was also conceived against what the Western managers saw as the rationale of the planned economy. The negative counterimage of the "looser" sketched out certain strategic attitudes that could have been rational for a manager in the planned economy in order to protect his position and his firm. For example, on receiving the plan's targets at the beginning of the year, it was useful for the manager in the planned economy to stress how unrealistic, problematic, and infeasible they were because this would prepare the field for asking for a plan correction later in the year. In the Socialist Competition, each brigade declared that it had made its ultimate efforts to fulfill the plan and pointed to the shortcomings of the other sections that hindered their achievements. Faced with a shortage of material and workers and the bad quality of the production machines, supplementary efforts were presented as improvised and a token of goodwill, and that quality cannot be perfect. In the face of all these difficulties, all the sections of the enterprise agreed that success would be relative and even unlikely.

The particular logic of the planned economy and the ways of acquiring influence and holding on to it were seen by the multinational company as a sign of irrationality, as an inextricable chaos that they had to clear. The functioning of the Muscovite enterprise was so nontransparent that HOCHINAUF sent in an experienced adviser to observe the running of the enterprise before proceeding to restructure it. In the Moravian firm, key positions in management were staffed with two people, an experienced Western manager and his Czech "twin" who was to learn from him how to run a capitalist firm and take over from him after two or three years. In East Berlin, the key positions in marketing, personnel management, and investment were attributed to West German managers. The first objective of the restructuration was to get a clear idea of the value of the firm in monetary terms. The Western managers discovered that the ways of accounting of the planned economy had little in common with a calculation of profit and loss or with the productivity of the enterprise.

The market economy brought for them the new experience of existential insecurity. Employees in East Germany, and increasingly also in the Czech Republic and Russia, had the feeling that they lost control of their material living conditions. Many of the people I spoke with in East Germany went so far as to use the term *death* to portray the economic collapse of the enterprise. To express the fear that one of their colleagues might be made redundant, they would say "He probably won't survive." On the one hand, workers felt exposed to the "world economy" or to "market trends" that lay beyond their control. Their superiors supported such fatalistic concepts. They referred to the world economy as if it were a metaphysical force and appealed for a joint effort to save the enterprise.

The task of the Western accountants was to reduce the complex criteria of socialist evaluation to a single one: profitability. All other criteria of evaluating the enterprise and its members were to disappear, such as political convictions, links of friendship, and animosities. The American mother firm organized the business politics of its European dependencies mainly through financial aspects. The productivity targets set for the HOCHINAUF factories in eastern Europe were, in the beginning, simply deduced from price provisions. However, the workers were not expected to answer the undisguised strive for profit of the capital holders with proportionate requests for a maximum reward for their labor.

In Moscow in 1993, the claim to increase productivity and maintain the level of salaries was met by the workers and the Muscovite management with utter incomprehension, despite the efforts of the German adviser to rephrase the enterprise philosophy. Thus, the manager responsible for work and wages was at the same time the representative of the trade union section in the enterprise. To link the two tasks seemed to her self-evident as she claimed to establish objective work norms according to scientific criteria. Trusting in her professional experience, she

fixed the norms on the basis of norm lists and technical drawings that
had not changed over the past fifteen years.

When salaries were doubled in September 1993 to adjust to infla-
tion, the planning department also doubled the prices. The German adviser who had been present only for a few weeks attempted to argue
against this automatic doubling of prices: "A lot of them here have not
yet understood that we will have competition one day. We can't just double the prices from one day to the next. . . . I also have to do something
about productivity. I give my people twice the salary or maybe even more
but I also expect that they produce in five hours what they had previously
done in ten. Only then I get something back from what I have spent."

The German adviser met with a "completely different way of thinking" among his Russian counterparts who did not aim at extracting a
maximum productivity for a minimal salary (Müller 1994). Persisting in
the rationality of perestroika, they measured productivity in rubles, rewarding an increase in output with an equivalent portion from the wage
fund. The adviser attempted to explain that the time needed for the
manufacturing of a product had to be reassessed and considerably reduced. Only the fastest and the best one survived in a competitive market economy and time norms thus had to be gradually tightened. The
task of fixing new work norms was transferred from the department of
work and wages to the technical department. The link between an increase in productivity and an equivalent increase in pay was broken up
and the way was opened up for the antagonistic relationship between
capital holders and workers prevalent in capitalism. More menacing still
for the workers in the Muscovite factory was the intention of the Western
management to transform the spare-parts factory into a service center
that would be buying the spare parts needed from other factories and
then reselling them to its clients. The plan had not been carried out,
though, as the suppliers proved unreliable.

In the East Berlin factory, which HOCHINAUF had bought in the
summer of 1991, workers insisted that time studies, made as the norms
according to which their productivity was judged, were deduced exclusively from the prices negotiated by the marketing department in West
Berlin. Between 1991 and 1993, five hundred of the one thousand members of the staff were laid off. The manufacturing department, restructured from the production of large series of lifts for socialist housing to
small batch production of specialized lifts, was struggling with the new
technical requirements and was unable to meet the time provisions. Although this did not cause the workers any material disadvantage, as they
were paid by the hour, it gave them the impression that time provisions
were a chicanery of the Western managers whom they suspected of want-

ing to show the East Germans how incapable and lazy they were. The Western managers who were employed to restructure the enterprise had the suspicion that the employed voluntarily held back their performance because they were not paid what they thought they deserved. According to the collective wage agreement prevalent for East Germany in the first years after the fall of the Berlin Wall, the salary of an East German worker or employee amounted to only 60 percent of the Western salary in 1991. It was only to be gradually adjusted until breaking even in 1996.

The result was a growing insecurity and frustration on both sides. The Western management was calling on the workers to work harder while the workers complained about the level of performance that was asked from them. They complained that although they now had to produce single items and fulfill a far wider range of tasks than before, they had less support from the production management and the design office. In the HOCHINAUF factories, skilled workers were expected to organize their production in a rather autonomous fashion but under a constant time pressure from management. Flexible work groups were paid by the hour and were responsible for the quality they were producing. The production instructions were less detailed and precise. The technical drawings the welders of the elevator frames, for instance, had been working with before the restructuring of production had indicated the welding and the mounting sequences and had even specified certain setups. These were not included in the drawings they received now from the design office in West Berlin. The lack of specification also meant that the responsibility for the work done lay more heavily on the shoulders of the workers as they could not blame the instructions given by a technician or an engineer. The abolition of formal time norms and the introduction of an hourly wage also had increased rather than reduced the pressure the workers were under.

In 1993, the mother company executed what some managers jokingly called the "German unification" on a small scale. HOCHINAUF united the enterprise it had bought in East Berlin with the production and service company it already owned in West Berlin. The production of luxury elevators mostly in glass and chrome was transferred together with its workforce and engineering from West to East Berlin and it was fused with the elevator production there. This fusion was intended by management to speed up the process of assimilation of the East Berlin workforce to the model of the multinational combine. The reorganization—it was hoped—should make the production more efficient and competitive in the face of growing competition from cheaper production units in eastern Europe that were part of the combine.[9] The decision to fuse production rapidly leveled the productivity of the mounting section.

The East Berlin workers entered into fierce competition with their West Berlin colleagues to show them and management that they were equally productive and that the difference in pay was therefore unjustified. The strategy of management was, to a large extent, effective in dividing the workforce into East and West Germans, into discriminated and privileged ones, and to increase overall productivity. When the salaries of East and West German workers finally reached the same level on July 1, 1996, the management of HOCHINAUF decided that production in Germany had become too expensive and should be moved to cheaper production facilities in eastern Europe. Without meeting any significant resistance from the disunited workforce, the factory in East Berlin was closed down and part of the production was moved to Moravia.

The HOCHINAUF factory in Moravia was, along with its director, the bogey for all the other HOCHINAUF factories in Europe. Production there had been restructured and the workforce reduced from thirty-five hundred to seven hundred between 1991 and 1996. As salaries were low and workers qualified, the threat to transfer production from other facilities to Moravia was taken seriously by other HOCHINAUF firms—"the internal competitors in the combine." At the initiative of the Czech management, the enterprise had even developed a cheap version of the standard HOCHINAUF lift that was competing with the standard product not only on the Eastern but also on the Western market. Despite the official discourse about the family spirit between the different branches of the multinational company, competition was fierce and indeed encouraged by the center as long as it did not inhibit the overall performance of the combine

The Western management invented elaborate payment schemes for keeping the basic salaries of the Czech workers at the barest minimum, offering them instead incentives in the form of paid overtime and exceptional bonuses. A constant hassling went on between the production manager and the workers: the former promising higher salaries if the workers increased their productivity; the latter refusing to do so as they did not trust the promises. Despite the workers' reluctance, productivity increased fourfold between 1993 and 1998, whereas the salaries increased only by two and one-half times. The workers preferred to work paid overtime at a relatively relaxed pace rather than accelerate the pace for an uncertain increase in hourly wages. This meant that they were spending long hours in the enterprise, up to five hundred hours in overtime a year, in order to earn not much more than a reasonable average salary.[10] While consciously withholding their productivity from being exploited by the multinational firm, and thus maintaining a certain control over their labor power, they sacrificed large portions of their time out of work.

## Conclusion

The change of factory regime from a socialist enterprise to a branch of a multinational company meant a radical break with the socialist past, when work had been at the center of social and political life and the worker the pillar of socialist society. Workers were confronted with the fact that they had ceased to be indispensable members of society. They could lose their jobs. The personal contribution they thought to make with their work to the well-being of society was no longer required. What counted now was the profit the enterprise could make thanks to their work. At the level of factory work especially, this had three effects: (1) the acceleration of time at the point of production, the higher turnover of goods through an efficient reorganization of the production process; (2) the pressure to increase the intensity of work without getting paid more in proportion; and (3) the emphasis on individual competition, measured in monetary terms at all the levels of the multinational company from the shop floor to the national company branches.

This new regime met with resistance among the workers of the three enterprises. In Moscow, employees in the administration and workers at the point of production refused to acknowledge the claim of the new management that work should be intensified without a relative increase in salaries. In Berlin, workers insisted on objective criteria to measure their performance and rejected diffuse pressures to accelerate their pace of work. In Moravia, workers preferred to work overtime rather than intensify the work effort, as they did not trust the promises that their salary would be increased if they produced more in a shorter time.

The attempt of the multinational company to make the new factory regime more acceptable to the workforce by offering them the thriving multinational company as a new identificatory frame was lost on the workers. Staff members did not equate their measure of personal success with the contributions they made to the success of the enterprise. As I have shown in this chapter, the compliance of the workers with the dominant political and economic system was never complete. They resisted and partially adapted to their political instrumentalization in the Socialist Competition and, later, offered resistance to the attempts of capitalist management to increase their productivity. For the workers, production in socialism and capitalism was largely external. Neither the necessity of fulfilling a centrally decided plan nor the principle of profitability allowed the workers to reflect on what is produced and for what purpose. However, while in the socialist system, the individual worker could pride himself or herself to make possible the survival of society, and to be thus indispensable, in the capitalist system he or she experienced that he or she became easily replaceable. The first generation of factory workers that experienced the introduction of capitalist work regimes did not internalize its work discipline. If they accommodated themselves to the new requirements, they did so out of fear of losing their jobs rather than trusting the promises of the multinational company that they would be part of the winners if they endorsed their economic aims.

## Notes

1. All names of enterprises are pseudonyms.

2. Neither the use of the term *productivity* in the socialist state industry nor in the capitalist company corresponds to the meaning Karl Marx (1977) gave to the concept in *Das Kapital.* Marx used "labour productivity" *(Arbeitsproduktivität)* as synonymous with productive power (*Produktivkraft*), defining it as determined by skill of the workers, the technological development, the organization of the production process, the scope and efficiency of the means of production and natural factors (54). The voluntary or reluctant effort the workers put in to increase the output of their work was called by Marx "labour intensity" *(Arbeitsintensität)* (431ff). In the enterprise philosophies of the planned and of the market economy that I studied, the two concepts of labor productivity and labor intensity are confused in the term *productivity.* Indeed, both ideological systems used the term mainly in a way of inciting the workforce to increase the intensity of their labor.

3. The research was carried out in the three factories at irregular intervals between 1990 and 1997. I would like to thank the Deutsche Forschungsgemeinschaft (German Research Foundation) for its generous support.

4. Kombinate grouped together enterprises of the same branch or of related levels of production.

5. "sozialistisch, leben, lernen und arbeiten."

6. The student Jan Palach immolated himself in 1969 in the center of Prague on Wenceslav Square to draw attention to the spreading of political repression after the Soviet invasion of August 1968. Thousands attended his funeral despite heavy police presence and monitoring by secret services.

7. For the present director of the firm, one of the few women to obtain such a position, the spirit of the Gorbachov era had been crucial for her suc-

cess. She had started to work in the factory as an unskilled worker and had improved her position in the enterprise through continuous schooling paid for and encouraged by the party.

8. Stachanov, a Soviet miner, was the more or less mythical hero of Soviet productivism.

9. A qualified worker from HOCHINAUF in West Berlin was guaranteed, in 1993, 27DM an hour, while a worker with similar qualifications would earn 5DM an hour in the Czech Republic

10. A skilled worker earned about 12000KC with overtime pay and primes on average per month.

# References

Bateson, G. 1996. *Ökologie des Geistes.* Frankfurt: Suhrkamp Taschenbuch.

Bendix, R. 1956. *Work and authority in industry.* Berkeley: University of California Press.

Braverman, H. 1974. *Labour and monopoly capital.* New York: Monthly Review.

Foucault, M. 1975. *Surveiller et punir. La naissance de la prison.* Paris: Gallimard.

———. 1986. Disciplinary power and subjection. In *Power,* edited by Steven Lukes. Oxford: Blackwell.

———. 1987. Wie wird Macht ausgeübt? In *Jenseits von Strukturalismus und Hermeneutik,* edited by H. L. Dreyfuys and P. Rabinow. Frankfurt: Athenäum.

Gorbachov, M. 1987. *Perestroika.* Munich: Droemersche Verlagsanstalt.

Honecker, E. 1984. *Arbeitermacht zum Wohl des Volkes.* Berlin: Dietz Verlag.

Marcus, G. 1992. Past, present and emergent identities: Requirements for ethnographies of late twentieth century modernity worldwide. In *Modernity and Identity,* edited by J. Friedman and S. Lash. Oxford: Blackwell.

Marx, K. 1977. *Das Kapital.* Vol. 1. Berlin: Dietz Verlag.

Méda, D. 1995. *Le travail. Une valeur en voie de disparition.* Paris: Flammarion.

Mejstrik, M., and J. Hlavacek. 1993. Preconditions for privatization in Czechoslovakia, 1990–1992. In *Privatization in the transition to a market economy,* edited by J. S. Earle, R. Frydman, and A. Rapaczynski. London: Pinter

Müller, B., with E. Mechtcherkina, K. Levinson, I. Cribier, and A. Onikienko. 1994. "Nous qui avons su ferrer une puce . . .": productivité et profit dans une joint venture moscovite. *Les Temps Modernes* 49(579): 124–155.

Thompson, E. P. 1967. Time, work discipline, and industrial capitalism. In *Past and present* 38: 56–57.

Vecernik, J. 1997. *Markets and people: The Czech reform experience in a comparative perspective.* Aldershot, Eng.: Avebury.

Verdery, K. 1996. *What was socialism and what comes next.* Princeton: Princeton University Press

Voskamp, U., and V. Wittke. 1991. Aus Modernisierungsblockaden werden Abwärtsspiralen—zur Reorganisation von Betrieben und Kombinaten in der ehemaligen DDR. *Berliner Journal für Soziologie* 1: 17–39.

# 8

# Redefining Work in a Local Community in Poland

*"Transformation" and Class, Culture, and Work*

MICHAL BUCHOWSKI

Agriculture and anthropological discourse about it is "a dying art form" (Abrahams 1991, 167) throughout most of western and northern Europe. However, in Poland 38 percent of the entire population, close to 15 million citizens, live in nonurban areas and the number of people employed in agriculture amounts to 3.5 million, one-quarter of the country's workforce (Turowski 1994, 151). Although some anthropological works on rural people in Poland have been done, most of them by Anglo-Saxon researchers in Malopolska, the southeast part of the country (cf. Hann 1985; Nagengast 1991; Pine 1998), they very rarely directly address the issue of existing labor relations (Pine 1993).[1] My field site is located in Wielkopolska (Buchowski 1997), the central-western region where, in comparison to Malopolska, agriculture has a unified land structure, a bigger proportion of large estates than in the Southeast (before the Second World War private, later nationalized), and a high productivity level despite the relatively low quality of the soil.

History left an imprint on this different land tenure. When the Polish commonwealth was divided into three political acts between Russia, Austria, and Prussia (1772, 1792, and 1795, respectively), Wielkopolska became a part of the latter. In Prussia, serfdom of peasants was abolished as early as in 1807, while in the Austrian part in 1848 and in the Russian part in 1863. The lower limit for a farm in the Polish part of Prussia was established at seventeen hectares and inheritance laws forbade a division of farmland between descendants. Alongside growing industry, land estates owned by Polish gentry and Prussian *Junkers* (squires), absorbed landless peasants and formed a class of rural proletarians. This kind of social relations was perpetuated in the reemerged interwar (1918–1939) Poland (cf. Nagengast 1991, 45–46). Nationalization of land and its distribution among peasants was one of the first acts of the communist authorities installed by the Soviets in 1944–1945. Part of the confiscated land was kept by the state and went into the building of socialist state farms. Despite intense attempts at collectivization of private farms into cooperatives during the period 1949–1956,[2] land was kept mostly private in socialist Poland; this was to become a hallmark of the country in the communist bloc.[3] In many rural areas in Wielkopolska and elsewhere, farmers and agricultural proletarians (former workers of the state farm) lived side by side. As industrialization went apace, part of them worked in industry; a fraction of the working class lived in the countryside.

Before I take up ethnography, I wish to explain some theoretical points and analytical notions. We should be wary of the notion of "systemic transformation." Change "is not a parade that can be watched as it passes" (Geertz 1995, 4) and it is up to researchers to catch glimpses of these phenomena. The years since 1989 have become a part of the reality of post-socialist societies, which have mysteriously tended toward "the ideal of Western societies."[4] The transforming of the economic and legal structural framework influences people's lives, but one may wonder if these changes should be described in terms of extraordinary happenings. The policies toward agriculture in Poland over the five decades of "real socialism" ranged from land reform through forced collectivization, decollectivization, "oppressive tolerance" in the 1960s and 1970s, favorable treatment in the 1980s, and, today, free market dubbed as "tolerant oppression." What appears to scholars as a systemic transformation, for rural people it is just a link in the chain of history.

I look at the work-related changes through the focus of different social groups called "classes." Social status shapes individual behavior rooted in customs as well as perception of group interrelations; human actions and views constitute class identity and at the same time are constituted by it. Classification parameters are culturally constructed and reproduction of class identity takes on a specific historical form, also in the post-socialist era. Socially determined individuals' cultural competence helps them to develop new strategies for survival in which "models are made and remade through use" (Gudeman and Rivera 1990, 15).

A class division is "an unequal and conflictive distribution of property, power and knowledge in a social system" (Wesolowski 1995, 301). It is "a structuring of subject positions within [a] differentiated field of value-power" (Kearney 1996, 168) that defines an appropriation of forms of capital and consumption of economic value and culture. Thus, *culture* is also an aspect of social relations that differentiates people. It does not "freeze differences," but rather it is an arena in which values, norms, and patterns of meanings of cultural actors are permanently negotiated, and social groups contest for influence. Culture and class combined assume dynamic significance in which the first functions as a variable conditioning social relations (Sider 1986, 10). Acting people, with habits related to their social status, modify social relations. The perception of work and labor, attitudes and values assigned to these culturally defined notions, are also factors creating social divisions and alliances.

*Work* means an engagement in activity designed to achieve a particular purpose and requiring an expenditure of effort through which individuals earn their living and can comprise a pursuit of a specified sort called "profession." *Labor* functions as an integral aspect of work understood as a production factor; it can be possessed, commodified,[5] and sold by its proprietors in exchange for wage or other values. Through these socially constructed categories, people identify themselves, classify others, and are described by the others. In the historical process, work and labor with ensuing work ethic and together with cultural values, marriage patterns, political views, educational aspirations, social ties, and everyday habits contribute to the formation of classes' ethos, that is, "a moral commitment of an individual that is anchored in the sphere of customs of a given community" (Fedyszak-Radziejowska 1995, 179). Let us see how "work and labor" and "class and culture" work together in the rural community in the post-socialist context.

## The Setting

Dziekanowice is a village located in an agricultural commune (*gmina*), Lubowo,[7] thirty-five kilometers northeast from Poznan on the road to Gniezno. Most of the roughly four hundred inhabitants are members of farming families. Forty-six farms in Dziekanowice cover more than six hundred hectares of arable land, two-thirds of the overall village territory. Farm sizes range between one and forty-three hectares, but an average farm comprises fourteen hectares and some farmers rent land in the vicinity. Farms smaller than five hectares are considered merely as a supplementary source of income. Most of the former state farm land (380 hectares) was given back to the church, sold to farmers, or to the museum and a portion of it is still owned by the state. Farm dwellers that have other ways of making a living constitute the category of "worker-peasants." A group of local white-collar workers comprised of administrative museum employees also live in Dziekanowice as well as in neighboring

Lednogora. Twenty agricultural workers of the local state farm were employed after its demise in 1994 by the local museum, which replaced the state farm as an employer, owner of farm buildings, and partly land. There are also other nonagricultural workers who have been employed for years in the museum and by other enterprises in the vicinity. A few try to establish themselves as small entrepreneurs, craftspeople, and as seasonal migrants abroad. Agricultural and nonagricultural workers today form a category of rural proletarians (working in nonagricultural sectors of economy, e.g., carpenters, and mechanics).

Having in mind that all categorization is imposed onto the fluid reality of social life,[8] I describe several classes in Dziekanowice, but I focus on the relations between farmers and rural proletarians. I distinguish these classes by looking at distribution of economic, social, and cultural capitals, namely, by the application of such criteria as ownership of means of production, marriage patterns, education, identity, and attitudes to work and perception of labor. Oppositions and partitioning between classes will be disclosed as they function in historical perspective.

## Being Hired or Retired

After the demise of the state farm and its partial takeover by the museum in 1994, the latter becomes the major employer in the community. A large group of white-collar workers is not indigenous to the village but some of its members settled in Dziekanowice, although most commute from Poznan.[9] Education, the social milieu they came from, the values they profess, the superior position they have toward manual museum workers, and their social and economic positions contribute to the creation of this class. Local people admit the importance of "culture and history," but it is past their understanding that "the state can afford so much money for such fancy things in a period when millions live in poverty." White-collar workers retort that this institution attracts tourists and employs many villagers. There are some tensions between white-collar workers and other groups, expressed, for example, in local folklore. The children of the first are nicknamed "relics" (*zabytki*) by their peers. In return, they call local people literally "aborigines" (*aborygeni*), a word that in Polish can also evoke pejorative connotations.

Power relations favor the white-collar workers in relation to hired workers. Manual workers are subordinated to pen pushers in the makeup of hierarchical dependencies. They have to be decent recruits if they want to keep their job. Salaries are granted by the state, but local power holders distribute them among the people. Managers make use of their cultural and social capital. This kind of dealing is not new in the Polish countryside and perpetuates even prewar relationships between the powerful and the dominated that also continued under socialism. Good relations with the top management grants, in the long run, jobs for other family members in the lucrative institution or licenses for small-scale commercial activities for tourists. There are whole "clans" working in or around the museum. Engaging rural proletarians and not the members of farming families has become a semiofficial policy of the decision makers. It is legitimized by the need to help the helpless, but also involves cultural images of who is fit for the jobs in which some give orders and others have to obey. Independent peasants are not considered suitable for such dealings.

Office work is not highly esteemed by the villagers; it is "artificial" and overpaid. Those who work physically for their living consider high incomes—by local standards—of the top administrators as unsubstantiated and legitimized merely by the unfair power structure that has become especially acute since 1989. "They" are a part of "the system" that underestimates previously more appreciated physical toil and privileges those "doing nothing but sitting in the offices and drinking coffee." The museum, as well as the state farm, with its managers, existed under communism, too, but disparities in incomes were not so striking.

The self-perception of the white-collar worker is exactly an inversion of that of the commoners—they think that their salaries are not a proper reward for their valuable work. Education as such should lead to steady employment in which the daily routine is very slow. "Etatization"[10] is so rooted in their minds that they perceive ample office employment as "natural" and the pace of work as given. Virtually nothing has changed in these culturally legitimized images. Nevertheless, the intelligentsia in Dziekanowice feels alienated and underestimated in relation to the commune's power holders and rising new rich.

Among rural proletarians, agricultural workers, that is, former state-farm manual employees, form a distinct group. Altogether around thirty families live in the four blocks of apartments, commonly called "Brooklyn," adjacent to the grange buildings of the former state farm—today, the home of the museum administration. Some are now employed by the museum and joined other workers who had been working there longer. Although there was a limited exchange of personnel between the state farm and the museum before 1994, the two factions differed because of their history under socialism and the status within the community.

The agricultural workforce in the Dziekanowice estate has existed for decades. Nationalization of land estate and the distribution of land in 1945 led to the creation of fifteen new farms, whose owners converted from proletarians to peasants. After a few years, together with some farms that existed in the prewar period, they were collectivized. Decollectivization in 1956 reestablished private ownership, but soon eleven from among the beneficiaries of land reform gave up farming, sold land cheaply to the state, and, with two exceptions, left the village. It facilitated, at the beginning of the 1960s, the creation of a state farm that, as time went by, was staffed by a mobile workforce coming mainly from the surrounding districts, the core of which was comprised of prewar rural proletarians.[11] State farms attracted people by offering free accommodation and quotas of potatoes, milk, and grain. Interestingly enough, the latter, called *deputat*, was an in-kind payment, the tradition of which reaches back to precapitalist times that the socialist state sustained. In the 1980s, most agricultural workers were satisfied with their jobs and overall life situation (Dzun 1991, 159–172). With the liberal reform of the 1990s, their economic situation declined rapidly and in 1992 their income was half the national average (Domanski 1995, 376), and today they are stricken by a high unemployment rate.[12] Thanks to the museum, the workers in Dziekanowice have not been so adversely affected.

The education of the elderly is mostly elementary. The younger generation completes vocational education such as house painting or carpentry, but it does not secure a job. The policy of the museum of bringing in former state farm workers as employees does not to have to be extended to their descendants who have difficulties in finding jobs. Only two unmarried young people among those able to work are employed. Hanging around has become a new style of living, bringing to mind the habit of urban underclass youngsters. Marriages are usually between partners coming from other manual workers' families. Often these young couples remain unemployed for years and we behold the emergence of permanent poverty. Very rarely, partners come from farming families having roots in the rural proletariat, that is, the beneficiaries of the land reform of 1945. I have never heard about a marriage between an agricultural worker and a "traditional" peasant.

The older generation that worked in the state farm relies today on pensions. In the 1990s, the state implemented programs that enabled many to receive early retirement benefits to help them get by until regular retirement age. Together with disability pensioners, they compose a large group of people not considered unemployed, but still depending on the help of the state. However, not all those eligible have taken full advantage of this program. Jakub,[13] for example, works as a stoker. For three years, he drew a temporary disability pension. He could have produced documents confirming that he had worked throughout, and thus received early retirement pension, but he failed to do so. Therefore, after the heating season, he receives unemployment benefits, the so-called *kuroniowka*[14] and half of the year wanders around.

For twenty former state farm workers, a job in the museum was a blessing. Encouraged by the distillery manager, they could have tried to establish a workers enterprise, but in his opinion, accustomed to obtaining everything from the state, they waited for manna from heaven: "They did nothing for so many years, so what can they do now?" As hired laborers they are still dependent on the state. Their job is considered lighter as they became guardians or manual workers in the museum. Job security, however, has decreased. In the past, they could find a job in the state farm easily and having it was taken for granted. Today, threats of staff reductions discipline the people and compels them to compete. Retirement and loss of job means that only one-quarter of the personnel "inherited" from the state farm still work in the museum. Satisfied with their relatively lucky fate, they complain that the deputat privileges have ceased and that they have been forced to buy out and pay rent for apartments.[15] The socialist state also extended deputat benefits to include occasional free holidays, excursions, and cultural events, such as a harvest festival. All of them, together with some products that one could easily "take home," are gone; therefore, "it was better under communism" (*za komuny było lepiej*).

Several people have been "forced" to find employment with local farmers, which is considered a bottom-line option. Farmers are called *babole* (slutters) and workers "do not want to serve slutters." Commenting on the situation of a young man who now works for the owner of the local chicken farm, one of the manual workers said, "What does it mean that he has to work there? Are prewar times coming back? Nothing compares to a job in a state enterprise." The low prestige that working on a private farm receives may be correlated with the low wages one gets there which in the summer of 1999 amounted to 3.5 zlotys (90 cents) per hour, extremely low even by Polish standards. The minimal payments for social insurance will result in small future retirement benefits. However, it seems that social perceptions play the most important role. Rural proletarians developed a strong feeling of independence from private employers and the state functioned as an abstract and exclusive employer. Under socialism, labor was both commodified and depersonalized. Today, this process has been partly reversed by a return to job relationships in which direct personal interactions with employers, real people living in the same community, are involved. It makes social hierarchy transparent and it is emotionally hard to sell labor to individuals considered babole who now determine work contracts. For rural proletarians, it is like selling a part of their souls, not just a commodity. Rooted in social relationships, feelings of degradation are supplemented with strenuous work. For instance, those employed by Pawel at the chicken farm "have to drink coffee while running." Agata, Jakub's wife, says that she does not want to work there since she "won't stand stinking air and endure staying there," so she works with the more appreciative employer, Rysiek.

Rysiek is a farmer who graduated to agricultural entrepreneur. He is successfully specializing in growing flowers, strawberries, and tomatoes in a very modern greenhouse. Ten people are employed there and several others are hired seasonally. His case is a spectacular example of class mobility. In three generations, the family has moved from the rural proletariat (his grandfather was a village butcher) to being a "peasant" (his father was a beneficiary of land reform) to agricultural entrepreneur employing a workforce. In contrast to Pawel, working relations in the greenhouse are described as "more humane." He and his wife allow breaks and prepare free coffee for the employees. This attitude retains features of traditional relations in which a person to whom one offers his labor repays in kind and kindness. Offering free drinks was even a habit at the state farm. Labor is paid in cash, but traces of traditional behaviors, as they sustained noncommodified relations, improve the content of the work relations today.

Some work *na czarno* ("on the black"). Administrative controls reduced illegal employment, but it still happens, particularly during seasons of intense work. However, it is less widespread than one might expect and the two mentioned entrepreneurs do prefer to use a permanent workforce. Agricultural proletarians are reluctant about serving farmers; those in turn favor mutual help among themselves over the hiring of rural proletarians as, along with other villagers, they do not perceive them as valuable people. Talking about the youngsters, Slawek, an outsider who married into a peasant family in the village and works in the museum, described them simply as "lazy and unable to learn." They all will end up badly. "Instead of going to work in the summer to farmers, when there is high demand for it, they prefer to lean against the walls and make boot marks on them. They could have earned some money and bought some jeans, but no, they prefer doing nothing and rely on their parents. They will barely complete some school and that's it."

There are few women who took up work with Rysiek or Pawel. "They immediately dressed up better, changed their hairdressing, wore earrings and look differently." One of the families living in the blocks of apartments, the Stachuras, managed to establish themselves as private entrepreneurs. As a former state farm worker, he works in the museum, while she, as a former employee in the shop in Dziekanowice that belonged to the Community Cooperative (Gminna Spoldzielnia) in Falkowo, enfranchised herself and has become an owner. In fact, with two sons they all are engaged in running the business, whose profitability is meager; their customers are few and rather poor. The older son worked for a carpenter, but quit the next day because "he won't toil and moil for 500 zlotys [$125 a month], and nobody will yell at him with his muzzle for that money," as his mother explained. He also went to Germany to work in the construction brigade, but "was there for a short time, since the work was hard for a young man and he is only twenty-three years old." Whether this behavior is a matter of weakness or pride remains unclear. Recently, however, he has found another job and the other son, after returning from military service, has been employed in the museum.

The economic status of affluent agricultural workers does not differ from the village proletariat. They own small houses or live in apartments purchased from the commune, and most have small garden plots. This diversified group is comprised of individuals coming from the agricultural workers, industrial workers, and even children of farmers. Most village proletarians are qualified as skilled workers and some teenagers go to vocational high schools. Under socialism the main source of income used to be employment in state companies outside Dziekanowice and in the museum supplemented by unregistered specialized services. Changing circumstances have forced people to pursue new forms of activity and seek a further multiplication of resources. Many decided to do things they would have hardly done in the past, for example, work abroad and for the farmers, or sell part of their plots for housing. Many are retired and receive disability pensions or unemployment benefits. The volume of this group's ventures is limited by the meager capital its members dispose of, and very small and hardly profitable businesses prevail. Several are doing relatively well and others are poverty-stricken. The latter move toward the stereotypic image of agricultural proletarians.

Village proletarians share differing ethos and resourcefulness. Adam is a good example of a person who represents this ethos appreciated in the community. A son of a single mother, he has been trained as a carpenter. Today, he commutes to work to the private enterprise in Gniezno and opened his own shop in Dziekanowice in which he works on weekends and in the afternoons. His determination is highly valued by the villagers and is in contrast to the young Stachura. Both men belong to different breeds: "post-state farm" and villager; in terms used here, that of agricultural proletariat and of village proletariat. For the residents of Dziekanowice, it matters.

## Being Self-Employed or Employer

The fact of having farmland distinguishes farmers from other classes in the classical sense. Managing the farm is a profession that defines everyday discourses, fields of shared meanings and interests, a feeling of community, and relations with other people. An awareness of class solidarity plays an important role. In this sense, they fit even Karl Marx's (1957) quite rigorous definition: Peasants live "under economic conditions of existence that divide their mode of life, their interests and their culture from those of the other classes, and put them in hostile opposition to the latter" (109). Therefore, despite internal divisions, farmers have their own class consciousness that translates into political preferences, and most of them vote for the conservative Polish Peasant Party.

Peasants in Dziekanowice are, in fact, farmers involved in an economic and social system completely different from precapitalist economies and are not called on to survive within a subsistence economy. Carole Nagengast (1991, 151–155) showed the inadequacy of Alexandr Chayanov's (1923) model with regard to Polish farmers during the communist period. Today, farmers participate in the process through which the "marketing system [is] penetrating into the community, and transforming all relations into single-interest relations of individuals with goods for sale" (Wolf 1966, 48). Attitudes to the structural changes of the 1990s differentiate very conspicuously the farmers of today—one from the other. The ethos of various factions within this class is evolving in divergent directions according to divisions related to their economic position. Simultaneously, the latter is partly defined, along with other forms of social and symbolic capital, by the ethos previously shared by individuals. The category of ethos appears as a part of cultural capital.

"Real peasants," a native category used by farmers, never buy on credit in the shop, do not rely on social welfare, and are opposed to the liberal policies of the state toward "lousy people." Farmers count on their own hard work and believe that everything they have they owe to their own sweat. They rarely get drunk, particularly in public. They drink vodka in the company of their equals, but never the cheap apple wine often drunk by *buraki* (literally "mangolds," a variety of beetroot used as cattle fodder, but having strong pejorative overtones, such as "country bumpkin"), men from the former state farm. The education of farmers in Dziekanowice varies from the elementary to the university level and all try to ensure at least vocational training for their children. Marriages are contracted with members of the same class or of higher standing. Exceptions occur only among those farmer families who stem from the prewar proletariat. In practice, every marriage in families of a long-standing farming tradition only connects partners of the peasant class.

This custom has various reasons. On the one hand, the question of dowry is involved, even if no one talks about it openly. An important, although immaterial, part of the dowry of a lifetime partner is her work habit since both partners must be accustomed to the hard toil of life on the farm. On the other hand, rural proletarians claim that it is not worthy to accept a way of life demanding such arduous labor. The mother of two young women told me she does not recommend that her daughters marry farmers because it means a life of drudgery. Besides, if a farmer marries a woman who is without a dowry, she will be reminded of it, sooner or later. Evidently, culturally defined boundaries work both ways.

Work on the farm is indeed hard and farmers sweat is in everything they have. Jan and Ula are an average farmer couple in Dziekanowice who own eleven hectares and rent an additional nine. They wake up routinely at five in the morning in order to feed their pigs and cows, and milk the latter—which is her job along with selling it to people coming from Brooklyn. These chores have to be done two or three times a day. She does all the kitchen-related labor: preparing breakfast for him and their five children, cook dinner, and serve supper. Daily shopping for basic items, cleaning house, washing, feeding hens, and tending the garden, as well as processing its products (making jam, jelly, sour or pickled cucumbers, tomatoes, cabbage, and so on) is all her responsibility. She also takes care of bringing up the children, which ranges from attending parent–teacher meetings to making sure that the youngest have washed before bedtime. He is in charge of all chores in the fields and pigsty. Commercializing the products, supplying inputs necessary for farm production, maintaining the house and grange buildings and the car and machinery, and taking part in public life (he is the *soltys*, i.e., village mayor and by rule attends the Commune's Council meetings) are his tasks. The older children help them quite often, although it is not the rule that they have to do tasks that children were expected to do in previous generations. Together, they go to Gniezno for the major shopping. Indeed, a "farmers' work is never done" and there is not much free time left, of what there is, most of the time is spent in front of the television set. Despite constant efforts, it has been difficult for them to make ends meet. She expressed a will to take a job in the museum, but because of the policy of rejecting farmers, she did not get it, but she recently managed to get a part-time job at the post office in Lednogora.

In the 1980s, "real socialism" ensured fixed prices for agricultural products and cheap credit making for relative prosperity. This situation changed radically after liberalization in 1990 when farmers jumped directly from the state-managed economy to the free market with few regulations. Paradoxically, private producers supposedly best fitted to competition (a "Trojan horse of capitalism in socialism") have had many problems. A "mild" market game in a nonmarket environment in the 1980s has been superseded by the "wild" contest in the 1990s. We have witnessed a process of subjugation of the former socialist agriculture to new capitalist conditions marked by the opening to the world markets. An adjustment to this new deal can serve as a criterion of adaptation in which habitus, class position, and possession of capital play a conspicuous role. Their combination places the individual in a different position on the scale between traditionalist and future-oriented farmers.

Those farmers who gravitate toward the pole of traditionalism react to structural changes in a way that does not work efficiently in a new situation. The market creates a situation "in which limits and 'incompleteness' of the rural folk's model become evident" (Gudeman and Rivera 1990, 15). These farmers want to remain in agriculture, but have difficulties in adapting. They exercise a kind of "wait-and-see policy": do not buy land or increase production. Several types of commodities—mainly pigs, poultry, grain, potatoes—are slightly increased or decreased in numbers according to fluctuations in the fragile market. Rationality demands that purchases and sales be adjusted to everyday transactions.

A similar rationale applies to all farmers. The capacity od producers to adapt to the new scheme differs according to their degree of foresight. Along with personal skills, the material situation prevailing when the changes began help to determine a successful adaptation. Unfavorable price relations can be alleviated by a larger turnover. The group of farmers able to undertake more advantageous economic plans has been formed. They are managing well in spite of the lack of stability in the business. Their starting capital enabled them to safeguard their economic and social status. Today, these families form a fraction of the traditionally well-off farmers moving to a free market.

Two farmers established themselves as rural entrepreneurs in Dziekanowice. Their attitude toward farming is decidedly prospective. One of them, Pawel, told me already in 1995 that his dream was to own several hundred hectares of land for larger scale production using hired labor force. This, he believed, was the future for making a decent living in agriculture. The dream of this young farmer came through. He developed a poultry enterprise the capacity of which has increased from 35 thousand broilers in 1995 to more than 100 thousand by 1999. In Falkowo he established a pigsty for thousand pigs. He owns and rents together 239 hectares and employs close to thirty people, many recruited from the rural proletariat in Dziekanowice. His venture is mechanized with gas installations and reservoirs, tractors and a butchery line. However by the villagers he is perceived as one who exploits people, demands too much, distances himself, is stingy and creates a tense atmosphere in the workplace. Not long ago, he was a regular farmer and an equal among his fellows. Today, he is a hardnosed entrepreneur who makes it visible who is a boss in the community.

## Labor, Class, and "New Deal"

The small community of Dziekanowice could have appeared at first sight as unified by language, religion, customs, many images, rural lifestyle, and even, generally, a negative attitude toward "transformation." However, it is deeply internally differentiated. Four social groups form classes that can be distinguished (but not essentialized) through a combination of economic, social, and cultural features significant for anthropological analysis. As Katherine Verdery (1998) says, "Property is about social relations. These include both relations among persons and the power relations in which people act" (180). Therefore, farmers differ from rural proletarians and white-collar workers from both of them in a very complex sense of the word. Social relations generate divergent identities that surface in the least expected circumstances. For instance, it is not mere coincidence that at village gatherings agricultural proletarians sit in one corner, close to them sit the village proletarians, and farmers sit separately. Social distance shows its symbolic power in a spatial distance that is also inscribed in a local topography that separates agricultural and rural proletarians, white-collar workers, and those farmers living in *huby* (scattered midfield homesteads). Village representatives in the Commune's Council and the mayor are almost virtually all farmers, too. Is it a coincidence that a person's choice of company reflects social divisions? If you ask someone What matters when people get married? you will hear that love is decisive. Interestingly enough, mutual love brings together partners from the same social strata.

Social borders are not always so visible. Behavior reproduces patterns rooted in culture. This explains why proletarians who have relied on the socialist state for decades smartly exploit the social security system today. All cunning or illegal forms of exploiting other venues in the struggle for survival are also accepted among them. In contrast, this raises contempt among strongly independent real peasants for whom the attitudes of proletarians would not be appropriate. Such silent barriers are created by every faction. White-collar workers from the museum are considered "relics" who will never fully understand local problems. They consider proletarians to be a deprived "gray mass." Even agricultural workers are perceived by village proletarians as an alcohol-abusing lower class. For farmers, agricultural proletarians and to some extent village proletarians are lazy jerks. For agricultural workers, farmers are slutters. And so on.

This brings us to the issue of labor. Buraki do not want to serve babole. Social barriers, strengthened by socialist ideas of production, have created a condition in which it is now difficult for proletarians to perceive their work at private enterprises as an ordinary contract between employer and employee. This is a negation of a notion of pride proletarians have held for years. An anonymous employer, the state, is considered much better than a private one. Martha Lampland (1995) writes that in Hungary it was the state that acted as a personalized subject in contrast to the depersonalized workings of the "hidden hand of a free market." This, in general, applies also to Poland where workers' strikes were addressed against "the party" and *przekleta komuna* (damned communism) was blamed for all misfortunes. However, for rural proletarians today, free market looms as an incomprehensible phenomenon, but what is visible and tangible is an employer who often comes from the same community and used to be on par with them. Socialist managers represented the state, but they were not the state itself and worked for it as hired workers as well. This is precisely what has changed, and the "invisible market" is personalized and within sight, embodied in a touchable employer, owner, and manager—all in one.

Postsocialist personalization of work relations raised worries that prewar social relationships, in which proletarians were little regarded, would come back. Memories of elders and communist propaganda have led to such a judgment in mythified form since there are very few people in the village who have actual experience of these times. According to oral accounts, prewar labor relation on big estates presented a mixture of capitalist and feudal relations in which proletarians sold labor to the landowners, partly paid in a deputat form, and the latter took responsibility for the housing and social security of the workers. Thus, a form of patronage was maintained. It was continued on the state farms, but the individual landowner was superseded by "the state." This status quo was appreciated, and, as already mentioned, in Dziekanowice most beneficiaries of land reform preferred to give it up to the state and work for it. "Etatized depersonalization" of work relations and further commodification of labor were welcomed. Prompted by industrialization, this took place during the period when massive migration from the countryside to urban areas occurred.[16] In times of industrial "emproletariasement" as it was acclaimed by propaganda,[17] work in agriculture was not very highly valued and city life was perceived as social advancement. In this milieu, being an agricultural worker was still a better option than working on one's own private farm. A reluctance to work hard on a farm is visible among rural proletarians today.

This resentment is observable in many ways. Legitimization of the barrier between proletarians and farmers to intermarry is probably the most remarkable one in which work functions as a crucial factor. Separation of the two classes seems to be rooted in the social history of the Polish countryside that defined them as culturally different and bearing discrete consciousness. Agricultural proletarians perceive the hard toil of peasants as futile in the long run and costing too much time and energy. Simply, it does not pay off. It has been easier to sell labor for money or services in kind and have "saint peace" (*swiety spokoj*). "Man worked and communism thought" (*czlowiek robil, a komuna myslala*), and the rule was that "whether you stay or lay, you deserve your pay" (*czy sie stoi, czy sie lezy, wyplata tak sie nalezy*). In the socialist relations, mere presence at work entitled employees who were totally unconcerned about the production process and its results to get their salaries nevertheless. Commodification of labor that was sold to the state and the significance of which was systematically diminished in everyday life ran parallel with the erosion of the work ethos. In theory, labor defined proletarians and for ideological reasons was even praised, but in practice it had little value, was even ridiculed, and as such could not establish itself as the major component of proletarians' identity.

Acceptance of the role of the state as generating income for those who lost their job due to changes in the 1990s has not caused a mental revolution. Devaluation of labor hit bottom and doing nothing has been as equally acceptable as that performed at the minimal level of engagement in the socialist process of production. The state has taken responsibility for the older and physically challenged, unable to readjust to the new structural framework, giving them earlier retirement privileges and unemployment benefits. Since 1994, the new state as a direct employer had been represented in Dziekanowice by the museum. On the one hand, it has withdrawn from many traditional responsibilities and forms of payment, such as free accommodation and deputat duties. On the other hand, the museum perpetuates former relations in many ways. As in the past, it hires rural proletarians that in many respects are treated in a way similar to the system of patronage. Recruitment depends now on benevolence and existing connections with families traditionally tied with the museum or those who managed to establish a good relationship with it recently. This policy is legitimized by the desire to aid the helpless, when they are deserving at the same time. With new patterns of work relations expanding in society and a depressed job market, managers are able to define conditions of employment. However, due to the relic of patronage practices, it does not produce labor relations ascribed within the ideal of a capitalist society, that is, fully commodified, but fosters relations of the patron-client type. The status of work, physical service in the state institution, has not changed very much. Although it is commodified, labor is not the only measure of one's quality. The very fact of "being there" defines the value of a person, even if one does not perform at work. In other words, for agricultural proletarians, commodification of labor does not go hand in hand with its appreciation as "the metric measure of value" (Biernacki, quoted in Lampland 1995, 10). It can be, however, the identifying gauge applied to proletarians by other social groups.

Much more visible changes in working relations in the period of transition occurred between employers and employees in the private agricultural sector. They have developed into full form only in the new circumstances. Under communism, farmers could not officially employ more than two people from beyond their family and in Dziekanowice this kind of arrangement did not really exist. New regulations opened a possibility for a free labor market and unlimited employment. The two major private job providers in the community are differently perceived through the lenses of traditional cultural values of proletarians preferring more "humane" and intimate relations between owners and workers. It has been difficult for them to sell their labor, the only thing they really possess, to employers coming from the same community in the first place. Still, today, their attitude follows the line of commodification of labor and partial but increasing "dehumanization" of work relations systematically reduced to the aspect of performance. The vegetable producer is better appreciated than the chicken farm owner because the former has retained some forms of traditional attitudes that soothe the feeling of degradation, while the latter has opted, intentionally or not, for a modern capitalist model. Socialist depersonalization and commodification combined with habitual attitudes would have fitted proletarians' ideals best.

It is difficult for them to grasp and to be confident about the capitalist model of work relations incurring further commodification of labor and commercialization of the work environment. These issues appear significantly different for peasants. In their ethos, work has always had high value. The attitude of farmers involves several elements that Lampland (1995), following Karl Marx, György Lukacs, and Richard Biernacki, treats as "unique to capitalism": "[It] is a material property of human actors, bearing physical, nearly tangible qualities. It is also the touchstone, the foundation, of subjectivity and morality" (11). Indeed, the labor and work ethics have extremely significant functions in the construction of the farmers' identity. The value of a person depends on their ability to work diligently and efficiently. Work is a measure that helps peasants distance themselves from the "others," both lazy jerks and *gryzi-piorki* ("pen biters"). A healthy individual who does not work is disqualified as a valuable human being at all. Nonphysical activity is hardly treated as a productive pursuit. Thus, labor is not only a matter of subsistence and prosperity, but also of honor, reputation, and distinction.

In the case of farmers, who are simultaneously owners and workers, commodification of labor is much more mystified and mediated as that in the other classes. It is essential that they work on their own. *Panskie oko konia tuczy* (owner's eye breeds the horse), as popular saying goes, confirms the superiority of private over collective property. First, although permanently swamped with work, they control it as well as the fruits of their toil that they partly consume themselves. This gives farmers a strong feeling of independence. They strongly oppose the appropriation of their labor and, as a result, of their self. However, such a feeling has been undermined by the free market relation penetrating agricultural activity. It is also true that in the past, a degree of their independence was determined by the state through administrative price regulations. At least during the period of the decline of communism, those rules were relatively favorable for farmers, but changed drastically in 1990. Free market means for them unpredictable fluctuation of prices and "price scissors." No wonder some poorer farmers would like "to hang Balcerowicz[18] on the withered bough." Labor input does not translate into profit, and moral capital into economic capital. The absolute value of labor and an appreciation for hard work wrecks on the rocks of invisible market forces. Accustomed to state intervention, an established "actor" regulating just labor relations, farmers from Dziekanowice blockaded the road that connects Poznan with Gniezno in a nationwide protest against unfair price relations in 1999.

Disruption of the direct and traceable relationship between physical labor and profit remains perplexing for most farmers. Although they participate in the market game, they cannot understand why their products are hard to sell when through the media they can learn about huge amounts of agricultural products being imported. They can also see them on the shelves in shops. "Don't we have our own cheese and sausages, or what?" This happens when "millions of hectares in Poland lay fallow and hundreds of thousands of people who worked in the former state farms rot in their dens," as Piatek, an owner of one of the medium-size farms, said. In this model, land and people are wasted, while the labor of those working hard is not rewarded. The "New Poland" means for farmers the depreciation of the core of their identity: diligent labor. It was recognized, at least at the ideological level, by communist propaganda. Today, sneaky or indolent people are backed. Businessmen, politicians, managers, and administration personnel form one mafia of those who "do nothing but money." These fortunes are made "on the backs of honest and hardworking people." In addition, "they feed all those jerks who do not work at all. When I need somebody to help me in the harvest season, it is difficult to find a single person. But they [former state farm workers] are first to get early retirement or line up for kuroniowka."

Still, despite difficulties, farmers stay in agriculture or are forced to do so. The most vigorous put themselves on a track to act as entrepreneurs. Alongside ownership of the farm, work ethos has acquired a function of the most conspicuous identity factor. It is one of the last strongholds of the peasantry. Being an owner of the means of production, working hard on one's own farm, and controlling labor and the process of production puts farmers in opposition to most social classes in the community, if not the whole society. As in the case of rural proletarians, encroaching capitalism has commodified the farmers' labor even further, but it is difficult for them to accept the capricious market gauge of the value of this work. For their identity, industriousness comprises a steady and faithful measure of selfhood and the value of a person. The same applies to newly established agricultural entrepreneurs. They work "round the clock," although their work moved from physical to managerial. They dared to take the risk of engaging in the market game and grasp principles of the "new deal" in which physical work, due to invisible market forces rules, does not convert literally into benefits in a kind of "one-to-one equation." In this model, one is also aware that the local economy is a part of the global economy. Both vegetable and poultry producers have their contractors nationwide and abroad.

It seems that today we are witnessing a process described by Charles Bettelheim (1969): "Inside social formations in which capitalism is predominant, this domination mainly tends to expand reproduction of the capitalist mode of production, that is to dissolution of the other modes of production" (297). This process, combined with globalization, is multithreaded and affects various groups differently. People faced with capitalism respond in ways rooted in historically defined meanings. Their practice is a result of the impact of the structural changes and their conceptualization of them entrenched in cultural meanings. In this way, they are not only transformed by the capitalist relationships of production, but also transform capitalism in its local form. The process of commodification of labor is caught up in a historical process that has different meaning for various classes. The rural proletarians and the intelligentsia are accustomed to selling their labor and serving as hired employees, but their social positions place them on different sides of the barricade as far as its conceptualization is concerned. The socialist depersonalization of work relations, meaning that the state was an abstract owner and employer and all coworkers, including managers, formed a class of hired people, causes these groups to have difficulties accepting the possibility that they sell their skills to private entrepreneurs, their fellow villagers. For farmers, diligent work is a major idiom of their identity that helps them also to distance themselves from the other classes. However, a mystified commodification of labor, strengthened through the obscure effects of market forces makes them confused about this traditionally absolute value of their ethos. They see that the traditional gauge for evaluation of a person does not function in the way they imagined.

The model of work that functions today bears both features of continuity and change. It continues to be perceived differently by various social groups and to function as social marker for these groups. As in the past, it lies at the heart of peasants' selfhood and is treated as an "external" factor in identity creation for proletarians. Simultaneously, capitalist relations have already forced people to redefine work relations within community and its perception in general. Socialist depersonalization of work relations connected with etatization has converted into more personalized relations. At the same time, labor relations have been further commodified and based on the principle of performance. In fact, it fits farmers' images about quality of man as a creative and busy person, and legitimizes commercialization of rural entrepreneurs' relations with proletarians. However, capricious free market forces are such that work does not always pay off and enable many people in a wider society to make effortless fortunes. This, inter alia, accounts for capitalism being so reluctantly accepted by peasants. The same processes make rural proletarians even more hesitant. They do not see work as the most important trait of a human being, but due to their meager economic, social, and cultural capitals are excluded from the market game, which is totally alien to them. Labor has become their sole capital that they have to sell in the new framework that puts them openly in a subordinate position to members of other groups in the community that used to be perceived as equal or even lower. It makes them feel degraded and offends their concept of dignity.

Change, according to Marshall Sahlins (1981, 6, 67), is failed reproduction. People in Dziekanowice try to reproduce their values, habits, ideals, and identities. Thanks to the fact that they "fail," we observe transformation within all those categories, of the people and of the social system. Entrenched in culture, the notion of work is the subject of similar change and at the same time a window through which we can look at this constant unfolding.

# Notes

The Centre Marc Bloch in Berlin supported the main part of the research in the village of Dziekanowice in 1994 and 1995. The Wenner-Gren Foundation for Anthropological Research financed the visit to the field in the summer of 1995. My fieldwork in the summer of 1996 was supported by the Alexander von Humboldt Foundation. Afterward, I have visited Dziekanowice each summer. I would like to thank to the people of Dziekanowice, especially Antoni Pelczyk and the Michalowiczs, whose compassion and hospitality made this research possible. For more ethnographic detail and theoretical arguments, see Buchowski (1995, 1996, 1997). In those works, Edouard Conte and Carole Nagengast helped me formulate my arguments. All translations of citations from Polish are mine.

1. Elizabeth Dunn (1996, 1998, 2001) published articles on industrial work relations in Poland.

2. Although state farms, called in Poland Panstwowe Gospodarstwa Rolne (State Agricultural Enterprises), and cooperative farms, called Rolnicze Spoldzielnie Produkcyjne (Agricultural Production Cooperatives), were counted as part of the socialist agricultural sector, their legal status was different. The state owned its farms and employed workers, while cooperatives were formally owned by its members who contributed their land to ventures and could hire a workforce. Profits were divided among "shareholders." In practice, both organizations supported by the state functioned in a very similar way.

3. In 1990, 76 percent of farmland in Poland was in private hands, 18.7 percent was owned by the state, 3.7 percent by cooperatives, and 1.6 percent by so-called Agricultural Circles. Farms below five hectares covered 52.8 percent (Maurel 1994, 99; Pilichowski 1994, 165–166). Since 1990, a proportion of private landownership and average farm size (today eight hectares) has been increasing systematically due to the privatization of state farms that are rented out or sold to private owners, and the systematic reduction of the number of farms.

4. Katherine Verdery (1996) writes:

A number of the stories of post-socialism have the knights of Western know-how rushing to rescue the distressed Eastern Europe. . . . The rescue scenario has two common variants: "shock therapy" and "big bang." The first compares the former socialist bloc with a person suffering from mental illness—that is, socialism drove them crazy, and our job is to restore their sanity. The second implies that (*pace* Fukuyama) history is only now beginning, that prior to 1989 the area was without form and void. (205)

In this chapter, I want to show, inter alia, that these scenarios have not much in common with the situation in central Europe.

5. I follow Martha Lampland (1995) in her understanding of commodification of labor. It is "the conflation of labor's objectification in particular acts of production with it[s] more general status as the source and arbiter of value" (11).

This emphasizes "the strange parallel of labor's acquiring a concrete, physical character while it takes on the general or dominant role in structuring social action and creating cultural value" (ibid.).

6. All data about the Lubowo commune was obtained at the Commune's Office, unless indicated differently.

7. Dating from the tenth century, the archeological site on an island in Lednica Lake together with open-air museum and Landscape Reserve comprise the Polish Piasts Museum (the museum hereafter), established in the 1970s.

8. Let me cite Pierre Bourdieu (1990a): "Concepts . . . remain open and provisional, which doesn't mean vague approximate and confused. . . . [T]his openness of concepts . . . is the essence of any scientific thought *in statu nascendi*" (40–41). At the same time our concepts become a part of the reality. This does not mean "that it's the symbolic structures that produce the social structures" (Bourdieu 1990a, 18). The significance of our statements increases if they can call out implicit phenomena, and throw a new light on them.

9. The museum employs almost ninety people, half of which are white-collars workers.

10. Katherine Verdery (1996) uses this term in relation to time in socialist Romania. It means literally, "the process of statizing" (40). I derive this term from Polish *etatyzacja*, which means an increasing "statization" of job positions.

11. Spatial division in the village combined with relative mobility of proletarians in relation to farmers contributes to the class oppositions by referring to such concepts as territorial belongings and the value of entrenchment. However, mobility of rural proletarians has been hibernated in the last period, they have lived in Dziekanowice for decades now and are not simply treated as "they" by the others, but as individual members of the group indigenous for the community.

12. At the end of 2000, the unemployment rate reached more than 15 percent in Poland (cf. *Sytuacja* 2001); in some former state farm districts, it oscillates around 30 percent. In addition, hidden unemployment in the countryside amounts to 600,000–900,000.

13. I use first names or nicknames for identifying people.

14. This folk term comes from the name of Jacek Kuron, an anticommunist dissident and the minister for social affairs in the first noncommunist government in 1989 under which unemployment benefits were introduced.

15. Apartments that in the past were free have had to be bought by the tenants although for an extraordinarily low price.

16. In the postwar period, the rural population decreased only slightly (from 16 to 14.5 million), while the number of urban dwellers rose threefold (from 7.5 to 24 million), mostly thanks to migration from the countryside (Eberhardt 1993, 34). However, in 2000, for the first time in the postwar period, migration

from towns to the countryside outnumbered the routine route by four thousand (*Sytuacja* 2001).

17. I invent this notion as a contrast to "embourgeoisement."

18. Then-minister of finance identified with austere market reform and famous for his "shock therapy."

# References

Abrahams, R. 1991. *A place of their own: Family farming in eastern Finland.* Cambridge: Cambridge University Press.

Bettelheim, C. 1969. Appendix I: Theoretical comments. In *Unequal Exchange: A Study of the Imperialism of Trade,* edited by A. Emmanuel. New York: Monthly Review.

Bourdieu, P. 1990a. *In other words: Essays towards a reflexive sociology.* Stanford: Stanford University Press.

———. 1990b. *The logic of practice.* Stanford: Stanford University Press.

Buchowski, M. 1995. Chacun laboure comme il peut. *Etudes rurale* (Special issue: "Paysans au-dela du mur," edited by E. Conte and C. Giordano): 138–140.

———. 1996. *Klasa i kultura w procesie transformacji.* Berlin: Centre Marc Bloch.

———. 1997. *Reluctant capitalists: An anthropological study of a local community in western Poland.* Berlin: Centre Marc Bloch.

Chayanov, A. V. 1923. *Die Lehre von der Bauerlichen Wirtschaft.* Berlin: Parey.

Domanski, H. 1995. Rekompozycja stratyfikacji spolecznej i reorientacji wartosci. In *Ludzie i instytucje. Stawanie sie ladu spolecznego.* Vol. 2, edited by A. Sulek, J. Styk, and I. Machaj. Lublin, Pol.: Wydawnictwo Uniwersytetu Marii Curie-Sklodowskiej.

Dunn, E. 1996. Managerial knowledge, privatization, and cultural change in post-socialist Poland. *Ethnologia Polona* 19: 7–25.

———. 1998. Slick salesmen and simple people: Negotiating capitalism in a privatized Polish firm. In *Uncertain transition,* edited by M. Burawoy and K. Verdery. Lanham, Md.: Rowman and Littlefield.

———. 2001. Audit, corruption, and the problem of personhood: Scenes from post-socialist Poland. In *Poland beyond communism: A critical perspctive on transition,* edited by M. Buchowski, E. Conte, and C. Nagengast. Fribourg, Switz.: Presse Universetaire.

Dzun, W. 1991. *PGR w rolnictwie polskim w latach 1944–1990.* Warszawa, Pol.: IRWiR PAN.

Fedyszak-Radziejowska, B. 1995. Spolecznosci wiejskie. Grabarz czy moderator panstwa liberalnego. In *Ludzie i instytucje. Stawanie sie ladu spolecznego.* Vol. 2, edited by A. Sulek, J. Styk, and I. Machaj. Lublin, Pol.: Wydawnictwo Uniwersytetu Marii Curie-Sklodowskiej.

Geertz, C. 1995. *After the fact: Two countries, four decades, one anthropologist.* Cambridge: Harvard University Press.

Gudeman, S., and A. Rivera. 1990. *Conversations in Colombia: The domestic economy in life and context.* Cambridge: Cambridge University Press.

Hann, C. 1985. *A village without solidarity: Polish peasants in years of crisis.* New Haven: Yale University Press.

Kearney, M. 1996. *Reconceptualizing peasantry: Anthropology in global perspective.* Boulder, Colo.: Westview.

Lampland, M. 1995. *The object of labor: Commodification in socialist Hungary.* Chicago: University of Chicago Press.

Marx, K. 1957. *The eighteen brumaire of Louis Bonaparte.* New York: International Publishers.

Maurel, M.-C. 1994. *La transition post-collectiviste. Mutations agraires en Europe centrale.* Paris: Editions L'Harmattan.

Nagengast, C. 1991. *Reluctant socialists, rural entrepreneurs: Class, culture, and the Polish state.* Boulder, Colo.: Westview.

Pilichowski, A. 1994. Chlopi w perspektywie strukturalnego przystosowania, *Kultura i Spoleczenstwo* 38(1): 163–173.

Pine, F. 1993. The cows and pigs are his, the eggs are mine. In *Socialism: Ideals, ideologies, and local practice,* edited by C. M. Hann. London: Routledge.

———. 1998. Dealing with fragmentation: The consequences of privatization for rural women in central and southern Poland. In *Surviving post-socialism: Lacal strategies and regional responses in eastern Europe and the former Soviet Union,* edited by S. Bridger and F. Pine. London: Routledge.

Sider, G. M. 1986. *Culture and class in anthropology and history: A Newfoundland illustration.* Cambridge: Cambridge University Press.

Sahlins, M. 1981. *Historical metaphors and mythical realities: Structure in the early history of the Sandwich Islands Kingdom.* Ann Arbor: University of Michigan Press.

*Sytuacja.* 2001. Sytuacja demograficzna Polski. *Rzeczpospolita* 39 (February 15), D6.

Turowski, J. 1994. Lud ność chłopska w strukturze społeczeństwa polskiego. *Kultura i Społeczeństwo* 38(1): 151–156.

Verdery, K. 1996. *What was socialism, and what comes next?* Princeton: Princeton University Press.

————. 1998. Property and power in Transylvania's decollectivization. In *Property relations: Reinventing the anthropological tradition,* edited by C. M. Hann. Cambridge: Cambridge University Press.

Wesolowski, W. 1995. Procesy klasotwórcze w teoretycznej perspektywie. In *Ludzie i instytucje. Stawanie sie ladu spolecznego.* Vol. 2, edited by A. Sulek, J. Styk, and I. Machaj. Lublin, Pol.: Wydawnictwo Uniwersytetu Marii Curie-Sklodowskiej.

Wolf, E. 1966. *Peasants.* Englewood Cliffs, N.J.: Prentice-Hall.

# 9

# Working in the West

*Managing Eastern Histories at the German Labor Market—The Case of Russian German Immigrants*

REGINA RÖMHILD

Russian German immigrants represent a specific segment in German "multiculture." Officially, they are perceived as late returning ethnic Germans from the former Eastern block (Bade 1992; Delfs 1993). Entering the German labor market, however, this privileged immigrant status conflicts with experiences of ethnicization, social devaluation and unemployment (Graudenz and Römhild 1996). In everyday social practice, the Russian Germans come to represent just another clientele of post-socialist Easterners, namely "Russians," who seek jobs in the "golden west." This chapter explores the ways Russian German immigrants react to this precarious situation and how they themselves try to make sense of their Eastern histories in relation to their presence in Germany. Their example can thus illustrate the interplay between ethnicization, ethnicity, and work precariousness in migration processes.

## Ethnicization at the Labor Market

I met Vladimir[1] at a workshop designed to assist Russian German academic professionals in integrating themselves into the German labor market. Along with him, other participants with similar backgrounds hoped for some information they could use for their daily occupational struggle: the German teacher from Novosibirsk, the agrarian engineer from Tashkent, the economist from a university in Kazakhstan. Vladimir, a man in his forties, used to work as a nuclear physicist in the former Soviet

Union. In Germany, it is difficult for him to find work at all, let alone a job adequate to his professional skills. When I met him, he had just taken over a job at the production line of the Volkswagen factory. Vladimir reported this experience to the other workshop participants in terms of a dramatic disillusion. The presenter of the workshop—himself a former professor of German language and literature in Omsk, Siberia—however, highlighted Vladimir's professional shift as an example of necessary and promising flexibility. Individual initiative and aplomb, he advised the participants, were the main requisites for successful adaptation to the German achievement society. Here, he continued, nobody could ever expect to be acknowledged for something that he has done before coming to Germany, unless he proved his individual abilities and his will to assert himself fundamentally. The lesson to be learned was that "we all have to overcome the socialist mentality we still carry with us—the mentality of falling in with the collective—and replace it by adapting actively to the necessities of the Western elbow individualism." Thus, a sharp contrast between eastern "collectivist" and Western "individualist" work values was constructed in order to explain and surmount the problems of Russian German occupational integration.

The Russian German immigrants share the fate of being degraded at the German labor market with other skilled immigrants and refugees from eastern Europe and the Third World. In general, missing language capacities and differences in professional training standards are made responsible for this maltreatment. More specifically, immigrants and refugees from countries outside the European Union confront problems of legalizing their residence. They are thus often forced to work in the low-skilled informal economic sector (Cyrus 1997, 1999; Miera 1997). Correspondingly, those German economies that rely heavily on the influx of a flexible, low-waged workforce have become central to eastern European immigration. The demands, for example, of the construction and the domestic work sector clearly neglect individual professional skills in favor of a gendered access to labor (Hess and Lenz 2001; Miera 1997). Moreover, the acknowledgement of immigrant skills is limited by way of ethnic and racial exclusion.[2] In the case of east Europeans (including the now "nationalized" East German citizens of the former German Democratic Republic), other ideological reservations resulting from the former confrontation of political systems add to this list: Easterners are often assumed to represent undemocratic, clientelist, or resourceless authoritarian work values due to their professional participation in socialist societies (see, e.g., Greverus 1999; Müller 1993). Russian German immigrants are similarly "Easternized" when they are criticized for their submissive and overadaptive "socialist mentality" or their unwillingness to invest in further education in favor of the "quick money" in low-skilled jobs (Herwartz-Emden and Westphal 1993).

Still, Russian Germans are differentiated from other Easterners by one decisive feature: they enter Germany on the legal status of the "late repatriate" (*Spätaussiedler*)—a category created for ethnic German immigrants from the countries of the former Eastern block (Bade 1992; Delfs 1993). The ethnic Germans in the East were the subject of a specific postwar repatriation program in which Germany presented itself as the national refuge for the persecuted "compatriots" locked up behind the Iron Curtain (Puskeppeleit 1996; Römhild 1999). Whereas only few could follow the call of the German "motherland" up to 1989, their numbers have increased dramatically since the frontiers to the West opened. Today, more than 2 million of these late repatriates live in Germany. Within German multiculture, *Spätaussiedler* are officially privileged Eastern immigrants: from their first day in Germany they are granted full German citizenship rights, and they are provided with specific integration assistance programs such as language courses or professional development training. Vladimir and his comigrants thus hoped for being welcomed in Germany as compatriots, on a par with the "native" Germans. The claim for ethnic equality, expressed in the wish to "live as German among Germans," is reported as a main motive for emigration in several surveys (see, e.g., Graudenz and Römhild 1996).

At the workshop, the proceedings started with a film. The scene of a small village in Kazakhstan emerged on the screen: the village square, untarred and full of muddy puddles, hosts a small group of women in scarves, apron dresses, and rubber boots holding up handwritten pasteboard signs reading "We Are Germans!" and "Where Is Our Homeland?" The small Russian German demonstration in front of running German television cameras marked the end of the film. After some silence, the workshop participants came up with one main question What does this have to do with us? Their backgrounds being the multiethnic urban settings of the former Soviet Union, they were not ready to identify with people they would rather devaluate as uneducated, hick *kolkhoz* (collective farm) peasants. Still, Friedrich, the presenter, advised them to consider that the film communicates the officially supported image of Russian Germans in Germany: that of an isolated and discriminated German minority having preserved the values and traditions of a remote Germanness against the centuries of tsarist and communist oppression. The publicly circulated image does not differentiate between the many histories of people with German ancestry in the former Soviet Union (Römhild 1998, 37ff).

Furthermore, the Spätaussiedler category lumps the Russian Germans together with ethnic Germans from other eastern European countries. On their arrival in Germany, immigrants from Poland, Romania, Hungary, the former Czechoslovakia, and the former Soviet Union are housed together in the narrowness of the provisional homes provided especially for the Spätaussiedler. It is only then that they realize they are being subsumed in a standardized ethnic pool linking up different people under the ambivalent notion of "alien Germans" (*fremde Deutsche*)—this expression being one of the most frequently used for Spätaussiedler in public discourse.

In everyday life, however, the late repatriates are perceived as aliens rather than Germans. The willingness of the German public to accept them as compatriots has as much decreased as their numbers have grown since 1989 (Puskeppeleit 1996, 101f). In contrast to official demands for national solidarity, the privileged Spätaussiedler status of being entitled to equal claims has fostered feelings of envy and competition not only among the "native" Germans, but also among long-term resident non-Germans who still have to struggle for being politically and socially accepted as cocitizens. In everyday public discourse, the legitimacy and the truthfulness of claiming rights of belonging by way of a remote German ancestry are heavily contested.

Hence, the Russian Germans find themselves clamped into an ambiguous process of "double ethnicization" in Germany. On one hand, they are distinguished and highlighted against other immigrants by way of being "Germanized" in accordance with a standardized traditionalist image of Germanness. From this perspective, they are welcomed as a highly adaptable and diligent reinforcement of the national workforce (Rürup 1989, 32ff). On the other hand, they are Easternized by conceiving of them as another subdivision of Russian refugees from post-socialism, thus reintegrating the Russian Germans into the general pool of eastern European immigrants. From this perspective, they are often considered not suitable and a further threat at the competitive labor market.

The ambivalence of being Germanized and Easternized at the same time is the initial experience of Russian German immigrants when entering the German society. This basic experience sets the scene for the revaluation of individual biographies and collective histories as well as the development of strategies within the struggle for recognition.

## Traveling Histories

Margarethe and Waldemar lived most of their lives in Kazachstan before they moved to Omsk in Siberia. From there, they came to Germany in 1993. When I got to know them in 1995 they had just managed to get out of the provisional home into a small apartment in Hanau, a middle-size city near Frankfurt. Both of them were in their fifties when they decided to start a new life in the West. Three grown-up children emigrated with them. Some siblings of Waldemar were already living in Germany when the family arrived.

The couple knew beforehand that it would not be easy to make a fresh start in Germany. Still, Margarethe finds it hard to accept that her qualifications as a schoolteacher do not allow her to work in the German educational system. Although she speaks German very well—better than most other Spätaussiedler—she has as yet not found any job at all.

Waldemar wonders why in Germany every step of the professional career has to be documented and stamped, whereas the actual work experience is not acknowledged in qualificational terms. In Kazachstan, Waldemar worked as a subsidiary physician—a position he tries to explain to me with the antiquated German word *Feldscher*. Actually, he was responsible for a small rural hospital with twenty-five beds and six nurses. The superior physician stopped by only once a week; meanwhile, Waldemar and his team handled the "normal cases" all on their own. However, this experience cannot be communicated as a specific qualification in Germany: there is no such professional status as Feldscher. Waldemar also had a hard time finding a job at all. Only with the help of a sympathetic civil servant could he manage to be employed at a hospital. However, being put on the same level as the young nurses who could be his granddaughters is hard on him. "I am paid like a beginner," he says,

> like a nurse with apprenticeship only. The girl gets as much as I get. I have a family, she is all on her own. . . . In Russia, a nurse is not supposed to make the beds. She only deals with medicaments, with injections. Here, the nurse does not deal with injections, that is done by the physicians exclusively. It is, for the most, service work: providing the food in the morning, clearing the tables.[3]

Waldemar is known as "the Russian" in the hospital. His German is full of antiquated vocabulary derived from the oral tradition of a specific Swabian-based Russian German dialect. For instance, he would use the word *Maul* (muzzle) for a human mouth, thus causing amused irritation among patients and colleagues. They, therefore, are not ready to perceive him as a native speaker but rather as an Eastern immigrant speaking some sort of "pidgin" German. Waldemar and Margarethe complain not so much about this misinterpretation but about the missing interest of their German environment to talk to them and move beyond the stereotyped impression once established in everyday discourse.

In sum, Margarethe and Waldemar do not feel well accepted in German society. They interpret their difficulties of being acknowledged occupationally and ethnically in terms of a severe devaluation. They had left the former Soviet Union for a better life in what they were obliged to see as their German motherland. When they were now looking back at the Soviet past from this German present, they could only find continuity rather than difference or improvement. Looking at me, the "native" German, Waldemar said:

> I always said: Why am I meaner than the natives? Is it my fault that my ancestors were so stupid as to move to Russia? Had they stayed here, I would be just one of you.
>     Also my children would be just like all the others! I am not the same, however, I am not like all the others. They look down on me.

As descendants of German-speaking settlers in tsarist Russia, Margarete and Waldemar were involved in the violent processes of ethnic exclusion in the Stalinist era when the Russian Germans were banished and exiled as traitorous "collaborationists" of the war enemy.[4] Margarethe told me about her life as a child under the *kommandantura* (military command) in a deportation camp in Kazakhstan:

> In wartime and the first time after the war everything was hard. It was so difficult to get food and bread. Once a day bread was brought from the neighboring village and sold. And there was a huge queue and many children—their mothers had to work, their fathers were away—we children had to go for the bread. The [Russian] women—their sons being killed in the war, and they knew I was a German—tore me out of the queue, pushed me into the dust and said: My children are dead, German children don't need to eat either!

Most of the elderly Russian Germans remember their youth in the early postwar Soviet Union in similar terms of incriminating ethnic antagonism. In response to the experience of ethnic exclusion, the Russian German families were rendered a place of subversive ethnic solidarity against a hostile outer world. Thus, a somewhat sharp separation emerged between the familiar sphere where being German was held up and cultivated, and the multiethnic public where cautious and inconspicuous flexibility was required in order to manage the daily coexistence with others. Waldemar described his way of sticking to and hiding Germanness at the same time:

> We learned that we had to continue doing everything the way our parents did. At home, we had to speak German. That was our tradition. In the streets, I was laughed and jeered at. However, when I started working in 1954 nobody realized that I was German: I was perfect in Russian, without any accent. Many noticed it, though, through my family name. Hence, I had to pronounce it differently. I added an "n" at the end to make it sound more Russian.

The disregarding of ethnic markers in everyday life led to some sort of "normalization" as my Russian German interview partners would put it. Still, the entry "German" in a passport could always be a source of discrimination, especially when it came to matters of education and professional career. "When Stalin was still there," Margarethe recalls, "the Germans could not even get near to a university." Russians and Kazakhs were put in the first place, "the Germans were the last for a long time." "For me," Waldemar said, "that was a problem. I was good in learning at school. If I had been a Russian, I could have made it to university." In spite of these obstacles, both managed to get a job appropriate to their interests: Margarethe worked as a Russian teacher in the village school; Waldemar became a medical assistant and head over twenty-five hospital beds. Still, the income of the couple—like that of many others—was not sufficient for a livelihood: "In the village, we had to have cattle. Coming from work, one had further work at home: some pigs, geese, calves. The meat was sold at the market."

Having lived for a long time in the small Kazakh village—in the area to which they and their parents were once deported—Margarethe and Waldemar decided to follow their grown-up children to the city of Omsk in Siberia where they invested their savings in a small house. Two years after the purchase, they were informed that the house was needed to make room for a new housing block. Alternatively, the authorities offered them only a small flat in one of the local skyscrapers but no further compensation at all. Waldemar took this as just one more act of chicanery in a lifelong list of discrimination due to his German ancestry. "I always felt like a second-class person," he summed up his biographical account. This last experience finally turned the scale for the family's decision to emigrate to Germany. There, they hoped, they could turn the disadvantage of being excluded as a German into the advantage of automatically belonging to the national majority, into being part of the mainstream instead of representing a marginalized minority.

Like Margarethe and Waldemar, many elderly Russian Germans reconstructed their biographical accounts around the key focus of being discriminated and ethnically excluded from the social agenda in the former

Soviet Union. Their direct experience of physical persecution and exile in the Stalinist era would again and again be revitalized by every discriminatory follow-up in their later lives. For them, it seems especially reasonable to interpret the present as a mere resumption of the past: as one more disillusioned expectation of escaping a fundamentally hostile history of ethnic alienation. Being degraded to the comparatively minor status of a low-skilled, resourceless guest worker from some remote East seems to be just one more variation of the same historic theme.

Other Russian Germans, particularly the younger ones, do not recall a collective history in mere ethnic terms. Those who remember the times of deportation and exile as a part of their families' histories but not as a part of their personal biographies are able to reveal other aspects of life in the former Soviet Union. They remember working and living in a multiethnic social landscape in which being German was only at times invoked as a discriminatory stigma. Others reported their lives in urban settings, some of them being involved in specific intellectual, sometimes dissident, networks that advanced, particularly in the deportation areas, far off the political center of power in Moscow. The past of the Russian German immigrants is thus composed of many histories, of different origins and positions within the wider social system; it is marked by severe ethnic antagonism and many forms of multiethnic communal life. Still, also the more "cosmopolitical" accounts tend to focus on the difference Germanness makes as soon as they draw nearer to the present. In these accounts, the crucial point is not so much the past collective trauma of deportation and exile but rather the present ethnic revival in the post-Soviet states that serves for individual redefinitions in ethnic terms. For most of my interlocutors, the uncertainty of whether they would be accepted as equal cocitizens in a "nationalized" Kazakhstan, Uzbekistan, or Russia was the main reason to move out for the better in Germany. Many experienced their being excluded from the participation in a common future and their being referred to Germany as their proper homeland. Lydia from Kazakhstan remembers her neighbors saying: "Go to Germany all of you! We shall live in our own houses, and we will shit in yours!"

It is in this process of renewed ethnicization that the many histories seem to be overtaken by a return of the hostile collective past. Elena, twenty years old when I met her in Germany, has lived most of her life under the impression of post-Soviet nationality politics. "I think that I am a German and not a Russian," she tells me. "Some think that one is a Russian because one is born in Russia—no! . . . From the blood you get what you are. . . . Nowadays, all of the [Soviet] nationalities strive for autonomy. There are many Germans in Kazakhstan, but there is no German republic in Russia. And where should the poor Germans go then?" Whoever decides to leave for a German homeland, then, has to prove his German ancestry when applying for the immigration status of a Spätaussiedler. The forms to be filled in require detailed information about the history and the ethnic composition of family and friends, about the knowledge and the use of the German language and German customs, the engagement in German communities and initiatives. Furthermore, they require a specific confession to Germanness (see Römhild 1998, 255ff). The process of applying for the Spätaussiedler status is thus another arena of re-creating ethnic differences: many of my interlocutors referred to this process in terms of being forced "to separate the inseparable." Not only are their marriages and families often ethnically mixed, but also the wider social web of their daily lives. The decision for Germany, then, is very often a decision against intimate others; a decision that split families, social communities, and individual biographies.

Those who go through this often-painful process do so for a better life in Germany, if not for themselves then at least for their children. Despite the tempting expectation of being welcomed and supported as compatriots in Germany, many Russian Germans are well aware that the reality may be different. Emanuel, a young family father from Kazakhstan, commented on his decision:

> I had a good job, a good place to live. However, I didn't see any future for my children. I thought: I am coming to Germany—I cannot speak German, my professional qualification is not admitted in Germany: I was trained to be a building plant engineer, in a specific Russian way, though. Still, I thought: a future for the children. They are able to learn something, they are still young.

## Contested Claims of Belonging

It is only after their arrival in Germany that the Russian German immigrants fully realize that they are not entering the "national refuge" they were called into but rather a multiethnic society in which Germanness is neither a properly defined nor an obligatory source of belonging. Those who had to prove their Germanness in full detail in order to be admitted to come to Germany, now find out that they are not clearly positioned on the side of the German "natives." Instead, they not only experience being considered "strangers" by the German residents but, moreover, that they actually have to compete for jobs and state-subsidized apartments with the non-German residents on the same social level. Thus, they are not only perceived as strangers but also made to share their social status.

In response to this downgrading, as the Russian German immigrants would have it, they rather insist on the once promised privilege derived from their German ancestry and try to make use of it in the competitive struggle for recognition. Like Peter, a young man from Kazazkhstan, many interlocutors put forth claims of a privileged immigration status:

> This Germany is no Germany. Wherever you go: Turks and Italians are everywhere. . . . Virtually, I do not see any Germany at all. . . . Indeed, it is like this: They are coming to Germany from all countries. And our Germans from Russia are not as able to come. The Italian buys a railway ticket and travels to Germany. . . . That is unfair. Our Germans over there now have to suffer a lot, and all other nationalities are invited to Germany. That is not good.

Waldemar felt reminded of the multiethnic past he just left behind: "I did not expect this situation. I thought it would only be like that in Russia. In Russia, the Kazakhs, the Uzbeks live in republics of their own, in their homelands. But here, in Germany, are living more 'dark people' than in Russia."

Compared to the expectations nourished by the long-term messages of the national motherland, the multiethnic and multicultural reality of Germany presents itself like an upside-down world. The traveling image of Germany the nation-state did not communicate the fact that Germany is, indeed, also an immigration country, a refuge for other work migrants and refugees as well. The former guest workers from southern Europe have settled down in Germany, their children and grandchildren now being native non-German residents. Their claims for belonging, however, do not refer to a German nation but rather to a transnational, multicultural society, thus challenging the internal and external borders of the nation-state. The Russian Germans do recognize the legitimacy of these claims since other immigrants have a longer history of positioning themselves in Germany. Whereas the Russian Germans can only demand for belonging by way of an ethnic communality, the long-term non-German residents are already an indispensable part of the social and cultural life in Germany. The naturalness with which they seem to move about in the society that seems so strange to many Russian Germans is a further source of uncertainty, particularly with respect to the problem of positioning oneself. "They do feel at home here more than we do," Waldemar noted in astonishment.

The confusion about the question who may legitimately claim for belonging on what grounds and with what success contributes to the tendency among Russian German immigrants to revalue Germanness as a qualitative differentiation. Self-defensive constructions of ethnic superiority are thus not so much "imported" but rather created during the migratory process and its struggle for recognition. Galina, a young woman from Tadzhikistan, provides a quite drastic, though not untypical example:

> There is a house right next to my workplace. A Turkish family is living in it—good grief, it's so dirty. . . . I said to my husband: Can't these people clear up their things, or what? This house, I said, give me this house! . . . Another woman who lives here [in the provisional home] has applied for an apartment, one that is state subsidized. She always made telephone calls and these people said that the flat is almost hers. . . . Then, the other man phoned and he was told: It's too late now, a Turkish family is already living there. . . . The Turkish family gets the place, and we always have to stay here."

Here, Galina employs stereotyped German virtues like tidiness and cleanliness in order to set herself and the Russian Germans as such off against the "dirty" Others. Although the ethnic exclusion of the Russian Germans from the "native" Germans and their inclusion in the marginalized pool of (Eastern) strangers renders them addressees of ethnic discrimination they are not ready to identify with and act on the basis of that positioning. Rather, they tend to become coproducers of ethnic discrimination themselves. Thus, ethnicization does not foster solidarity but furthers ethnic antagonism among the discriminated.

Furthermore, the new focus on Germanness as a means of delimitation is applied to the coimmigrants. Also, within the ascribed category of Spätaussiedler, the performance of proper Germanness is rendered a decisive feature for contesting claims of belonging. Many interview partners criticized those who "continue to speak Russian only" long after their arrival in Germany. Others were accused of having emigrated under the false pretense of a German ancestry. These coimmigrants were not only excluded from the solidarity of a collective "We" but also made responsible for the reservations of the German public to recognize the Russian Germans as homecoming compatriots. This suspicion, originally grounded in the public discourse on the legitimacy of ethnic German immigration, is thus applied and turned against one's own Others.

Again, the ethnicized generalist category of Spätaussiedler does not create common identification and solidarity but further competition on ethnic grounds among the categorized. In the provisional homes that most Spätaussiedler live in after their arrival in Germany, the forced community of different people from all over the East leads to the invention of ever new differences rather than any forms of sustainable communality. In this internal discourse of delimitation, the decisive questions may refer to whether one comes from Poland or the former Soviet Union, from Kazakhstan or Uzbekistan, from a city or a village, whether one was a "simple worker" or part of an academic intelligentsia. These different origins and backgrounds are evaluated with respect to their inherent potentials for making one's way in Germany. Young Nina from Kazakhstan counts herself among the "workers from the countryside" and sets herself off against high-skilled Russian Germans:

> All of these people—whether they have been engineer or professor—lack the language. And this may be the reason why they are angry about us: For the people in the countryside do speak a little German. However, the people who have grown up in the city lack this ability. We workers are easy in getting contact with other people. And therefore, they are angry about us: Look at her, the worker—and she has a German friend already! . . . In the past, they have been big, and we were small. . . . It doesn't make a difference to a worker what kind of work he has to do. I have to work anyway, I have to earn money. I worked in Russia, I can work here as well. The others, however, those who have been engineer or director for example, they wait and wait. What are these people doing? I don't know.

According to Nina, the migration process turns the inner social relations upside down. Those who once occupied the advantaged social positions, those who used to look down on the rural kolkhoz workers far off their own urban lifestyle now have to struggle with the disadvantage of overqualification and social degrading. What is more, the workers with the more traditional Russian German background, gained in the villages, experience that they do fit in better with the image of the "ethnic German" created by the official immigration discourse. From this perspective, their language abilities, their value performance, and their visible lifestyle renders them "more German" than the high-skilled city dwellers.

Along similar lines, an antagonistic discourse emerges with respect to the second largest group of Spätaussiedler, that of the Polish Germans. Among the Polish German immigrants it is common to characterize their Russian counterparts as provincial and old-fashioned (Graudenz and Römhild 1996, 58). In this case, it is the Russian German "traditionalism" that is made responsible for the alienation of the Spätaussiedler in the German public. Right to the contrary, though, the Russian Germans themselves value traditionalism in terms of proper Germanness and thus an advantage in the struggle for recognition. They, in turn, devaluate the "individualism" of the Polish German immigrants as expressions of egoism and greed, contrasting it to Russian German countervirtues like modesty and diligence. Still, as Nina put it, compared to the timid restraint of the Russian Germans the "cleverness" among the Polish Germans seems to be more promising in the German "elbow society":

> They [the Russian Germans] are always anxious. The Polish people say what they think. And our people keep it to themselves, say it "at the heart." . . . They don't argue against something, they agree, the main thing being that they have some work, earn money. They are always anxious about saying something, that's their problem. . . . It's exactly like that when it comes to finding an apartment. They don't go to the social security office and say: I need an apartment, or so. They say: If I get in trouble with that office, then I will not get an apartment at all. It's better that I stay quiet, make a phone call once in a while—then I'll get the apartment, otherwise I will not.

In this aspect, at least, the strategies of the Russian German immigrants to assert themselves in the competitive struggle for recognition do not seem to work out. According to a survey, 25 percent of Polish German respondents, but only 4 percent of Russian German respondents, managed to leave provisional housing for an apartment of their own during the first two years of their stay in Germany.[5] Still, some of the interview partners would interpret their longer-lasting willingness to stand the crowded life in the small rooms of the provisional camps as an expression of thrift and modesty—virtues that would, again, be understood as symbolic capital in the interethnic struggle for recognition.

## Recapturing Socialist History: Values of Work and Life

The counterrelated processes of ethnicization and ethnicity tend to produce notions and practices of self-isolation among the Russian German immigrants. Experiences of exclusion from the mainstream society correspond to practices of self-exclusion from non-German and German comigrants. In this situation, many Russian Germans increasingly rely on their families, on their private lives, as a resource of mutual support and confidence. At the same time, the family is rendered the central locus of evaluating the migration process from the different viewpoints of its members. These discourses between children and parents, men and women, reveal and foster alternative perspectives on the past and alternative levels of comparison between former and present lives.

Galina, the young woman from Tadzhikistan, emigrated to Germany together with her husband, two children, and her parents-in-law. When I met her, she had already lived for two years in the provisional home where the whole family was allocated two small rooms. In their case, it was the husband rather than herself who decided to emigrate. Galina misses her work, her friends, and her parents, all of which she had to leave behind.

> My mother said: I want to live in Germany as well. She is German, but my father is Russian. He said: No, I'll live here in Russia. I want to stay with my mother, brother, and sister. . . . I said: Father, what do you want from this home country? That's not possible—no food, no things. I cannot send so many goods to you, I don't have so much money. He said: No, I want to live here, leave me alone.

For Heinrich, the husband, emigration meant reuniting with his family in Germany, the place where his brother and his sister already lived. Galina, however, had to decide whether she would stay with her parents or leave with her husband. From this background, she develops a more critical view on the present in Germany, contrasting it sharply to the family's expectations for a better future but also to the commemoration of a lost past. "There," she said with respect to her former life in Tadzhikistan, "it was very good, but here—I don't know. I sit at home the whole day. I have to get up so early and go to work, then I have to go home again and cook. Then I have to go to the kindergarten to take my son home. Then I sit at home again waiting for my husband, eating. It's the same every, every day."

In contrast to the isolated monotony of the present, Galina remembers a past network of friends, neighbors, and colleagues in which she felt both integrated and free to act on her own. She used to work as a lab technician in a big chemical plant: "There [in the plant] we had a great club where we organized parties and festivities. In our city, we knew everyone. We went in the streets, always saying hello, always, always." Nina, who lives next door in the provisional home, corroborates Galina's view on the past by remembering her village in Kazakhstan: "In our streets—nobody would ever be sitting on a bench all on his own. . . . In our village, the streets and the yards are crowded when the people come home from work. A bench is found in every yard, there the people sit together. And then you pass by, others pass by as well—in the end, it is a garden full of people."

Statements like these reveal a rather different, if not idealized perspective on the (post-)socialist past. Furthermore, they refer to contrasting experiences in Germany. Many Russian Germans criticize on the tendency of "cocooning" in private isolation among the "native" Germans and on the sharp differentiation between the private and the public in general. In the Soviet Union, as they remember it, the workplace was a central locus of social life, thus serving for connecting the locals beyond their occupational cooperation. At the chemical plant where Galina used to work, she directed courses in dancing and aerobics and organized parties and events. In Germany, she experiences the retreat to the narrowness of the one-room family life as a forced isolation. Sometimes, though, she makes room for her feelings: "Then I play some music and dance on my own. I said to my husband and my children: Go out of my house, my room! I have to dance here now. I cannot only sit around all the time."

Work was a resource of social gathering and social recognition. In spite of all ethnic antagonism, many Russian German interlocutors highlighted the workplace as the space where they felt most accepted and integrated in the Soviet society. It is thus particularly hard on them to find that their workforce is neglected or degraded at the German labor market. As a source of acknowledgment and self-esteem, work—rather than profession—is a value in itself. It is for this reason also that the Russian Germans tend to accept working in low-skilled jobs rather than investing in the search for adequate employment. In particular, many of them cannot stand to stay away from work during the first year in Germany when they are expected and financially supported to participate in full-day language courses. "Our people," Nina says, "just can't do that: stay at home and do nothing."

This holds especially true for Russian German women. In the socialist system of the Soviet Union, women were fully integrated in the labor market. In contrast to the circulated image of the "traditional" Russian German, the modern lifestyle of a fully employed woman was a general feature in the biographical accounts of the female interlocutors. In fact, the pattern of being engaged as a housewife and mother only, as it is traditionally employed in Western bourgeois lifestyles, was virtually unknown to them. Russian German women even tend to be higher qualified than their male counterparts. In my survey (Römhild 1995, 232), 74.4 percent of the female respondents had a midrange or a higher education, but only 41.4 percent of the male respondents had the same education. With respect to the women, the problem of entering the German labor market comes as a gendered experience. As a further obstacle against realizing their expectations, they are confronted with new difficulties of reconciling the demands of work and family. Galina found herself a job in the local post office where she sorts the letters every morning. Being fond of her work abilities, the head of the post office offered her a full-time job. However, Galina is likely to refrain from this opportunity: "Our oldest son goes to the kindergarten. My mother-in-law stays with my younger son. If she is allocated an apartment in a different town I have to stay at home with my little son."

In Germany, the social infrastructure is not as compatible to the needs of fully employed mothers as it was in the former Soviet Union: "In Russia, it was very easy with the kindergarten. They can stay there the whole day from half past seven until seven in the evening. They sleep and eat in the kindergarten. We pay for it, of course, but it is not so expensive: twelve or thirteen roubles." Furthermore, the women could more easily rely on the extended family, where the retired grandparents would look after their grandchildren while both father and mother were off to work. In Germany, the state-subsidized apartments usually do not fit the size of an average Russian German extended family. Hence, the families are often split up geographically. This creates problems for the expectations of the younger, but also of the elder, women who feel deprived of participating properly in family life. Lydia comments on her experience from the perspective of a grandmother:

> We had applied for an apartment. I wanted my son, my daughter-in-law to stay with us. But there, where we had to apply for it, they said: That is not possible in Germany. The young have to live on their own, and mother and father have to live on their own. I said: Why should I sit in the room on my own all day? We are not used to this. . . . We had a house of our own, such a nice, big house, our son stayed with us. But you here don't have the children living together with the parents.

The experience of a state-subsidized social security system that does not fit their needs fosters the tendency among Russian Germans to strive for autonomy. In particular, many dream about building or buying a house of their own. Still, quite a few manage to realize that dream due to resolute thrift and personal contribution. Here, the many skills necessarily gained from the daily improvisation in the socialist and post-socialist life worlds pay off. Furthermore, the reservations about dependencies from state institutions also reflect the general distrust of authorities as a historically invested experience.

It is through these experiences of social and cultural difference that the Russian German immigrants begin to revalue their other history of having been an active part of a multiethnic (post-)socialist society.

Whereas the ethnic differences created by the specific conditions of their immigration tend to foster, in response, ethnic antagonism and retreat to the family, the detection of this social history may well lead to opening up the ethnic borders to former and present Eastern compatriots, working in the West as well. Finally, the notion of a common past also becomes part of the present in the migratory process. "We have been amidst of that life," Lene told me. "I don't know any Russian German who has come to Germany and is not sad about everything he left behind. . . . One had a home and a life there, built up a house and everything necessary, a job. . . . At our age, one has achieved many things with great effort . . . and then it hurts even more."

Olga and her husband have not given up their apartment in Omsk although they emigrated to Germany. "We haven't really separated from Russia," she said. "We would be so happy if things would improve there again." Their decision to keep a door open may point to a new alternative: Russian German immigration, designed as the national repatriation of ethnic Germans, may develop in a more transnational direction, thus connecting rather than separating East and West across ethnic borders.

## Notes

This chapter is based on ethnographic research with Russian German immigrants in Germany from 1990 until 1996 (Römhild 1998). In those parts of the research project that included a comparison with Polish German immigrants, I enjoyed and gained much profit from the collaboration with my psychologist colleague Ines Graudenz (see, e.g., Graudenz and Römhild 1996). The collaborative project (1990–1992) was funded by the Deutsche Forschung gemeinschaft. I have already focused (Römhild 1995) on some of the aspects that are dealt with in this chapter.

1. All names of interview partners have been changed according to the usage in Römhild (1998).

2. The current German discourse on the economic necessity of high-skilled green-card immigration from Third World countries neglects the fact that this type of immigration is not at all a new phenomenon: Many of the refugees and immigrants already living in Germany are equally high-skilled professionals. Since they were not provided with green card opportunities they are rarely found as appreciated specialists in the German high-tech economy but rather working in sweatshops, fast-food kitchens, or for the public refuse disposal companies. The idea that the Indian or the Pakistani selling newspapers in the streets may be a teacher or an engineer is still far from being present in German public discourse.

3. All personal quotations have been taken from recorded interview material and translated from (Russian) German into English by the author.

4. For the history of foreign settlement in Russia under tsarist rule, see Bartlett (1979) and Kappeler (1992); for early Russian German history in particular, see Long (1988); for Russian Germans in the Soviet Union, see Pinkus and Fleischhauer (1987). An ethnographic account of Russian German reconstructions of collective histories is presented in Römhild (1998, 163ff).

5. See Graudenz and Römhild (1996). The study was conducted in 1990–1991. We consulted 253 Russian German immigrants and 184 Polish German immigrants with a semistandardized questionnaire asking for their expectations and emigration motives as well as their experiences during their first years in Germany. With respect to the Russian German sample, the quantitative data was accomplished with twenty-two narrative biographical interviews (Römhild 1998, 163ff).

# References

Bade, K. J. 1992. Fremde Deutsche: "Republikflüchtlinge"—Übersiedler—Aussiedler. In *Deutsche im Ausland—Fremde in Deutschland: Migration in Geschichte und Gegenwart*, edited by K. J. Bade. Frankfurt a.M.: Büchergilde Gutenberg.

Bartlett, R. P. 1979. *Human capital: The settlement of foreigners in Russia, 1762–1804.* Cambridge: Cambridge University Press.

Cyrus, N. 1997. Grenzkultur und Stigmamanagement. Mobile Ethnographie und Situationsanalyse eines irregulär beschäftigten polnischen Wanderarbeiters in Berlin. *Kea. Zeitschrift für Kulturwissenschaften* 10: 83–104.

———. 1999. Im menschenrechtlichen Niemandsland. Illegalisierte Zuwanderung in der Bundesrepublik Deutschland zwischen individueller Rechtlosigkeit und transnationalen Bürgerrechten. In *Angeworben, eingewandert, abgeschoben. Ein anderer Blick auf die Einwanderungsgesellschaft Bundesrepublik Deutschland*, edited by K. Dominik et al. Münster, Ger.: Westfälisches Dampfboot.

Delfs, S. 1993. Heimatvertriebene, Aussiedler, Spätaussiedler. Rechtliche und politische Aspekte der Aufnahme von Deutschstämmigen aus Osteuropa in der Bundesrepublik Deutschland. *Aus Politik und Zeitgeschichte. Beilage zur Wochenzeitung das Parlament* B48: 3–11.

Graudenz, I., and R. Römhild. 1996. Grenzerfahrungen. Deutschstämmige Migranten aus Polen und der ehemaligen Sowjetunion im Vergleich. In *Forschungsfeld Aussiedler: Ansichten aus Deutschland*, edited by I. Graudenz and R. Römhild. Frankfurt a.M.: Lang.

Greverus, I.-M. 1999. Poetics within politics: Towards an anthropology of the own. *Anthropological Journal on European Cultures* 8(2): 7–26.

Herwartz-Emden, L., and M. Westphal. 1993. Bildungserwartungen und Berufsmotivation von Aussiedlerinnen aus der Sowjetunion. *Unterrichtswissenschaft. Zeitschrift für Lernforschung* 21(2): 106–125.

Hess, S., and R. Lenz, eds. 2001. *Geschlecht und globalieserung. Ein kulturwissenschaftlicher streifzug durch tranationale Räume.* Königstein, Ger.: Ulrike Helmer.

Kappeler, A. 1992. *Rußland als Vielvölkerreich. Entstehung, Geschichte, Zerfall.* Munich: Beck.

Long, J. W. 1988. *From privileged to dispossessed: The Volga Germans, 1860–1917.* Lincoln: University of Nebraska Press.

Miera, F. 1997. Migrantinnen aus Polen. Zwischen nationaler Migrationspolitik und transnationalem sozialen Lebensräumen. In *Zuwanderung und Stadtentwicklung,* edited by H. Häußermann and I. Oswald. Opladen, Ger.: Westdeutscher Verlag.

Müller, B. 1993. The wall in the heads: East–West German stereotypes and the problems of transition in three enterprises in East Berlin. *Anthropological Journal on European Cultures* 2(1): 9–42.

Pinkus, B., and I. Fleischhauer. 1987. *Die Deutschen in der Sowjetunion. Geschichte einer nationalen Minderheit im 20. Jahrhundert.* Baden-Baden, Ger.: Nomos.

Puskeppeleit, J. 1996. Der Paradigmenwechsel der Aussiedlerpolitik—Von der Politik der "nationalen Aufgabe" zur Politik der "Eindämmung der Zu- und Einwanderung und der Konkurrenz- und Neidbewältigung." In *Forschungsfeld Aussiedler. Ansichten aus Deutschland,* edited by I. Graudenz and R. Römhild. Frankfurt a.M.: Lang.

Römhild, R. 1995. Les Allemands de Sibérie sont de retour. *Études rurales* 138–140: 227–238.

———. 1998. *Die Macht des Ethnischen: Grenzfall Rußlanddeutsche. Perspektiven einer politischen Anthropologie.* Frankfurt a.M.: Lang.

———. 1999. Home-made cleavages: Ethnonational discourse, diasporization, and the politics of Germanness. *Anthropological Journal on European Cultures* 8(1): 99–120.

Rürup, B. 1989. *Wirtschaftliche und gesellschaftliche Perspektiven der Bundesrepublik (Schriftenreihe des Bundeskanzleramtes, 7).* Munich: C. H. Beck.

# Contributors

**Michal Buchowski** is professor of social anthropology at the University of Poznan (Poland) and of comparative central European studies at the European University–Viadrina in Frankfurt/Oder, Germany. He has held research fellowships and has been visiting professor in the United Kingdom, the United States, France, and Germany. His principal interests include anthropology of central European societies and culture, rural anthropology, and modes of thought and systems of beliefs. Among his latest publications in English are *Reluctant Capitalist* (Berlin: Centre Marc Bloch, 1997), *The Rational Other* (Poznan: Humaniora, 1997), and *Contesting Transition, Rethinking Transformation* (Poznan: Humaniora, 2001).

**Sophie Day** is senior lecturer in anthropology at Goldsmiths College, London University. She has conducted research with sex workers over a number of years in the United Kingdom and in Europe, much of which has been based at St. Mary's Hospital, Imperial College where she set up the Praed Street Project with Helen Ward. She has conducted other research in medical anthropology and completed a doctorate on spirit possession at Ladakh, North India. She is one of the editors (along with Michael Stewart and Evthymios Papataxiarchis) of the book *Lilies of the Field: Marginal People Who Live for the Moment.* (Boulder, Colo., Westview, 1999).

**Richard-Michael Diedrich** is lecturer in social anthropology at the University of Hamburg and Heidelberg, Germany. He did fieldwork on ethnicity in North Wales and on gender relations and unemployment in South Wales for which he received a Ph.D. from the University of Hamburg. He is the author of *You Can't Beat Us! Class, Work, and Gender on a Council Estate in the South Wales Coalfield* (Hamburg: Staats- und Universitätsbibliothek; available: http://www.sub.uni-hamburg.de/disse/878/dissertation.pdf).

**Birgit Müller** is a senior researcher at the Laboratory of Institutions and Social Organizations, Centre National de la Recherche Scientifique in

Paris. She has worked extensively on social movements and societies in rapid transformation: on riots in colonial Nigeria, alternative movements in West Germany, Nicaragua during and after the Sandinistas, and post-socialist transformations in East Germany, the Czech Republic, and Russia. Her focus is on institutional change, mechanisms of domination, and the unintended and intended consequences brought about locally by political and cultural contestation and economic struggles. Among her books are *Toward an Alternative Culture of Work: Political Idealism and Economic Practices in West Berlin Collective Enterprises* (Boulder, Colo.: Westview, 1991) and *Political and Institutional Change in Post-Communist Eastern Europe* (Canterbury, Eng.: CSA, 1999).

**Susana Narotzky** is Professor Titular of social anthropology at the Universitat de Barcelona, Spain. Her research has focused on issues about women, work, and the construction of cultural hegemonies in Europe. Narotzky tries to underscore the need for a historical framework in order to understand present-day tensions, struggles, and cultural constructs. She has done fieldwork in Catalonia, Valencia, Spain, and Lombardia, Italy. Among her publications are *Trabajar en familia. Mujeres, hogares y talleres* (Valencia: Edicions Alfons El Magnànim, 1988) and *New Directions in Economic Anthropology* (London: Pluto, 1997), as well as several articles in edited books and journals.

**Italo Pardo** was granted his Ph.D. in social anthropology by the University of London. At the present he is Honorary Research Fellow at the University of Kent. He has carried out long-term independent research in Britain and Italy (1978 to the present). His research interests include urban anthropology, morality and thought, work, organization and power, legitimacy, the elite (1990 and continuing), and hunting with hounds (in progress). He has published extensively in refereed journals and also in mainstream periodicals. Publications are in English and Italian. He is the author of *Managing Existence in Naples: Morality, Action, and Structure* (Cambridge: Cambridge University Press, 1996) and *Morals of Legitimacy: Between Agency and the System,* (Oxford: Berghahn Books, 2000).

**Angela Procoli** is anthropologist at the Laboratory of Social Anthropology of the College de France in Paris. Her research is focused on the study of work in relation to cultural representations and social change in French contemporary society. From 1991 to 1995, she was lecturer at the Ecole du Louvre and at INALCO, Université Paris-Dauphine. She is the author of *Anthropologie d'une formation au CNAM. La fabrique de la competence* (Anthropology of a Professional Training at CNAM. Making Up Competence)

(Paris: l'Harmattan, 2001). At present she conducts research on the work of French researchers in genetics.

**Regina Römhild** is assistant professor at the Institute of Cultural Anthropology and European Ethnology in Frankfurt, Germany. She has worked ethnographically in the fields of tourism, ethnic and national identity politics, and, more recently, transnational relations. Her publications include *"Histourismus." Fremdenverkehr und lokale Selbstbehauptung* ("Histourism." Recreational Traffic and Local Empowerment) (Frankfurt: Kulturanthropologie Notizeu, 1990) and *Die Macht des Ethnischen: Grenzfall Rußlanddeutsche. Perspektiven einer politischen Anthropologie* (The Power of Ethnic Discourse: The Case of the Russian Germans) (Frankfurt, a.M.: Lang, 1998). She currently conducts fieldwork on transnational relations between Greece and Germany as well as—in a collaborative project with students—on processes of transnationalism and cultural globalization in the Frankfurt area.

**Sandra Wallman** is professor of anthropology, chair of "urban change," at University College London. She has taught in a range of anthropology departments in Europe and North America. Her publications as editor include *Social Anthropology of Work* (London: Academic, 1979) and *Contemporary Futures* (London: Routledge, 1992); and as author, *Eight London Households* (London: Tavistock, 1983) and *Kampala Women Getting By: Wellbeing in the Time of AIDS* (London: James Currey, 1996). Her present research in Turin, Italy, extends Europe–Africa comparisons of urban systems as they effect migrants: host options, cultural compression, and identity processes.

# INDEX

221